Romance and Rights

Romance and Rights

The Politics of Interracial Intimacy,

1945–1954

Alex Lubin

University Press of Mississippi
Jackson

www.upress.state.ms.us

The University Press of Mississippi is a member of the Association of American University Presses.

12 11 10 09 08 07 06 05   4 3 2 1

Library of Congress Cataloging-in-Publication Data

Lubin, Alex.
 Romance and rights : the politics of interracial intimacy, 1945–1954 /
Alex Lubin.
  p. cm.
 Includes bibliographical references (p.) and index.
 ISBN 1-57806-705-7 (alk. paper)
 1. Miscegenation—United States—History—20th century. 2. United States—
Race relations—History—20th century. I. Title.
 E185.62.L83   2005
 306.84'6'097309044—dc22   2004010078

British Library Cataloging-in-Publication Data available

Contents

Acknowledgments

THIS BOOK PROJECT began as a graduate seminar paper for a class taught by David Roediger at the University of Minnesota. During the time it has taken to transform the ideas I first presented in that seminar into a dissertation and book, I have received invaluable help from a number of teachers, classmates, colleagues, and archivists.

I have been fortunate to have had two fabulous professors guide me through graduate school and the writing process. Judith Smith was, and is, a dedicated mentor whose suggestions are always brilliant and helpful. I feel immensely fortunate to have worked toward my M.A. with Professor Smith at the University of Massachusetts Boston. David Roediger, my dissertation adviser at Minnesota, was generous and inspirational.

At Minnesota, my work benefited from helpful suggestions and observations by classmates. Marjorie Bryer, Katherine Griffin, Tiya Miles, and Meredith Wood pushed my thinking on this project in ways they may never fully realize. The University of Minnesota's Dissertation Fellowship was welcome support during the final year of writing.

Archivists at Michigan State University's Nye Popular Collections Library, at Emory's Woodruff Library, and at Yale's Beinicke Library were extremely helpful in guiding me through a huge amount of materials.

During the postdissertation phase of this project, I was greatly assisted by graduate students at the University of New Mexico, including Elizabeth Swift, Asako Nobuoka, and Margie Montañez, each of whom provided invaluable research assistance. Various students in my Interracialism in America course at the University of Colorado Boulder and at the University of New Mexico have helped me rethink my own research on the subject. My junior faculty research group at New Mexico—Amanda Cobb, Alyosha Goldstein, and Rebecca Schreiber—read and helped improve chapter 1.

Peggy Pascoe and Rachel Moran gave extremely useful suggestions for how to rethink the major argument of my project, and for this I am grateful.

Their respective essays and books on interracial intimacy were invaluable in helping me contextualize my own study. John-Michael Rivera gave helpful direction whenever it was needed.

The editors at the University Press of Mississippi have been wonderful. Seetha Srinivasan has been an active and responsive editor. The not-so-annonymous reader (James Hall) was immensely knowledgeable and helpful. His suggestions and comments made me think about my project in new ways.

It is no secret to anyone who has written a dissertation and a book that the work is mostly lonely and involves years of stress with only brief moments of joy. My brother, Charlie Lubin, has always been an inspiration to me, especially during the construction of this project. More than anyone else I know, Charlie suggests the hopeful possibilities of taking risks and crossing all sorts of boundaries.

In both the stressful and joyful parts of this process, Kelly Gallagher has been a compassionate partner who made me realize that a book is just that. It is to her, and our newest joy, Eyob, that I dedicate this book, and so much more.

Introduction

IN THE SUMMER OF 1942 the black actor, singer, athlete, and political activist Paul Robeson walked onto the stage of the Brattle Street Theater in Cambridge, Massachusetts, portraying the role of William Shakespeare's Othello. In doing so, Robeson became the first black actor to assume the role of Shakespeare's "dark Moor" in an interracial production in the United States. Although there had been all-black off-Broadway productions of *Othello* prior to World War II, white audiences did not view these productions. Prior to Robeson's performance, white actors had played Othello in various shades of blackface. In the pre-1942 productions, Othello had been stripped of his nobility in favor of a more hostile and irrational version that confirmed the myth of the black male rapist. Robeson's performance was significant, therefore, not only because Robeson was black but also because he recast Othello as a noble man.

Robeson's costars were Uta Hagen, a popular stage actress who played Desdemona, and her husband, José Ferrer, a Puerto Rican American actor who played Iago. Despite the play's multiracial cast, it was Robeson, the play's black actor, whom producers worried would not be accepted; after all, *Othello* is the story of an interracial romance ending in Desdemona's death at the hands of Othello. In selecting Robeson as Othello, the producers challenged the color line in a society that outlawed black/white interracial marriage in thirty-one states and that lynched African American men for imagined indiscretions toward white women.

Perhaps even more important than Robeson's role in the play were the political uses the play served for its audiences. Critical praise of this production of *Othello* reveals telling evidence about the importance of the interracial cast and romance both to the ways racial boundaries were managed and to the politics of civil rights. Audiences in Cambridge and around the United States saw this production as evidence that racial equality could exist in the United States. The interracial cast and the interracial romance, it seems, fit quite nicely into American wartime discourse that cast the United States as the bastion of democracy and freedom.[1] The day after the first performance, a Boston critic suggested that Robeson's Othello was "a great artistic achievement" and that the ovation was "abundantly deserved." The *New York Times* wrote that Robeson had shown "a Negro actor is acceptable, both academically and practically," and that Robeson's "heroic and convincing" performance had "captured all the facets of Othello's layered personality." *Variety* argued that "no white man should ever dare presume to play the role [of Othello] again."[2]

The black press, during one of the rare moments when it concurred with the mainstream media, viewed Robeson's portrayal of Othello as a civil rights victory. One publication declared that "the production [was] a milestone in race relations." Walter White, president of the National Association for the Advancement of Colored People (NAACP), who himself would enter an interracial marriage with a white woman, wrote, "It is one of the most inspiring and perfectly balanced performances I have ever seen . . . the playing of a Moor by a Negro actor has given [blacks] hope that race prejudice is not as insurmountable an obstacle as it sometimes appears to be." For White, the 1942 production of *Othello* not only had desegregated the theater but, as importantly, had placed a black body in the position of a noble leader, capable and deserving of affection from anyone, including the white Desdemona.[3]

In the national edition of the *Chicago Defender, Ebony*'s editor, a white man named Ben Burns, similarly praised Robeson's performance as a civil rights victory that would herald a new dawn of race relations in America. "History is being written by the great Paul Robeson these nights. . . . It is more than theatrical history. It is epoch-making, precedent-shattering American history that is a happy omen of a new world acomin' in the U.S. race relations."[4]

The critics' reception illustrates how the play's use of Robeson and its subject-interracial intimacy-served as a place of convergence for foreign policy matters and domestic civil rights activities. The play emerged during a moment when interracial intimacy was thought to have a favorable impact on black, domestic, and international politics. Hence, even as a majority of states legally prohibited interracial marriage and during a moment when interracial romances were seen as dangerous throughout the nation, critics and audiences made *Othello* the most popular play in Broadway history up to that point. Interracial romances were safe onstage—especially if they ended in tragedy—while interracial couples continued to have their intimacy regulated and scorned offstage. What are we to make of the favorable reception of Robeson's Othello alongside the public and legal prohibitions on interracial intimacy? Was Robeson's performance a civil rights victory? At the core of these questions lies the issue of whether interracial intimacy was considered a public act or a private matter.

This book argues that interracial intimacy, during the period marked by the end of World War II and the 1954 *Brown v. Board of Education* decision, sparked an important debate over the relationship of intimate matters to civil rights activism in the public sphere. In framing interracial romance and sexuality as matters of private choice and not as rights to be demanded in the public sphere, mainstream American culture limited the kind of political transformation interracial intimacy could engender. At the same time, civil rights leaders and activists struggled to move the presumably private matter of intimacy into the realm of the public sphere and, in so doing, threatened to expose previously obscured layers of racism in American society.

Disagreements over the meaning of interracial intimacy and its relationship to civil rights demands shows how the public and private spheres were racialized in the years after World War II. At a time when postwar culture located the nuclear family within the private sphere, containing the radicalism of women, workers, and black people, interracial romances threatened to place sexuality within the public domain of rights discourse. Yet placing sexuality within the realm of rights challenged the dominant view that sexuality ought to be contained fully within the boundaries of the nuclear family. Interracial sexuality and marriage thus threatened to expose the very public and political discourses of the nuclear family—a discourse that lent financial and psychological support to white heterosexuals—at the very moment that exposing racism became a foreign and domestic policy problem. By looking at debates over interracial romance and sexuality in postwar court cases, popular culture, and black politics and culture, I argue that romantic racial border crossings threatened the postwar assumption that the nuclear family was a private sphere by turning the family into a public, race-defined, civil rights discourse. At the same time, however, postwar courts and popular culture attempted to contain the politically explosive matter of interracial romance and sexuality by directing matters involving interracial intimacy to the seemingly private realms of the family and romantic choice.

Taken as a whole, this study reveals the mobility of interracial intimacy between and within the spaces of postwar society. At stake in such mobile

politics was the meaning of civil rights and the appropriate spaces of desegregation. Although the contest over civil rights and race reform was not just
a discursive struggle over the meaning of interracial intimacy, such rhetorical debates over the implication of interracial intimacy shaped the possibilities for and responses to various forms of civil rights activities. Moreover,
my focus on legal, social-historical, and cultural instances of interracial intimacy suggests that one can only begin to comprehend the complex politics
of interracial intimacy by examining how it shaped multiple spheres of public and private life.

Interracial romance has always been politically explosive in the United
States. Yet the location of such politics in the public sphere has changed over
time. Among the first laws passed in the American colonies were those regulating interracial sexuality. In the period after the Civil War, attempts to
regulate interracial romance and sexuality inspired the creation of the Ku
Klux Klan and the related rise in public lynchings of black men in the early
twentieth century. At the outset of World War II, more than half of the states
had laws prohibiting interracial marriages between black and nonblack people. Underlying the politics of interracial marriage and romance has been
the assumption that racial categories, as Michael Omi and Howard Winant
argue in *Racial Formation in the United States: From the 1960s to the 1980s*,
are presumed to be fixed and immutable. Hence romantic crossings of the
color line have historically called into question the meaning of race itself.
Such relationships challenge the presumed incommensurability of white
and nonwhite bodies. Especially problematic to the system of race are the
mixed-race offspring of interracial sexual relations. Such bodies trouble the
presumed naturalness of racial difference and the presumption that white
bodies always reproduce whiteness.[5]

During the era of Robeson's performance, a number of political and intellectual transformations made interracial intimacy especially contentious.
The United States entered World War II under the pretense of fighting fascism and racism. This motive made racial discrimination embarrassing and,
for a time, potentially dangerous to an American foreign policy mission that
relied on framing the United States as a place of pluralist harmony. Adverse
race relations came under intense scrutiny during and after the war both by
civil rights activists and by foreign policy makers. As foreign policy makers
struggled to win over the minds, and ultimately markets, of the Third World,
they chose to juxtapose racial diversity and tolerance in the United States

with totalitarianism in the Soviet Union. Prohibitions on interracial intimacy threatened to undermine this foreign policy mission.[6]

Linking domestic race relations to foreign policy strategy required foreign policy makers to actively shape the story of American race relations for foreign audiences, making sure to stress the improvements in race relations made during the war. Part of this rhetorical feat required federal participation in efforts to improve race relations. Consequently, during the war foreign policy makers began to advocate and advertise civil rights reforms, such as the creation of the Fair Employment Practices Committee (FEPC)—a federal organization established to monitor and prevent employment discrimination in federal manufacturing jobs—as evidence that the government was actively challenging racism. Moreover, during the war black judges and lawyers were appointed to prominent positions in the Departments of State and War. Further, foreign policy makers could cite the bravery of black, Asian, American Indian, and Mexican American soldiers who fought to protect American ideals during the war as evidence of smooth race relations at home.

After World War II, as the cold war began to simmer, civil rights became more central to foreign policy concerns. The United States desegregated its armed forces amid intense criticism from the radical leader of the Brotherhood of Sleeping Car Porters, A. Philip Randolph, and black soldiers who had fought in the war. Moreover, the federal government took an active role in postwar Supreme Court cases that held the potential to make public to international audiences American racial attitudes. In 1954, for example, the federal government filed a brief encouraging Supreme Court justices to overturn *Plessy v. Ferguson* in its *Brown* decision. Mary L. Dudziak shows that the international context of the postwar era made the *Brown* decision potentially explosive because the whole world was watching the outcome. In its amicus brief supporting the claims for desegregation, the United States argued that racial discrimination threatened the image of the nation abroad:

> *The existence of discrimination against minority groups in the United States has an adverse effect upon our relations with other countries. Racial discrimination furnishes grist for the Communist propaganda mills, and it raises doubts even among friendly nations as to the intensity of our devotion to the democratic faith. . . . During the past six years, the damage to our foreign relations attributable to [race discrimination] has become progressively greater. The United States is under constant attack in the foreign press, over the foreign radio, and in such international*

bodies as the United Nations because of various practices of discrimination against minority groups in this country. As might be expected, Soviet spokesmen regularly exploit this situation in propaganda against the United States, both within the United Nations and through radio broadcasts and the press, which reaches all corners of the world. Some of these attacks against us are based on falsehood or distortion; but the undeniable existence of racial discrimination gives unfriendly governments the most effective kind of ammunition for their propaganda.[7]

If international awareness of racial discrimination in the United States threatened American foreign policy makers, so, too, did the growing radicalism of black civil rights groups. The civil rights politics of the NAACP and black leaders like A. Philip Randolph and W. E. B. Du Bois were equally influential in shaping the new federal commitment to civil rights reform. During the war, black civil rights leaders focused on the right to work without discrimination and to serve in the armed forces. The rhetoric of World War II made available to black civil rights leaders new leverage within the federal government. As soldiers and as workers, black people were needed by a nation that had historically treated blacks as less than human.

The postwar years signaled a transformation for black politics. While the nation would still rely on black labor and soldiers, the end of the war invited a period of retrenchment, when leaders in the federal government would sort out the implications of wartime labor and civil rights activism. Furthermore, as the United States became engaged in a cold war with the Soviet Union, racism became a national issue, threatening to undermine U.S. prestige abroad. Hence, although federal leaders would attempt to contain the gains made by black activism during the war, they would, as Dudziak shows, similarly attempt to create limited civil rights reforms that would solve the problem of racial violence that was broadcast to American allies and enemies abroad.

The context of World War II made available to many black people a new kind of politics centered on bodily closeness with whites. As a result of interracial workplaces and European and Asian battlefields, interracial romantic and sexual relations developed that threatened to undermine the racial order in the United States. The postwar years, then, brought the black struggle for desegregation but also a different kind of battle over the right to be intimate across the color line. This less-publicized struggle was potentially explosive, threatening to alter race relations and to challenge affiliations within black communities. The fight for black civil rights after the war raised potentially debilitating questions about the role of interracial intimacy in desegregation struggles. At the heart of the matter was whether marriage was fundamentally a private choice or a public institution. And if marriage was primarily a public contract, then should it be considered part of the fight for desegregation?

As cultural arguments about the meaning of race replaced older scientifically based understandings of race, American society increasingly transformed its presumption that racial categories were biologically fixed. In so doing, Americans, according to Omi and Winant, began to view race as a cultural identity that functioned similar to ethnicity. One consequence of such an ideological shift was the consensus within many 1940s and 1950s courts that pre–World War II biological arguments about racial superiority were outdated and disproved. Even more radically, many postwar courts and ordinary Americans argued that older biological arguments about racial difference and superiority were un-American.

Although the war beckoned a new era of race relations in the United States, the matter of interracial sexuality remained taboo, and federal attempts to improve race relations did not extend to the realm of marriage. The exclusion of interracial intimacy from the realm of civil rights discourse after the war illustrates what Peggy Pascoe has called "modernist racial ideology." Pascoe argues that since the 1920s, cultural anthropologists influenced dominant race thinking in ways that linked ending racism to a "deliberate non-recognition of race." Cultural anthropologists were brought into antimiscegenation cases to undermine the scientific racial argument that shaped race thinking up to that time. Citing social scientific studies that showed that race was cultural, and not biologically fixed, anthropologists eventually convinced judges that the legal basis for antimiscegenation laws—that is, the scientific racial argument that racial bodies were biologically different—was a fiction. By the 1960s, argues Pascoe, the Supreme Court

concluded that ending white supremacy required abandoning [racial] categories. In de-emphasizing racial categories, they joined mainstream mid-twentieth-century social scientists that [sic] argued that because culture, rather than race, shaped meaningful human difference, race was nothing more than a subdivision of the broader phenomenon of ethnicity. In a society newly determined to be "color-blind," granting public recognition to racial categories seemed to be synonymous with racism itself.[8]

The nonrecognition of race was a way for courts to ignore the matter of antimiscegenation laws, and it was also a way to allow for multiple forms of racially based federal programs that privileged whites. As George Lipsitz has argued, postwar housing and bank lending policies invested material and cultural capital in white opportunities at the expense of people of color. Further, Lipsitz argues that the postwar housing boom created suburban social spaces that helped white ethnic groups reduce their ethnic differences and assimilate into a white identity. Federally sanctioned housing discrimination and racial covenants ensured that the suburbs would be a place for white assimilation and black exclusion. Yet policies that allowed the entrenchment of whiteness could exist alongside a federal commitment to the rhetoric of color blindness. Looking at legal and cultural representations of interracial intimacy reveals how terms like "pluralism" or "diversity"—much like "color blindness"—could operate in tandem with prohibitions on interracial romance and sexuality.[9]

In the same year that the Supreme Court overturned *Plessy v. Ferguson*, thereby affirming the color blindness of the Constitution, it refused to decide a case concerning a state antimiscegenation law. The Court was concerned about the potential backlash it would face had it found an antimiscegenation law unconstitutional. In the ten-year period prior to the *Brown* decision, only one state antimiscegenation law was found unconstitutional; after *Brown*, the Court waited thirteen years to hear another miscegenation case, when it overturned Virginia's antimiscegenation law in the 1967 *Loving v. Virginia* decision. The reluctance of courts to hear antimiscegenation cases suggests that interracial sex, marriage, and romance were the sites at which one could find the limits of the new postwar racial politics. While Robeson's Othello contributed to a body of evidence that foreign policy makers used to wage their arguments about America's tolerance for racial diversity, this use of interracial intimacy obscured deeply held desires in American society to prevent racial border crossing by carefully delineating what issues could enter the public-sphere debates over civil rights. In many cases, interracial intimacy was excluded from the public sphere altogether.

Historians usually date the beginning of the modern civil rights movement to the mid-1950s, with the landmark *Brown* decision often cited as the beginning of major civil rights reform. In looking at racial politics prior to *Brown*, this study examines racial, gender, and sexual politics during a time when these categories were not as solid as they would become after 1954. Moreover, my choice to focus on a relatively short period of time after the war is strategic, as it allows me to examine how the politics of race and sexuality shaped the strategies of civil rights activists after *Brown*. The period between the end of World War II and the 1954 *Brown* decision marks a liminal moment in race formation. During this moment, debates about the role of interracial intimacy in civil rights activism were central to black Americans' vision of full democratic inclusion. In this way, this book builds on recent historical studies, such as Renee Romano's *Race Mixing: Black-White Marriage in Postwar America* and Randall Kennedy's *Interracial Intimacies: Sex, Marriage, Identity, and Adoption*, by focusing on the historical and political dimensions of interracial intimacy after World War II. Romano's *Race Mixing* examines the changing social and political meanings of interracial intimacy during the second half of the twentieth century. By considering how interracial couples describe their experiences, Romano is able to show change over time in the ways Americans treat issues of interracial marriages. Although rates of interracial marriage are increasing, Romano cautions against viewing this increase as racial progress. Instead, Romano wants to show the ways that race continues to structure courtship and marriage rituals. Kennedy's *Interracial Intimacies* seeks to expand the discourse of interracial romance beyond the legal regulation of marriage to the social and cultural meaning of interracial adoptions and families. Like Romano, Kennedy documents the rise and fall of legal regulations on interracial intimacy. *Romance and Rights* adds a new wrinkle to these fine books by considering how understandings of public and private spheres shaped how Americans understood the relationship between interracial intimacy and civil rights. This focus allows us to see civil rights politics in a new light and to rethink what kind of politics interracial intimacy could engage.

In order to fully understand the implications of Robeson's performance and what it represented, we first must challenge one of the main assumptions guiding historical studies of gender and sexuality in the postwar era. Scholars of the post–World War II decade have generally understood this era in terms of ideological containment. This scholarship appropriately locates the ways that corporate liberalism and the international imperatives of the cold war effectively moved political activism from the public sphere to the private sphere of the home and the nuclear family. This framework reveals how the nuclear family and its assumptions about men's and women's roles served to assuage fears of the atomic age and of Communist "others." While this concept has allowed us to understand how ideas about men's and women's roles were in part determined by national and international politics, it has largely overlooked what the nuclear family imperative meant for people of color. Although the "domestic imperative" was an attempt to undermine the political efficacy of women and workers in the public sphere, it allowed for a level of privacy that was unavailable to people of color. The privacy accorded to the nuclear family was thus a privilege most fully realized by white heterosexual couples. The sexuality of gays and lesbians and people of color was generally forced into a public sphere in which all sorts of public policies could regulate and prohibit that which was protected–though contained— for white heterosexuals. The framework of "containment culture" and its attendant "domestic imperative" reveals very little about how antimiscegenation laws regulated the presumably "private" behaviors of people of color.

The relationship of Robeson's performance in an interracial play to the public-sphere matter of civil rights requires that we complicate containment frameworks by focusing on public and private spheres, both of which, I contend, are always operative in determining rights. For example, southern lawyers and judges who sought to undermine and contain the explosive potential of interracial sexuality argued that the legal regulation of interracial marriage ought to be determined by the state and not by the federal government. This antifederalist argument posited the state as the most appropriate public for the regulation of sexual matters. In this instance, the "public" refers to a belief about sovereignty and jurisdiction—in this case, the state's right to regulate "its" social relationships. As southern states attempted to defend their right to regulate marriage and sexual relations within their states, they attempted to define interracial sexuality—or miscegenation—as a regional matter, best regulated by local courts and state courts, not by the federal government. Hence, while some antimiscegenation laws were overturned after the war, a legal consensus developed that interracial marriage would not fall under civil rights reforms; it was therefore excluded from the public sphere.

While postwar courts attempted to contain the civil rights implications of antimiscegenation laws by consigning interracial intimacy to the local/ regional sphere, postwar culture attempted to confine the explosive potential of crossing the color line by discursively containing interracial intimacy to the domestic sphere of the family. In this case, the space of domesticity— although highly politicized—was defined outside the public sphere in which civil rights debates took place. By looking at postwar comic books and movies, we can see how the political implications of interracial sexuality were limited through narrative techniques that turned such relationships into family melodramas and made interracial romance a matter of private choice rather than public politics.

While mainstream popular culture and law contained the possibilities of interracial intimacy to the state or to the nuclear family, black magazines and newspapers publicized and celebrated interracial intimacy in an effort to make interracial sexuality a public-sphere matter. Debates within black communities over the relationship of interracial intimacy to civil rights activism were implicitly discussions of the meaning of "public." When, for example, the nation's black press decided to advertise and celebrate cases of interracial romances and marriage, these editors were attempting to introduce sexual and racial matters into a public realm denied by postwar courts and culture. The reason for this has to do with the context of civil rights and the creation of a new black public sphere represented by John Johnson's black magazine empire. Johnson's *Ebony, Jet, Tan Confessions*, and *Negro Digest* were integral to black public-sphere politics after World War II. These magazines regularly featured stories about interracial intimacy that revealed tensions over whether such matters were primarily public or private matters.

Perhaps the most public form of interracial intimacy involved black soldiers' conflation of civil rights activism and the struggle to have their interracial romances and marriages to European brides acknowledged and respected. The U.S. Department of War and the NAACP debated the appropriate spheres of interracial desire that shaped the European and Asian theaters of operation in ways that suggest the importance of locating the public sphere at the center of this story.

Making interracial intimacy a public-sphere issue was also fraught with limits, however, for such an effort relied on notions of "appropriate" interracial intimacy. A comparative analysis of black responses to black/white intimacy and black/Asian intimacy shows that only some forms of interracial intimacy, and only some idealized types of womanhood, could enter the politics of black interracial romance and marriage. Furthermore, writers such as William Gardner Smith, Ann Petry, and Chester Himes attempted to obscure the boundaries between the public and private spheres as a means to reveal the material consequences of interracial intimacy and as a way to challenge the limited discourse of racial belonging that structured black understandings of interracial intimacy. These writers made the politics of interracial intimacy central to their fiction in order to expose the contradictions inherent in making the politics of interracial intimacy public-sphere matters.

Throughout the book, I use the term "interracial intimacy" to signify practices and representations of interracial sex, marriage, and romance. In grouping together these cultural, social, and personal practices, I do not mean to ignore the ways that they are different. Although interracial intimacy signifies a wide array of social and cultural practices, I want to place these practices in dialogue and suggest that each gained meaning from the other. A study of interracial romance, sex, and marriage, however, must tread carefully around the very categories it employs. I do not want to reify race itself by labeling some relationships "interracial," thereby naturalizing the very categories I hope to complicate. I have tried to be sensitive to the fact that race is an ideology and not a biological fact; hence interracial intimacy is also a social construct that names a kind of relationship between racially marked bodies. It was Othello (Robeson) and Desdemona's (Hagen) romance, after all, that raised concern, not the actual marriage between the white Uta Hagen and the Puerto Rican American José Ferrer. The former relationship was called interracial, while the latter was not, suggesting that the term "interracial" is itself an ideological construct.

While interracial intimacy describes relationships between people who are marked as racially different, most of this study focuses on black/white interracial marriage and romance. I have struggled to understand race by moving beyond the black/white binary. Nonetheless, my sources continually brought me back to black/white relationships. Every antimiscegenation law targeted black/white couples, although many western states also constructed prohibitions on who Asians—and in some states, Native Americans—could marry as well. Moreover, I do not want to imply that Mexican Americans' absence from antimiscegenation statutes means that Mexican American/white interracial intimacy was not a powerful social taboo in many places. One only needs to study the Zoot Suit Riots that erupted in Los Angeles during World War II to recognize white fears of Mexican American male sexuality. Yet in one of the most important postwar antimiscegenation cases, a Mexican American woman named Andrea Perez was legally categorized as white. This shows the complexities of Mexican American racial formation—especially in California after World War II—and illustrates the reliance of antimiscegenation laws on white bodies. Without exception, the kind of interracial intimacy that most concerned policy makers, the NAACP, and cultural workers after the war involved white bodies. Hence, while I do not limit the definition of interracial intimacy to white/black relationships, much of the study engages black/white racial categories.[10]

During the production of *Othello*, Robeson and his married costar, Uta Hagen, began an illicit affair. While it is remarkable that such a "real" affair would mirror the "represented" affair in the play, it is also interesting to wonder how the adulterous affair between Robeson and Hagen would be received by an audience all too eager to make the play represent racial progress and uplift. Although this question cannot be fully answered, my task in *Romance and Rights* is to begin to lay out the complexities of such relationships and to suggest that the publicly performed romance of *Othello* cannot be easily divorced from the "private" affair that took place backstage.

Romance and Rights

Chapter 1

Legislating Love

Antimiscegenation Law and the Regulation of Intimacy

W HEN CRITICS AND AUDIENCES celebrated Paul Robeson's performance in the 1942 production of *Othello* as a civil rights achievement,
they rearticulated the meaning of interracial intimacy in American society.
Robeson's casting in the role of Othello, in addition to the play's interracial
romantic plot, moved the matter of interracial intimacy into public view
and potentially into the realm of civil rights. In order to understand the significance of this performance and its location within the public sphere, we
must first examine how the politics of interracial intimacy developed in the
United States. From 1661 to 1967, U.S. citizens in certain states were subject
to laws regulating their intimacy and marriage choices on the basis of race.
Antimiscegenation legislation was among the first type of laws passed in the
newly formed colonies.[1] Not until the Supreme Court found Virginia's antimiscegenation law unconstitutional in its 1967 *Loving v. Virginia* decision
were interracial heterosexual couples free to marry in every state. Although
antimiscegenation laws have been a staple of U.S. history, the uses, intentions, and outcomes of such laws have varied based on local circumstances,
historical contexts, and political situations. At times, antimiscegenation laws
were deployed to regulate social relations between black slaves and white
servants. At other times, the same antimiscegenation laws were used to
determine the status of grandchildren descended from interracial grandparents. Hence one must analyze the legislation of interracial intimacy cau-
tiously, making sure not to reify only one underlying cause of its origins.

What is most important for our purposes are the ways that, historically,
the regulation of interracial sexuality has signified competing notions of

publicness. First, the creation of antimiscegenation laws in the seventeenth century signified the earliest attempt to limit the privileges of privacy to certain forms of sexuality. Yet having defined interracial sexuality as a public-sphere concern, lawmakers and judges have not agreed about which public sphere ought to have the sovereign right to regulate interracial intimacy. As I will discuss below, prior to the Civil War interracial sexuality was treated as a local, regional relationship that could, in a sense, be protected as a private relationship. Local courts, and not the state, would regulate intimate relations. As a result, although there existed state laws regulating interracial intimacy, such laws were sporadically enforced and only entered local public-sphere politics when interracial sexuality affected property relations. Even though interracial intimacy among slaves and mulattoes were especially vexing to the antebellum South, the legal regulation of interracial intimacy remained a local concern.

After the Civil War, however, interracial sexuality was no longer treated as a local matter that could be tolerated and largely ignored by political entities. Former slave-owners made the politics of interracial intimacy central to their claim that the North had victimized the South. Such a claim moved the regulation of interracial intimacy into a larger public sphere, from local community to region. Interracial intimacy became part of national politics after the Civil War because of the ways that the South framed its conflict with the North in terms of its fear of racial amalgamation. Interracial intimacy was at the crux of national remembrance of the Civil War through the 1930s. Furthermore, increasing immigration and urbanization at the turn of the century led to new strategies of sexual regulation that further publicized intimate matters.

During the 1940s, the regulation of interracial sexuality once again signified tensions over competing definitions of the public sphere, as southern states argued that federal civil rights legislation ought not influence their right to regulate marriage relations. The modern civil rights movement made the politics of interracial intimacy a national issue. Southern courts thus attempted to contain matters of sexuality and race as local relationships, rather than state or national ones. Such spatial arguments allowed the states to maintain a level of sovereignty at a time when the federal government was increasing its power over the nation.

This chapter traces the history of antimiscegenation legislation in order to show how competing definitions of publicness shaped the politics of interracial intimacy. After World War II, the need to make race reform public—because of international concerns and because of the civil rights movement—came into conflict with American society's attempt to contain the political implications of interracial intimacy. For southern states, asserting state sovereignty was an attempt to limit how the politics of interracial sexuality would be treated as a public-sphere issue. Yet even as southern states and the federal government argued over the appropriate jurisdiction for regulating interracial intimacy, they ultimately agreed that marriage and sexuality, regardless of where they were regulated, were not civil rights issues.[2]

As early as 1661 the Maryland colony enacted the first law in British North America to regulate interracial sexuality. This law was created to manage relations between white servants and black slaves. Historians have argued that there was little distinction between the status of white indentured servants and black slaves in the early colonial era.[3] Colonial officials were concerned over how to regulate the status of white women who sought to marry black slaves. The preamble of the legislation began,

> *And forasmuch as divers freeborn English women, forgetful of their free condition, and to the disgrace of our nation, do intermarry with Negro slaves, by which also divers suits may arise, touching the issue of such women, and a great damage doth befall the master of such Negroes, for preservation whereof for deterring such free-born women from such shameful matches, be it enacted: That whatsoever free-born women shall intermarry with any slave, from and after the last day of the present assembly, shall serve the master of such slave during the life of her husband; and that all the issues of such free-born women, so married, shall be slaves as their father were. . . . And be it further enacted: That all the issues of English, or other free-born women that have already married Negroes, shall serve the master of their parents, till they be thirty years of age and no longer.*[4]

This legislation was intended to solve a problem for slave-owners; namely, what to do with slaves who were married to freeborn white women. The law enslaved white women who married a slave for the life of her husband, thus increasing the property holdings of the master. Moreover, the law enslaved "all the issues of such free-born women"—that is, the mixed-race children of interracial unions.

The Maryland legislation confounds many contemporary assumptions about antimiscegenation law. First, the legislation suggests that in the early colonial era, free white women, already disempowered and disenfranchised, could be made slaves, thus undermining the association between race and status. Even more telling is the absence in the legislation of condemnation for interracial sex itself. In fact, shortly after passage of the Maryland statute, colonial lawmakers revised the legislation when they learned that many slave-owners, in the wake of the 1661 law, actively encouraged their slaves to marry white female servants because such relationships increased the owner's property. Hence in 1681 the Maryland statute was revised to exclude from punishment any white women who married a black slave under the supervision or encouragement of the slave's master. What seemed most abhorrent to Maryland legislators was the falling status of free white women, not their sexual choices. Thus, while antimiscegenation legislation would become a tool to protect notions of racial purity, the earliest law was not about interracial sex, nor was it about racial purity; it was about slavery and property. Equally important here is how the matter of interracial sex could be viewed as a private, local matter, only entering the public sphere when questions of property arose. Despite the existence of colonial laws regulating interracial sex, the matter of interracial sexuality could be viewed as a private matter so long as such relationships did not confuse property or patriarchal relationships.

The historian Martha Hodes argues that even as laws like Maryland's were passed throughout the American colonies and in the early republic prior to the Civil War, American society largely tolerated interracial romances and marriages between black men and white women. For example, as Hodes notes, when "Irish Nell," the governor of Maryland's servant, married a slave named Charles Butler, the governor and many other whites—though with considerable disdain—attended the wedding and offered their best wishes to the newlyweds. Nell's choice led to her enslavement and to the enslavement of her and Charles's children. Although Maryland society seemed surprised that Nell would degrade her status by marrying a slave, Hodes argues that it tolerated the marriage and was not dismayed by the possibility of interracial sexuality.

It would be nearly a century later that Irish Nell's interracial marriage became a legal problem. In 1787 Nell and Charles's grandchildren petitioned a court to win their freedom. The Butler descendants claimed that because their mother was white, they ought not be enslaved. In the mid-eighteenth century, status had been clearly attached to color; hence the Maryland law enslaving white wives of black slaves seemed antiquated and contradictory. Consequently, although the Maryland law clearly enslaved Irish Nell and contemporary law stipulated that children follow the status of their mother, eighteenth-century contemporaries were unwilling to admit that a white woman could be enslaved. The Butler grandchildren were therefore emancipated despite the fact that their parents and grandparents were legally slaves.

What had changed from the time of Nell and Charles's marriage to the late-eighteenth-century case of the Butler children was that color had been firmly associated with status. If Nell and Charles could be regarded equally as slaves in the mid-seventeenth century, this would not exist for long because as slavery took hold in colonial America, color became the dividing line between free and slave. Furthermore, Nell's case became an issue because of the ways antebellum society made white women's sexual practices public issues, while offering the safe haven of privacy to white male slave-owners, many of whom were regularly involved in illicit and often violent interracial sexual relations with black women.

Prior to the Civil War, antimiscegenation laws were common, yet they were deployed infrequently to address matters usually outside the nexus of interracial marriage. For example, antimiscegenation laws were frequently deployed to regulate inheritance and divorce proceedings. Children of illegal interracial marriages became legal bastards without the right to inherit their parents' wealth. During divorce proceedings, antimiscegenation laws were used to annul marriages and to undermine black claims for property and wealth earned during a marriage. Moreover, in making the regulation of interracial intimacy a local matter, Southern society was able to hide the regular sexual abuse of black women by white slave-owners.

Toward the end of the Civil War and throughout the period of Reconstruction, interracial sex moved from a local to a national matter. Throughout the 1860s, whites' fears of black political power were often framed in terms of fears of interracial sexuality. For example, in the election of 1864, Southern politicians sought to represent the Republican Party as comprised of politicians who, if elected, would facilitate the ability of freed blacks to engage in interracial sexual relations with white women. A political hoax, hatched to undermine the political power of Northern Republicans, coined the term "miscegenation" to describe black-white sexuality as "mixing genes."[5]

In the election of 1864, Democrats knew that Abraham Lincoln, the Republican nominee running for reelection, would win the presidency.

Two editors of the Democratic-run *New York Globe* developed a political strategy to force Republican views—as they constructed them—about interracial romance and civil rights into the open. In a pamphlet called *Miscegenation: The Theory of the Blending of the Races, Applied to the American White Man and Negro*, the anonymous authors advanced a theory, based on pseudoscientific facts, that an improved race of people could be developed through the intermixture of black and white genes. The authors combined the Latin word "*misce*" (to mix) with "*genus*" (genes) to coin the word "miscegenation." They argued that it was a fact "well established in history" that "the miscegenetic or mixed races are much superior, mentally, physically, and orally to those of pure or unmixed."[6]

The pamphleteers, posing as Republicans, claimed that the Civil War was about human progress, best achieved through interracial intimacy.

> *It is idle to maintain that this present war is not a war for the Negro . . . it is a war, if you please, of amalgamation . . . a war looking, as its final fruit, to the blending of the white and black. . . . Let the war go on. . . . Until church, and state, and society recognize not only the propriety but the necessity of the fusion of the white and black—in short, until the great truth shall be declared in our public documents and announced in the messages of our Presidents, that it is desirable the white man should marry the black woman and the white woman the black man.[7]*

The authors sent *Miscegenation* to a number of abolitionists for comment. After receiving comments that were, according to Sydney Kaplan, "admiration tempered with cautious enthusiasm both for the substance of the pamphlet and for the timeliness of its publication," the authors began to circulate their pamphlet in England. The pamphlet ultimately made its way to Democratic editors in the United States, who readily blamed Republicans and abolitionists for writing it.[8]

Although Democrats were not able to use the miscegenation issue to derail Lincoln's reelection, they planted the seeds of an argument that would be common after the Civil War and beyond—that black freedom threatened white women and, by extension, white men's ability to control white women and black men. Moreover, the hoax made Republicans cautious about advocating black civil rights. The miscegenation issue in the election of 1864 had started a troubling precedent of undermining black civil rights by invoking the fear of the rape of white women by black men. Interracial intimacy came to signify not just a threat to white womanhood and the purity attached to white femininity but also a threat to the patriarchal system through which men controlled female and black bodies. Interracial intimacy had moved from a local, private matter to the public sphere of national politics.

State antimiscegenation laws that prior to the Civil War were invoked sporadically were followed religiously after the Reconstruction era.[9] Moreover, concurrent with a renewed interest in using antimiscegenation laws, the post-Reconstruction rise of Jim Crow legislation led to changes in the criteria of who could be legally called "white."[10] Most telling in this regard are the changing definitions and blood quantum used to define the category "mulatto" in Virginia. In 1705 the colony deemed "mulatto" any person containing any "Negro" blood. In 1785, after a couple of generations of interracial sexuality, Virginia changed the legal definition of "mulatto" to those with "one-fourth part or more of Negro blood." As A. Leon Higginbotham and Barbara Kopytoff remark, "Thus, by implication, those of one-eighth Negro ancestry (one Negro great-grandparent), who by the 1705 statute had been mulattoes, were now legally white."[11] The 1785 definition created a wider definition of whiteness than the definition developed in 1705. As James Hugo Johnson has argued, "It would appear that the lawmakers of the early national period feared that a declaration to the effect that the possession of any Negro ancestry, however, remote, made a man a mulatto might bring embarrassment to certain supposedly white citizens."[12] This would be the only time that Virginia loosened its definition of whiteness. In 1910 one had to have less than one-sixteenth "Negro blood" in order to be classified as white. In 1924 any "Negro blood" precluded entrance into the white race.[13] As racial categories became more fixed, interracial sexuality posed even larger problems for questions of property because such relationships threatened to further blur racial, and hence political, boundaries.

During the early twentieth century, interracial sexuality was at the forefront of the national debate over the collective memory of the Civil War and the public debate about how to deal with southern and eastern European immigrants. In 1915 the young filmmaker D. W. Griffith produced his wildly popular silent film *The Birth of a Nation*. The film was based on southern novelist Thomas Dixon's *The Clansman: An Historical Romance of the Ku Klux Klan* (1905), which romanticized the growth of the Klan. In Dixon's historical romance, the Klan was framed as a civic organization that saved the Union from the ineptitude and violence of black politicians, newly enfranchised during Reconstruction. Dixon was a southern politician, a Baptist minister, and a staunch white supremacist. Griffith, whose grandfather had served in the Confederate army during the Civil War, was an obvious choice to represent Dixon's novel. Moreover, Griffith was the nation's most innovative filmmaker; he used new technology to represent black sexuality in especially damaging ways.[14]

The Birth of a Nation represents the Civil War as a war of Northern aggression against the communities, and especially the white women, of the South. Griffith suggests that a few carpetbagger Republicans forced the Civil War on the nation. In the process, Griffith's film suggests, the South's peaceful institutions were disrupted and ultimately destroyed. The greatest violence of the Civil War, however, was not the war itself but the Reconstruction era that followed the war. In Griffith's representation, Reconstruction placed lust-driven free blacks in power in the South. Sylas Lynch, the mulatto "leader of the blacks" during the Reconstruction era, is consumed by sexual urges. Griffith used new film techniques to juxtapose Lynch's demonic gaze with the purity and aloofness of Southern white women. In so doing, he successfully equated the politics of remembrance with the fear of interracial sex.

Griffith's mastery over his medium allowed him to represent history through a complex love story between Elsie Stoneman, the daughter of a Northern carpetbagger, and Colonel Ben Cameron, a Southern Confederate. Although the story is often recounted, we should focus on how the romance cemented interracial intimacy as a public-sphere matter. The young couple overcomes their parents' ideological differences and finds romance, thus symbolizing the impending reunification of North and South. Yet this reunion depends on casting black bodies outside of the public sphere. The climax of *Birth of a Nation* is when Sylas Lynch turns his gaze toward Elsie. Griffith represents Lynch's lust as a threat not only to Southern male patriarchy but also to Northerners' ability to control their daughters and to the Republic itself. Lynch and his black followers ultimately corrupt the political system in the South at the very moment that Lynch attacks Elsie. For a brief moment, the freedmen have political control over the institutions of the South; but it is the fear of their control over white female bodies that causes Northern and Southern white men to unite in opposition to Reconstruction. Stoneman's father, the Northern general leading the Reconstruction effort in the South, ultimately realizes the futility of black freedom, and he hopes for an organization that can challenge the predatory sexuality of his protégé, Silas Lynch.[15]

Meanwhile, *Birth of a Nation* shows that the only organization capable of saving the nation is the Ku Klux Klan. Organized by dispossessed Southerners, the Klan is cast in the film as saviors. The Klan organizes primarily to save white femininity from black masculinity. The film concludes with the Klan's victory and the reunion of Elsie Stoneman and Ben Cameron. The "birth of the nation," it would seem, meant a complex wedding between whiteness and patriarchy; the nation was saved because white men were able to reassert power over black men and white women.

In the decade after *Birth of a Nation* disgraced the silver screen, interracial sex was becoming a more common occurrence in northern urban cities. According to historian Kevin Mumford, the migration of black workers to burgeoning urban centers during the First World War, concurrent with the growth of social-reform organizing, created social spaces in which there were opportunities for consensual interracial intimacy. As Progressive Era reformers created discrete vice districts as places of prostitution and other illicit activities, some white and black couples found a modicum of privacy in these public places. Although some new black migrants could find work only as prostitutes in the newly created northern vice districts, other black workers created an urban milieu in which white and black often interacted socially and intimately. As a consequence, interracial sex moved into the public sphere in the North.[16]

In Harlem, the renaissance of artistic productions made that space a site of interracial desire. Mumford argues that many white New Yorkers indulged in Harlem's jazz clubs, speakeasies, and house parties. Often white participants in Harlem's nightlife reinscribed the color line within Harlem. For example, the famed Cotton Club became a space of black performance solely for the entertainment of white clientele. Moreover, white participation in 1920s Harlem was often understood as "slumming." The logic of slumming meant that white participants in interracial social activities were only indulging in certain forbidden pleasures. Yet even as slummers admitted to desiring the taboo, they nevertheless maintained their commitment to a social order that made black bodies different, aberrant, and devious. In other words, slumming allowed whites to indulge their desires without extending political rights to blacks.[17]

Places like Harlem and Chicago afforded blacks the opportunity to participate in interracial relationships. It would be a mistake to consign these interracial spaces, or "interzones" as Mumford terms them, as only places of white racism, for in these spaces black migrant workers controlled, for a while, their economic destiny. White participation in black communities during the 1920s created wealth for black businesspeople, including night-club owners, musicians, writers, and artists.[18]

The interracial vice districts created by Progressive Era reforms and by black migrants to the urban North underlines the paradox of interracial intimacy during the 1920s; at the very moment that black/white sexuality became a northern vogue, it was being cast as threatening to the nation on screen. This paradox, containing desire and revulsion over black sexuality, constitutes a central theme of interracial intimacy throughout American history. During the 1920s, Americans simultaneously engaged in new inter-racial practices while the birth of America's largest mass-mediated art, the movie, was based on a film that cast black/white sexuality as deviant and suicidal to whites. The public sphere thus offered possibilities even as the publicness of interracial intimacy caused panic and intense police efforts to contain it.

One way in which the new publicness of interracial sex was contained was through political campaigns centered on the fear of "white slavery," the term given to the abduction of young white women for illicit sexuality or prosti-tution. Historians argue that the "white slavery" hysteria was inspired partly by the growing number of rural migrants to urban cities during the 1920s and the conflation of urban space with blackness. Some young white women resorted to prostitution as a means to support themselves in a harsh urban milieu. Sometimes these white prostitutes based their operations in the inter-racial vice districts described by Mumford. The "white slavery" crusade emerged as a discourse to redeem young rural white females caught up in sex work in urban cities; white prostitutes were made slaves, they did not consent to their status. Yet the term "white slavery" is unmistakably racialized, evok-ing the fall of white females into black slavery. And indeed "white slavery" reformers often targeted black men as the "masters" of "white slaves," thereby excluding from their reform efforts the plight of black women, who remained vulnerable to sexual violence.[19]

One such accused "master" was the black prizefighter Jack Johnson, who bragged about his ability to conquer white foes. He flaunted his masculine prowess to such an extent that he openly touted his ability to attract white women. Whites were threatened by Johnson's seemingly unrestrained mas-culinity; they focused their concern on the attempt to find a white boxer to de-throne Johnson and on their disdain for Johnson's interracial romances. Using legislation inspired to prevent "white slavery," authorities went after Johnson. Representative James Mann authored the White Slave Traffic Act in 1910, a law that regulated the transportation of women across state lines for the purpose of sex work. Using the Mann Act, federal authorities prosecuted Johnson for his relationship with a white Chicago prostitute named Belle Schreiber, although the prosecution was inspired by Johnson's marriage to Lucille Cameron, another white woman.[20]

Moving interracial sexuality from the regional realm of local communities to the larger public realm of national politics allowed whites to discursively regulate black bodies in public through legal and representational strategies. Yet such a shift also threatened to expand the sphere of civil rights. World War II signified the moment when civil rights leaders marshaled the power to make demands for civil rights in the public sphere. At the moment that such demands were made, American society responded by attempting to return interracial sex to the private sphere of antebellum days, a time when interracial intimacy was not a national issue.

World War II fundamentally changed racial formations in the United States and in so doing made interracial intimacy especially charged. First, American entry into the war was framed in terms of a fight against totalitarian regimes in Japan and Germany and as a struggle for democracy and against racism. These motives made practices of racial discrimination on the home front contradictory. Moreover, black activists from labor unions and the NAACP exploited the contradictions in war rhetoric and practices of racism. Black leaders such as W. E. B. Du Bois, Walter White, and A. Philip Randolph struggled to ensure that wartime patriotism would not overshadow the struggle for racial justice; indeed, the war made calls for racial justice more powerful because the audience for these demands was international. As Mary Dudziak has argued, black leaders voiced their protest to international audiences, knowing that within the United States the leaders of the war effort needed to present an image of the United States as antiracist and democratic. Black leaders had new leverage during the war to make their protests heard, and the federal government responded by allowing increasing numbers of blacks to enlist in the armed forces and by passing legislation to monitor employment discrimination at home.[21]

Some black leaders cautioned their communities to avoid getting swept up in the patriotic fervor of the war and insisted that participation in the war effort should not deter the struggle for racial justice at home. A. Philip Randolph wrote an article in *Survey Graphic* during the early stages of the war in which he asked, "What's the difference between Hitler and that 'cracker' Talmadge of Georgia? Why has a man got to be Jim Crowed to die for democracy? If you haven't got democracy yourself, how can you carry it to somebody else?"[22] Walter White, the head of the NAACP, pushed blacks to critique the national rhetoric of wartime mobilization when he argued that "declarations of war do not lessen the obligation to preserve and extend civil liberties here while the fight is being made to restore freedom from dictatorship abroad."[23] In 1939 W. E. B. Du Bois wrote in the *Crisis*, "If Hitler wins, every single right we now possess, for which we have struggled for more than three centuries will be instantaneously wiped out by Hitler's triumph. If the Allies win, we shall at least have the right to continue fighting for a share of democracy for ourselves."[24]

In 1941 Randolph organized black working-class people to demand fairness in employment and in the selective service. Randolph threatened to organize a march on Washington that would expose practices of racial discrimination in the United States during a time when doing so would undermine the rhetoric of democracy that drove the war effort. Randolph sought to organize a march to demand equal employment. "To this end we propose that ten thousand Negroes march on Washington for jobs in national defense and equal integration in the fighting forces of the United States."[25]

The threat of a massive march on Washington, in addition to other civil rights activism, had profound implications for the federal government's management of the war. Fearing a mass movement for black civil rights, Congress passed the Selective Service and Training Act on September 16, 1940. The act committed the government to recruiting black soldiers and to expanding the number of black units. Additionally, Franklin Delano Roosevelt appointed the dean of Howard University's law school, William H. Hastie, as an aide on African American affairs to the secretary of war and promoted Benjamin O. Davis to brigadier general. Perhaps most important, the kind of protest that led to the March on Washington movement prompted Roosevelt to issue Executive Order 8802 on June 25, 1941. Roosevelt created the Committee on Fair Employment Practices "to receive and investigate complaints of discrimination in violation of the provision of this order [and] to take appropriate steps to redress grievances that it finds to be valid." Black activism had contributed to tangible changes in federal employment and to black opportunities in the military.[26]

Black leaders recognized the contradictions inherent in blacks' participation in the war, yet most argued that the war could make new opportunities available. Aware of the precarious relationship of blacks to the war effort, Robert L. Vann, the editor of the *Pittsburgh Courier*, spoke of the possibility of a "double victory," one against racism in Europe and the other against racism in the United States. The call for "double victory" suggests the unstable relationship of blacks to the nation during the war; at the same time that black GIs fought in the U.S. armed services, they were fighting against egregious forms of racism and segregation in the United States.[27]

Moreover, because of the wartime conditions, black workers were needed in unprecedented levels. Black migrants to the West Coast and Midwest found lucrative manufacturing jobs. Black workers, in addition to white women, were needed for the war effort, and the federal government actively recruited black men and women and white women to enter the workforce. Yet these new wartime workers brought their racial consciousness to the plant with them. In her study of the social relationships between black men and white women in wartime manufacturing plants, Eileen Boris found that white workers often protested against working next to black workers. Boris argues that white men and women attempted to use their racial privilege to distance themselves from their black coworkers. White workers and often their union leaders policed the spaces of manufacturing plants during the war to ensure that black and white bodies would not come too close. For example, union leaders terminated union social gatherings that involved dancing. And white female workers in one company protested to prohibit black women from using the same restroom facilities as white women. Even the toilet, Boris argues, became a site of social struggle.[28]

One aspect of the racialization of the World War II era was American society's attempt to undermine the very public and national issue of interracial intimacy at a time when the politics of interracial romance and marriage converged with the civil rights movement. Legal strategies that asserted the sovereignty of state governments and, alternatively, that marriage was a human and religious right moved the politics of interracial sex away from the sphere of federal civil rights. The rhetoric of the nuclear family was central here, for in containing all sexuality to the domestic—though highly politicized—realm of the private home, rights demands focused around interracial sex could be undermined. Attempts to contain the politics of interracial sexuality—even when advocated by opposing political entities—politically contained the scope of civil rights claims to nonintimate matters. In sum, while state and federal courts debated their sovereign right to oversee social relationships, they agreed that civil rights demands could not extend to the bedroom.

Miscegenation cases provide a crucial lens through which to examine the attempt to exclude the politics of interracial intimacy from the federal sphere of civil rights demands. Although local, state, and federal judges and lawyers vehemently debated and disagreed over the constitutionality of antimiscegenation laws during the 1940s and 1950s, all sides of this debate shared an assumption that interracial sexuality was a distinct political issue, outside the realm of federal civil rights. Some state courts argued that marriage was too important to be a federal matter, while others maintained that marriage was solely a local and regional relationship. The consensus surrounding the role of interracial marriage and sexuality in federal civil rights shaped the possibilities for civil rights demands.

The deployment of antimiscegenation legislation after 1940 was not certain in every interracial marriage case or in every place that had such a law. An interracial couple in Alabama might be prosecuted under an antimiscegenation law only if a child was produced as a result of their relationship or, more likely, if an adulterous interracial romance was discovered. Moreover, the justification for using antimiscegenation legislation differed depending on region and circumstance. Questions concerning wills and other property considerations were often decided by employing antimiscegenation legislation to determine the legitimacy of certain filial relations.

That antimiscegenation laws during the 1940s and early 1950s were invoked sporadically and inconsistently is not historically significant; as we have already seen, such laws have always been used in such unpredictable ways. What did change during the 1940s was the influence of court decisions on national politics. Because of changes in racial ideology from scientific racial discourse to modernist racial discourse, defenders of state antimiscegenation laws could not as easily rely on the common prewar defense that interracial sexuality yielded inferior biological subjects. Hence defenders of antimiscegenation legislation increasingly relied on states' rights arguments and antifederalism to defend antimiscegenation legislation. Such arguments attempted to contain interracial sex and marriage as local and even state matters, not national ones. In this way, such cases excluded interracial sexuality from the jurisdiction of the federal government and, in so doing, limited the sphere of interracial intimacy. Judges and attorneys who defended antimiscegenation laws argued that the federal government had no right to regulate how the states determined appropriate marriages. These arguments would attempt to limit federal oversight of intimate matters, especially after the Supreme Court's 1954 *Brown v. Board of Education* decision mandated school desegregation throughout the country. For its part, the Supreme Court, during the period of this study, was willing to ignore the constitutionality of antimiscegenation legislation in order to win consent for other civil rights struggles.

The scope of attacks on antimiscegenation legislation also changed after the war. Because of the new climate of racial discourse and the rhetoric of democracy that had shaped the war, lawyers and appeals court judges were able to challenge antimiscegenation laws as un-American. At times judges connected their critique of antimiscegenation laws to the global context of the war and the need to protect the image of American prestige abroad. Further, the context of postwar race thinking made available to judges and lawyers the argument that racial classification was arbitrary. Some lawyers attempted to undermine the ease with which their client's race could be determined, thereby questioning the very categories upon which antimiscegenation legislation relied.

In the following discussion of antimiscegenation court cases, I want to show how the context of World War II shaped the possibilities for the legal fight against antimiscegenation laws by turning this debate into one over whether interracial sex should be located in the public sphere. At stake in this argument were the limits of civil rights reform as a public matter and the designation of which public had jurisdiction. This discussion will show that although new arguments were used to challenge antimiscegenation laws, legislation banning forms of interracial intimacy remained intact throughout the decade after the war.

In 1948 California's supreme court was faced with the first major antimiscegenation case in the post–World War II era. Amid a context of American triumphalism and modernist racial ideology, the court would have to decide whether to compel W. G. Sharp, the Los Angeles County clerk, to issue a marriage certificate to Andrea Perez, a Mexican American woman legally classified white, and her fiancé, Sylvester Davis, who was classified "Negro." Sharp refused to issue Perez and Davis a marriage license because of California Civil Code section 69, which stated, "All marriages of white persons with Negroes, Mongolians, members of the Malay race, or mulattoes are illegal and void." This section of the state's Civil Code was first established in California's

1872 antimiscegenation law. Denied a marriage certificate, Perez took her case to the state supreme court. Perez argued that the statute was unconstitutional because it violated her free exercise of religion. Perez and Davis were Catholics who were given consent to marry by their parish. Perez argued that the state, in prohibiting the marriage, had interfered with her religious freedom. The case hinged on whether marriage was fundamentally a private, religious contract or whether it was primarily a public contract enacted within the civic sphere. Furthermore, Perez's case forced the California justices to consider whether California's antimiscegenation law relied on arbitrary racial categories and was therefore unconstitutional.[29]

The politics of World War II shaped the deliberations. After the nation had fought a war for democracy and against fascism, how could a state supreme court uphold a law that resembled the racial politics of Germany? In a bold majority decision by Justice Roger J. Traynor, the California supreme court overturned its state's antimiscegenation law by a four-to-three margin. Traynor's opinion reads as a manifesto against California's antimiscegenation law during a time when the United States waged war for democracy. At the heart of Traynor's argument was his belief that marriage was a "fundamental right of free men," something more than a civil contract. For Traynor, marriage was neither a purely private nor public matter but a bit of both and more. "The right to marry is as fundamental as the right to send one's child to a particular school or the right to have offspring." For Traynor, marriage was both a civic right and a natural right that could not be abridged by law.

Even more powerful than Traynor's argument about marriage, however, was his claim that race should not shape public policy except in cases of national security. In making this case, Traynor documented the shift in racial formations from the pre- to the postwar years. If the prewar society viewed the offspring of interracial sexuality as less fit than "racially pure" bodies, Traynor argued that new research in cultural anthropology undermined this argument. No evidence, he argued, supported that claim that interracial offspring were inferior or that Caucasians were smarter. "The fact is overwhelming that there has been a steady increase in the number of people in this country who belong to more than one race, and a growing number who have succeeded in identifying themselves with the Caucasian race even though they are not exclusively Caucasian."[30]

Having argued that marriage is a fundamental human right and that antimiscegenation laws rely on spurious racial categories, Traynor's majority opinion concluded that the regulatory codes that fell under California's antimiscegenation law "are not only too vague and uncertain to be enforceable regulations of a fundamental right, but that they violate the equal protection of the laws clause of the United States Constitution by impairing the right of individuals to marry on the basis of race alone and by arbitrarily and unreasonably discriminating against certain racial groups."

In an equally emphatic concurring statement, Justice Jesse W. Carter suggested California's antimiscegenation law was all too reminiscent of Hitler's racial policies. For Carter, the contradiction between California's law and the nation's rhetoric upon entry into World War II was clear. "Let us not forget that this [Hitler] was the man who plunged the world into a war in which, for the third time, Americans fought, bled, and died for the truth of the proposition that all men are created equal." Anticipating the need to protect American prestige abroad, he argued, "The rest of the world never has understood and never will understand why and how a nation, built on the premise that all men are created equal, can three times send the flower of its manhood to war for the truth of this premise and still fail to carry it out within its own borders."

For Justices Traynor and Carter, Andrea Perez's religious freedom was less important than her right to marry. The fundamental assumption shaping both justices' arguments was that marriage was neither a public nor a private relation but both, and something that could not be interfered with by the state. In this sense, the justices distinguished between a civil right that could be given or taken away and a human right that stood outside the state's control. This view was shaped perhaps as much by the context of World War II rhetoric, and its racial ideologies, as it was by theories of marriage and rights. Yet Traynor wrote for a slim majority in *Perez v. Sharp*. Throughout the nation, especially in the South, state supreme courts were unwilling to argue that marriage should not be regulated by the state. Although the U.S. Supreme Court had not yet ruled in *Brown v. Board of Education*, many state court justices feared that civil rights reforms at the federal level would undermine state sovereignty. While this argument was most powerful in southern states, some of the California supreme court justices also feared the implications of civil rights on states' rights.

Justice John Shenk wrote a scathing dissent in *Perez* in which he argued that "the power of a state to regulate and control the basic social relationship of marriage of its domiciliaries is here challenged and set at naught by a majority order of this court arrived at not by a concurrence of reasons but by the end result of four votes supported by divergent concepts not supported by authority and in fact contrary to the decisions in this state and elsewhere." Although Shenk vehemently disagreed with the majority decision, he shared its assumption about the relationship between marriage and *federal* oversight. While the majority argued that marriage was extrapublic, that is, outside the realm of state regulation, Shenk argued that the state did have the right to regulate marriage. In this way, both states' rights arguments and the majority decision concurred that marriage was not a federal issue. Consequently, and probably unwittingly, both decisions implied that only some civil rights demands deserved federal oversight.

In a lengthy dissent, Shenk argued that antimiscegenation laws were within the state's authority and that marriage could be regulated based on race. Citing scientific racial arguments about racial degeneracy through interracial breeding, Shenk clearly established the precedence of antimiscegenation laws in his state and in thirty-one other states in 1948. For Shenk, marriage was "more than a civil contract between them, subject to their will and pleasure in respect of effects, continuance, or dissolution. It is a domestic relation having to do with the morals and civilization of a people. It is an essential institution in every well organized society. It affects in a vital manner public welfare, and its control and regulation is [sic] a matter of domestic concern within each state." Just as a state has the right to proscribe the age at which a couple may marry, argued Shenk, so, too, a state may determine the race of people who may marry. As we will see later, Shenk's argument that marriage could be regulated by the state constructed marriage as a public institution. In doing so, Shenk had unwittingly placed the regulation of marriage under the scope of desegregation legislation and court decisions. Had he argued, as many southern judges did, that marriage was a Christian relationship or a contract under God, he would have lent support to the notion that desegregation orders did not apply to the private covenant of marriage. Shenk recognized marriage as a public issue; yet he sought to contain the scope of "public welfare" to the state and not the federal government.

Although Shenk was in the minority of the California supreme court in *Perez*, his argument remained powerful in many other states. Moreover, as I will argue below, the U.S. Supreme Court did not view *Perez* as a precedent-setting case. Instead, it viewed the case as unlike similar cases involving southern couples. Especially after its landmark *Brown v. Board of Education* decision, the Supreme Court was cautious not to appear overly liberal. For more than twenty years after *Brown*, the Supreme Court refused to consider antimiscegenation cases. This neglect allowed judges like Shenk and his southern peers to argue that *Brown*'s sweeping conclusions about the unconstitutionality of official segregation did not apply to the state's ability to regulate marriage. Yet even as states' rights arguments, like the one articulated by Shenk, became more popular in the wake of civil rights reforms, it was in no way predictable how southern courts would rule in miscegenation cases.

Just as illicit sexual relations could be treated with a level of toleration in early colonial society, interracial sexuality was not always the most relevant fact determining the outcome of postwar antimiscegenation cases. Because of the new climate of civil rights activism in America, southern appeals courts were careful to limit their own power over local sexual matters. Whenever a southern court used antimiscegenation legislation to decide a case, it risked making its own power to determine sexual matters the subject of federal oversight. When states deployed antimiscegenation laws to regulate social relations, they did so only when such use would not incur too much unwanted federal participation.

In *Stevens v. Oklahoma*, for example, a state antimiscegenation law was used to prevent the probate of a will. Although the case was prosecuted in a state appellate court, the trial turned on local relations between William Stevens, a black man, and Stella Sands, a Creek Indian living in the Creek territory of Oklahoma. In this way, the case contained the explosive potential of interracial sexuality by focusing instead on cultural definitions of racial status. The constitutionality of the antimiscegenation law was not questioned because the case turned on whether a black man was actually "black" and whether a Creek Indian woman was actually "Indian." Although racial indeterminacy was at the core of many prewar antimiscegenation cases, such issues became especially vexing given the changed atmosphere of racial formations after the war. If race was no longer thought to be based in biology but instead in culture and behavior, then it would be difficult to prove racial identities in court.

Oklahoma's state antimiscegenation law prohibited black intermarriage while permitting interracial marriages between whites and Native Americans. Western states often constructed Native American/white marriages as permissible, and even beneficial to Native Americans and whites, but prohibited black/white marriages. Yet changing definitions of race in the wake of World War II confounded the regulation of black/white marriages, especially in Creek territory. If blackness and whiteness could no longer be biologically determined, but only culturally determined, then enforcing antimiscegenation laws in cases in which race was difficult to determine was arbitrary and contradictory. Although pre–World War II antimiscegenation cases often turned on racial ambiguity, *Stevens*'s focus on racial categories amid postwar racial formations made this case especially important.

When William Stevens proposed marriage to Stella Sands, the couple knew that they would have to wed outside of Oklahoma. Stevens, a black man living in Creek territory, could not legally marry Sands, who was registered as a "full-blooded" Creek. On November 17, 1936, Stevens and Sands wed in Independence, Kansas. The couple returned to Creek territory after their wedding, where they lived together for nearly five years in obscurity. Ten days before their fifth wedding anniversary, Stella Sands died. William assumed that, as Stella's widower, he would be the beneficiary of his deceased wife's modest estate of a house and $3,000. Yet before William could collect his wife's property, Stella's sister, Lorna Thomson Minyard, sought a legal injunction against him. Minyard claimed she was the rightful benefactor of Stella's estate because under Oklahoma state law her sister had never been legally married to William. There is no available evidence about whether Stella was close to her sister or how Stella's sister felt about William. What we do know is that Minyard hired a lawyer to argue in front of an Okmulgee County judge "section 7499 O.S. 1931, in force at the date of said purported marriage, and continued in force at this time, prohibits the marriage of a person of any other race with a person of African descent and expressly declares the same to be unlawful."[31]

William Stevens's case, although not the only or the most influential postwar antimiscegenation case, illustrates how antimiscegenation laws legislated property relations through race and sex ideologies. But the case is useful for other reasons as well; it offers a rare look into the logic employed in the early 1940s to understand racial categories and to contain the politically explosive matter of interracial sex. In deciding whether William Stevens could inherit a modest sum of property, a district court would have to determine the definition of blackness and American Indianness in a context in which blacks and American Indians had lived together and intermarried for nearly a hundred years. In fact, William Stevens was enrolled in the Creek nation as a "freedman," which was the category used to label black descendants of the

Creek nation's black slaves. Within the Creek territory, black freedman were given the same rights as "full-blooded" Creeks. Hence Stevens could rightfully claim some kind of American Indian status in his defense.[32]

The U.S. Department of the Interior claimed jurisdiction over the case because William and Stella lived in Creek territory. On April 20, 1943, William Stevens was denied the right to inherit Sands's estate because, according to the court, "the decedent, Stella Sands, left surviving no husband, nor issue, nor father or mother." William and Stella's marriage had been erased from history. Moreover, the court found that the marriage between Sands and Stevens "is void and of no force for the reason that said William Stevens is enrolled as a Creek-Freedman . . . and is a Negro and a person of African descent."

William hired a local white lawyer to wage his defense. A. L. Emery used numerous arguments in his attempt to defend Stevens. He argued that Oklahoma's antimiscegenation law should not apply to the Creek nation because doing so would violate Creek sovereignty. According to Emery, antimiscegenation laws "were enacted after statehood and were never made applicable to the Five Civilized Tribes by an Act of Congress, and therefore, said statues have no application in this proceeding." Moreover, Emery argued that antimiscegenation laws relied on racial categories that could not be easily determined in the case of William and Stella; hence, even though Stella's parents were enrolled as "full-blooded Creek," Emery had evidence that they were of partial "African descent." Thus, even if Oklahoma's antimiscegenation law should apply to the Creek Nation, there was reason to believe that William and Stella had not violated it. Emery created enough confusion about the case that the Muskogee judge gave Stevens a continuance and moved the case to a state appeals court.

A year later William Stevens's case had ramifications for other state antimiscegenation laws and the politics of World War II itself. Stevens's case had the potential to reveal the paradox of antimiscegenation laws in a country that was fighting a war to protect democracy and defeat Nazi racism. Yet what may have been most explosive about Stevens's case was its potential to reveal the fiction of racial categories. Emery's defense relied on racial indeterminacy; that is, that William's and Stella's racial status could not be determined. This argument raised troubling concerns for a society that created laws assuming clear racial categories.

In the federal district court, William Stevens testified that he viewed himself as part American Indian. William based this belief not only on his registration in the Creek nation but also on his understanding of his ancestry. "I have Indian blood. . . . I do not consider myself to be a person of African descent; I am mixed, Indian and colored and I live in the colored part of Okmulgee." In order to corroborate Stevens's testimony, Emery invited Creek residents of Okmulgee County to testify about their perception of Stevens's and Sands's racial status. This testimony sought to determine racial categories on the basis of phenotypical traits, like hair color and texture, or on the basis of William's and Stella's friendships with locals.

Philip McNac was a Creek resident of Okmulgee who testified that Stella was partly of African descent. According to McNac, Stella's father was "an Indian, and was very dark, and had wavy hair, so maybe he was a mixed-blood . . . apparently he was of colored blood but I wouldn't say how much blood, he was dark, his hair was black but on cloudy days his hair would curl up." McNac further suggested that Stella's mother "was mixed up with colored blood; she was rather light complected, more yellow, wasn't too dark or too light, her hair was wavy—she looked like Stella; the only way I could judge what blood Stella was, her mother was mixed blood." McNac concluded his testimony by illustrating the arbitrary nature of classifying people on the basis of race. "All Indians have dark hair and some of them have wavy hair too but that is the case of mixed blood, if not, they wouldn't have wavy hair at all. . . . With wavy hair bound to be mixed blood."

If, for Philip McNac, wavy hair signified mixed-race identity, for Samuel Anderson skin color was far more telling. Anderson, a Creek Indian, argued that Stella's skin color suggested that she was not a "full-blood" Creek Indian. "[She] didn't look like a full blood typical Indian. Mixed with some other blood, could have been Spanish, French, German or Negro blood in them. . . . Stella had more of a banana color, or cream color, wasn't dark or white, wasn't red, and her head was just round, wasn't like an Indian head at all. Stella's hair was short, wasn't kinky, kept it well greased all of the time, or oiled." Like Philip McNac's testimony, Anderson's testimony helped Emery establish doubt about Stella's "full-blooded" status. If Emery could convince the court that Stella was partly of African descent, then the judge could conclude that Stella and William had not violated Oklahoma's antimiscegenation statute.

Unfortunately for William and his lawyer, William's and Stella's guilt could be confirmed using the same logic employed by the defense. The arbitrary nature of racial categories could be used to uphold William's and Stella's racial difference. Sands's family argued that William and Stella were indeed racially different, and like Emery, their counsel relied on local testimony to prove his case. W. H. Yeager, a white citizen of Okmulgee, testified that he saw "full-blooded" American Indians all the time, "and I am familiar with their looks." According to Yeager, "Stella Sands looked like a full blooded Indian, she had black straight hair, she was known in the neighborhood as an Indian, and she was buried in a white cemetery." M. F. Minyard, Stella's brother-in-law, argued, "I have lived in Oklahoma for thirty-five years and I sure know what a full blood Indian looks like and I would say Stella was a full blood Indian." Leah Taylor, a local Creek Indian, testified, "I always believed [Stella] was a full blood Creek Indian, her hair was like mine and mine is straight and black." Ella Perryman, a "full-blood" Cherokee, argued that Stella's "hair was straight and dark and she had the features of a typical Indian."

William Stevens lost his right to inherit his deceased wife's estate because the Oklahoma court erased from state records the fact of his marriage. Most telling here is how a case about whether a state antimiscegenation law was constitutional and whether such a law should apply to a sovereign nation turned on a debate over the phenotypical markers of racial identity. By making this case about hair color and racial indeterminacy, Oklahoma's right to regulate interracial marriage and sexuality was protected.

Even when racial categories were not the subject of antimiscegenation court cases, postwar courts attempted to shield themselves from federal oversight. In 1952, the year that Congress eliminated racially based immigration restrictions, Han Say Naim, a Chinese immigrant, sought to use his marriage to an American woman to petition for U.S. citizenship. Han Say wed Ruby Elaine in North Carolina in order to evade Virginia's antimiscegenation law. Yet after their return to Virginia, for unknown reasons Ruby Elaine no longer wanted to be married to Han Say. In order to annul the marriage, Ruby Elaine invoked Virginia's antimiscegenation law. Even though her marriage took place outside of Virginia, Ruby Elaine argued that she and Han Say had broken Virginia's racial purity law.

Virginia's racial purity law was one of the oldest in the United States. In 1955 the law read:

It shall hereafter be unlawful for any white person in this State to marry any save a white person, or a person with no other admixture of blood than white and American Indian. For the purpose of this chapter, the term "white person" shall apply to such person as has no trace whatever of any blood other than Caucasian;

but persons who have one-sixteenth or less of the blood of the American Indian and have no other non-Caucasic blood shall be deemed to be white persons. All laws heretofore passed and now in effect regarding the intermarriage of white and colored persons shall apply to marriages prohibited by this chapter.[33]

Virginia's law defined whites as those persons who have one-sixteenth American Indian blood or those with full "Caucasian blood." These criteria for whiteness were stricter in 1955 than they were at the turn of the century, when the criteria for being classified white was that a person had no more than one-eighth nonwhite blood.[34] Couples who violated Virginia's "racial integrity law" were guilty of a felony and confined in the penitentiary for one to five years.

Han Say and Ruby Elaine's marriage was annulled in a Virginia court. As a result, Han Say feared that he would no longer be permitted to reside legally in the United States. In 1955 he appealed the Virginia decision in front of a state supreme court. At stake in the appeal were whether Virginia had a right to annul a marriage that was legal in North Carolina and whether the state's antimiscegenation law was unconstitutional.

Fundamental to the state's defense was its argument that "intermarriage of the races is harmful to good citizenship. The prevention of miscegenetic marriages is the proper governmental objective." Here Virginia argued that marriage was a relationship properly regulated by the states, not by the federal government. Appealing to states' rights was a common move in southern courts, where federal civil rights legislation increasingly undermined social relations. In *Naim v. Naim*, the Virginia supreme court argued that marriage is subject to the control of the states. Yet in maintaining that marriage was a civil contract enacted under the regulation of the state, it unwittingly placed marriage under the jurisdiction of a public-sphere institution subject to federal desegregation policies. In order to evade *Brown's* scope, the Virginia court stated:

In this State marriage is treated as a civil contract, but it is more than a mere civil contract. It is a public institution established by God himself, is recognized in all Christian and civilized nations, and is essential to the peace, happiness, and well-being of society. The right, in the states, to regulate and control, to guard, protect, and preserve this God-given, civilizing, and Christianizing institution is of inestimable importance, and cannot be surrounded, nor can the states suffer or permit any interference therewith. If the federal government can determine who may marry in a state, there is no limit to its power.

If marriage is a religious contract ordained by God, the Virginia court argued, it is outside the scope of federal regulation because God, and God's rightful assistants, the states, already regulate it. Hence the Virginia court asserted that *Brown's* sweeping challenge to racial segregation could not apply to antimiscegenation statutes.

> Brown v. Board of Education *reached its conclusion that segregation in the public schools was contrary to the Equal Protection clause on the basis that education is perhaps the most important function of State and local governments, "the very foundation of good citizenship," and that the opportunity to acquire it, "where the state has undertaken to provide it, is a right which must be made available to all on equal terms." No such claim for the intermarriage of the races could be supported; by no sort of valid reasoning could it be found to be a foundation of good citizenship or a right that must be made available to all on equal terms. In the opinion of the legislatures of more than half the States it is harmful to good citizenship.*

The Virginia court argued that if public education was "fundamental to good citizenship," marriage was an entirely different social contract and that interracial marriages were in fact "harmful to good citizenship."

Han Say Naim did not challenge Virginia's use of arbitrary racial classifications to punish certain marriages. His own racial status may have been uncertain, but it was certainly not 100 percent Caucasian. Nor is there evidence to suggest that Naim challenged his wife's racial classification as white. In the end, the Virginia supreme court upheld the lower court's annulment of Han Say and Ruby Elaine's marriage. Naim took his case to the U.S. Supreme Court, where Justices Earl Warren, Hugo Black, William O. Douglas, and Stanley Reed were willing to hear the case. Yet as legal scholar Rachel Moran argues, Justice Felix Frankfurter "feared that any decision in *Naim* would jeopardize the Court's ability to implement school desegregation. To avoid confronting the antimiscegenation issue, Frankfurter worked with Justice Tom Clark to draft a per curium opinion asking the Virginia Court to clarify the legal basis for its jurisdiction to annul Naim's marriage." The Virginia supreme court quickly declared that Naim's marriage, though contracted in North Carolina, was subject to Virginia's antimiscegenation law.

Despite Justices Warren's and Black's desire to hear *Naim,* "another Justice summed up the rest of the Court's view with respect to desegregation and antimiscegenation: 'One bombshell at a time is enough.'" Han Say Naim's marriage was annulled, and Virginia's antimiscegenation law would remain intact until 1967, when the Supreme Court finally found the courage to find it unconstitutional.[35]

In a number of cases brought in front of southern appeals courts, local jurisdictions used antimiscegenation laws to regulate gender and racial relations. In a context of popular antifascism and shifting racial formations, southern appeals courts worked diligently both to contain the explosive potential of interracial sexuality and to limit the regulation of interracial intimacy to local and regional jurisdictions. Hence, while the specter of amalgamation and interracial sex haunted the segregated South, many southern appeals courts overturned local antimiscegenation convictions in order to preserve their state's ability to regulate illicit sexual relations.

When John Benjamin Watts, a white man living in Monroe Country, Alabama, left his entire estate to a black woman named Nazarine Parker, local townspeople and distant relatives thought that Watts had gone insane, and they invoked Alabama's antimiscegenation law to prevent Parker from inheriting Watts's estate. Though there was no evidence that Watts and Parker had a sexual relationship—which would have violated the state's antimiscegenation law that covered fornication as well as marriage—it was an assumed fact. Yet the antimiscegenation prosecution developed in Watts's case (*Dees et al. v. Metts et al.* [1944]) was not primarily about interracial sexuality but was instead about the range of legal rights extended to white male patriarchs and the maintenance of white wealth through inheritance customs. In giving his estate to Nazarine Parker, Watts had broken a cherished tradition of passing family wealth on to surviving family members and thereby challenged one of the bases of white racial privilege; Watts undermined what George Lipsitz has termed the possessive investment in white racial skin privilege by moving wealth from white hands to black hands.[36]

Nazarine Parker's ability to inherit a white man's wealth was challenged when Watts's surviving relatives invoked Alabama's antimiscegenation law to claim that Parker and Watts's relationship was illegal. Given that Watts, now deceased, could not testify as to his "real" intentions, a Monroe County court would have to determine whether antimiscegenation legislation could prevent the probate of a white man's will. Even more important, the lawyer for Watts's scorned relatives argued that Parker must have exerted undue influence over Watts; in trying to explain how it was possible for Watts to ignore his blood relatives and to leave property to a black woman, he argued that Parker was to blame for Watts's irrational behavior. A Monroe County court agreed and refused to probate the will, showing that antimiscegenation laws could be used to police economic relations outside the nexus of romance and intimacy.

In an Alabama appeals court trial, Watts's lawyer, Loxley Dees, appealed the lower court decision. In his appeal, Dees suggested there were competing issues at stake in this case. While the local court sought to regulate the presumed—yet never proved—illicit relationship between Parker and Watts, the issue in front of the appeals court was whether a local court could challenge a white man's dying wish to pass his wealth on to whomever he chose. By appealing the case on these grounds, Watts's lawyers transformed the case from a miscegenation case to one about the protection of white male privilege. In turning a miscegenation case into a case to preserve white male patriarchy, Watts's lawyers gave the Alabama appeals court a way to scorn interracial intimacy while maintaining its contention that romance, marriage, and sexuality were local matters, best left to county courts.

The evidence in the lower court trial was clear and uncontested. Watts's lawyers testified that Watts was of sound mind when he wrote his will. Moreover, the probate lawyer indicated he had never met Nazarine Parker and that she had played no part in drafting the will. Watts was aware of the scorn he would face when his relatives learned of his will. He told his lawyer, "I want to leave what I have for this Negro woman that has been taking care of me all the time. You know how white people are about Negroes, and I want to be sure this thing is handled right because I want her to have what I've got. All my own people have ever done for me was to borrow money and never pay it back. I want to see that she gets it, and I want to see that some white man sees that she does get it." Watts knew that white men held all the meaningful power in Alabama. Hence he made sure that his attorney would fulfill his wish as executor of his will.

The Monroe County court was asked to annul the will solely because of the charge that Watts and Parker had violated the state's antimiscegenation law. There was no evidence, however, that Watts and Parker were actually romantically or sexually involved. In Watts's own testimony, he refers to Parker as someone who helped him with chores and took care of him.

Despite the lack of evidence linking the two romantically or sexually, in a four-to-three majority opinion of the Alabama appeals court, Chief Justice Lucien D. Gardner argued that Watts and Parker had violated the state's antimiscegenation law. The appeals court affirmed the Monroe County court's contention that Watts and Parker had committed a crime. Yet the appeals court also affirmed Watts's ability to control his economic destiny by arguing that the state's antimiscegenation law "forfeits no right to ownership of property of either of the guilty parties, nor challenges the right of free disposal thereof." The appeals court thus overturned the lower court decision annulling the will. In this way, the appeals court affirmed the state's antimiscegenation law while reversing a lower court miscegenation conviction.

In his majority opinion, Justice Gardner argued that Watts and Dees had committed a serious sin. "It is reprehensible enough for a white man to live in adultery with a white woman thus defying the laws of both God and man, but it is more so, and a much lower grade of depravity, for a white man to live in adultery with a Negro woman." In an even more powerful statement, Gardner located his decision within the context of World War II rhetoric. He argued that Americans had the freedom to make their own choices about how to live, and this freedom extended, he argued, to the right to choose sin.

> However boldly he may have defied the laws of our State and its public policy, and the recognized traditional racial distinctions, organized society took no steps to interfere. Freedom of religion, so sacredly guaranteed to us, and which we cherish so highly, is freedom not only to worship according to the dictates of one's own conscience and to follow whatever religion one desires, but it is also a freedom, if one chooses, to have no religion at all. And so far as one's conscience is concerned (and this, of course, is wholly aside from the violation of our State law), there is a freedom also in the moral world for one to choose his own way of life. Ben Watts chose the evil way. But whatever may be said in condemnation of his manner of life, and however disgraceful and reprehensible it may have been, the courts must not lose sight of the fact that his accumulated estate, valued at some $3,500, was his own; and it is clearly shown from this record, beyond the peradventure of a doubt, that he wanted this estate to go to Nazarine Parker.

Gardner's opinion allowed him to affirm his commitment to freedom, to overturn an antimiscegenation conviction, and to support his state's antimiscegenation legislation. In this way, Gardner shielded his state's antimiscegenation law from a federal appeal, while affirming a lower court's ability to employ antimiscegenation law.

Gardner's negotiation of postwar racial politics did not convince all of his appellate court peers. In a spirited dissenting opinion, Justice Virgil Bouldin was less forgiving of Watts's choices. He argued that Watts had undermined two cherished southern institutions: racial purity and patriarchy. Bouldin argued that Watts must have been unduly influenced to give up his racial and gender privilege. He made this case by suggesting that Nazarine Parker had assumed a "dominant" position in her relationship with Benjamin Watts.

> *Keeping up such criminal relations at such a price may be considered by the jury in connection with all the evidence, and found to support a reasonable inference that the man has become so infatuated with his Negro mistress as to render her the dominant party in matters of special interest to her. Her alleged declarations above quoted carry reasonable implication of her activity in procuring the will and deed, and also of her sense of power to get what she wanted; the role of a mistress, rather than that of acquiescence or servile submission to the dominant will of the man.*

The majority and the minority in this case were in agreement that Benjamin Watts and Nazarine Parker had violated Alabama's antimiscegenation law. Moreover, each side believed in the validity of the law. Yet the majority was willing to validate a white man's desire to leave money to whomever he wished and to make Watts's violation of the state's antimiscegenation statue a secondary matter. The minority also sought to protect the interests of a white man by arguing that he had become temporarily insane because of his intense infatuation with a black woman. Although Parker ultimately inherited Watts's estate, her voice was completely absent from the trials. While Watts's will was eventually probated, Parker's reputation had been questioned and disparaged.

A similar drama of miscegenation occurred in a local Mississippi court in 1949. The case involved a World War II veteran whose racial status as white was called into question by a distant relative. In this case, a local authority successfully waged an antimiscegenation prosecution only to have the state's appeals court overturn the decision. In ways similar to the Watts case, the Mississippi appeals court would have to determine how to regulate interracial intimacy within its jurisdiction without bringing unwanted federal observers into the case. This case was especially vexing to the Mississippi court because the man accused of illegally marrying a white woman was a World War II veteran, a respected representative of the nation. Changing this soldier's racial status from white to black would have made this case a national embarrassment, as the NAACP and black newspapers monitored the case.

In 1946 Davis Knight returned after the war to his home state of Mississippi and married his sweetheart, Junie Lee Spradley. Knight and Spradley's honeymoon was short-lived, however, because a distant relative of Knight's, angry at the Knight family for unknown reasons, accused his relative of breaking Mississippi's antimiscegenation statute. This distant relative claimed that Knight had more than one-eighth "Negro blood," making him ineligible to marry a white woman in Mississippi. In a lower court, Knight was convicted of breaking the state's antimiscegenation law under a charge "that being a mulatto with 1/8 or more of Negro blood, he married a white woman."

The only damning evidence against Knight in the lower court trial was his relative's testimony. In the appeals court, Knight brought evidence that his grandmother, who in the lower court was alleged to have been a mulatta, was actually white. Witnesses testified that Knight's grandmother, Rachel Knight, "was of a ginger-cake color, did not have kinky hair and did not possess the distinct racial characteristics by which all pure Africans are identified." Hence, although Rachel had dark features, she surely was not black. Genealogical information could often provide spurious evidence regarding race. It was nearly impossible to determine racial ancestry given the shifting definitions of whiteness throughout the nineteenth- and early-twentieth-century South. Moreover, Knight's grandparents were no longer living in 1949. Thus, in order to "exonerate" himself and prove his whiteness, Knight would have to show that he "acted white."

Knight's lawyers argued that Knight upheld the time-honored racial boundaries of the segregated South by associating only with whites. "The State did not undertake to show that at any time in his entire life he had ever associated with Negroes or conducted himself in such a manner as to indicate to the public that he considered himself a Negro, nor did it undertake to prove any statement that he had ever made to any person that he was a Negro." Moreover, Knight's defense argued that he had served as a white person in the U.S. military during the war and that such service to the nation should shield Knight from any damage to his reputation.

When he registered for the draft during the late war, he registered as a white man at Camp Shelby in this State. Having been inducted he was chosen for naval service and served in the Navy with white troops and as a white man. Having served honorably, he was discharged as a white man. Being once again in civil life, he married a white woman as a white man, his physical appearance being such that his race was not questioned by the official who issued the license or the one who performed the marriage ceremony.

Knight's military service, it would seem, earned him a level of respect within the appeals court, and it made Knight's case the target of national attention. Ultimately, the appeals court overturned Knight's conviction in such as way as to affirm Knight's whiteness and the state's antimiscegenation law.

Dees et al. v. Metts et al. and *Knight v. State of Mississippi* were two antimiscegenation cases in which the matter of interracial sexuality was only a secondary or tertiary concern. At stake in these cases was how well Ben Watts and Davis Knight behaved as white men. Watts was viewed as a failed white man because he had associated with a black woman and because he had broken the inheritance chain of white wealth. Watts's racial status as a white man was never questioned, however, and the appeals court, though scornful of his association with a black woman, nevertheless upheld his right as a white man to control his economic destiny. Similarly, Knight was accused of being an imposter. In his case, antimiscegenation law was used to disallow his access to a white woman because he was accused of defying race lines in Mississippi. Yet Knight's military service, in addition to his propensity to "act white," helped him convince an appeals court that he was indeed white. Both cases held the potential to explode postwar racial categories. In both cases, however, the question of whether antimiscegenation laws were appropriate and constitutional was secondary to other questions. In this way, these cases effectively contained the explosive potential of illicit sex by focusing on matters of patriarchy (for Watts) and racial identity (for Knight).[37]

If directing antimiscegenation court cases away from the matter of illicit sex and toward matters of patriarchy and racial identity was a strategy for Dees and Knight, such a strategy was not available in cases in which white women were prosecuted for illicit sex. When white women were accused of violating an antimiscegenation law, they posed a problem for southern states that were struggling to maintain their sovereignty over matters of illicit sex. While white men like Watts and Knight could employ their white manliness to protect themselves from a miscegenation prosecution, white women did not have the same protection. Yet southern states, in all illicit sexual matters, had to be careful when prosecuting antimiscegenation cases concerning white women because such prosecutions threatened to expose the state's ability to regulate sexual relations to federal intervention.

In 1951, for example, a white woman named Luby Griffith sat in front of the court of appeals of Alabama seeking to overturn her lower court conviction for committing "adultery or fornication with each other, against the peace and dignity of the state of Alabama." Griffith's seven-year sentence was based on a jury's decision that she had violated the state's antimiscegenation law when she was caught having—or presumed to have had—an adulterous relationship with Nathan Bell, a "Negro." At issue for the appeals court was whether Griffith could be convicted under the state's antimiscegenation law even though her prosecutors had shown no evidence of a sexual relationship between herself and Nathan Bell. Importantly, the appeals court considered the appeal only in terms of how to use the state's antimiscegenation law and not whether such a law was unconstitutional.

Neither Griffith nor her prosecutors contested the facts presented in the lower court. Luby and her husband owned a general store in a black neighborhood. Nathan Bell, a black man, was a frequent customer in the Griffith store. Witnesses testified that Luby and Nathan often left the store together for long periods. Nathan was seen kissing and hugging Luby in her car. Despite this evidence, Luby claimed that she was just being kind to Nathan, that she was someone who liked to help her black customers by driving them home and mending their clothes. No witness had ever seen Luby and Nathan having sex.

The most damaging evidence in the case came when some of Luby's friends and neighbors testified about an incident in which Nathan was seen having a sexual relationship with a black woman named Miley Moore. When Luby learned than Nathan was involved with Miley, she went into a rage and threatened to kill Nathan and Miley. This fact confirmed the jury's suspicion that Luby had romantic feelings for Nathan.

The appeals court affirmed the lower court's conviction, and Luby Griffith was sent to jail for seven years. The Alabama appeals court judges did not share the California court's belief that antimiscegenation laws seemed contradictory given the context of World War II. Luby had presumably violated Alabama's racial boundaries, but she also undermined the assumption of patriarchal control within marriages. In this way, perhaps the state thought that Luby needed to be made an example of deviant white womanhood. Moreover, Luby's "crime" of adultery probably made her a "safe" target of an antimiscegenation prosecution because she had violated patriarchal as well as racial boundaries.

Luby Griffith was made an example of because she crossed racial lines and because she undermined her husband's patriarchal authority. But in a similar Alabama case in 1951—*Agnew v. State of Alabama*—Agnew, a black married man, and Vena Mae Pendley, a white married woman, were jointly indicted on the charge of miscegenation. In his appeal, Agnew argued that Pendley's race was ambiguous, that she may have been partly American Indian. Hence, Agnew argued, if Pendley were indeed part American Indian, then they had not violated Alabama's antimiscegenation law, which regulated black/white relationships but not black/nonwhite relationships. During his appeal, Agnew's lawyers argued, "a woman who is part Indian cannot be classified as a white person within the miscegenation statute."

The appeals court had to determine the legal criteria to decide Pendley's race. Agnew and his wife lived in close proximity to Vena Mae Pendley and her spouse. Several witnesses saw Agnew at Pendley's house and in her bedroom. In 1950 Pendley gave birth to a child who, according to witnesses, possessed "Negroid characteristics." Pendley argued that her child was white and related to her husband. Such a claim sought to solidify her reproduction as *intra*racial and to confirm her own whiteness. Pendley was undoubtedly aware of the contradictory nature of racial ideologies that allow, as Barbara J. Fields notes, for a white woman to give birth to a white or black child but disallow the possibility of black women giving birth to white children.[38] If Pendley's baby was white, then Pendley had to be white, too. Yet Pendley's testimony was challenged by witness testimony that a number of Pendley's relatives were dark complexioned "due to Indian blood, and that Pendley herself was either one-eighth or one-sixteenth Indian." Such evidence that Pendley was not white would help Agnew reverse his lower court conviction, yet it would convict Pendley of something far worse than miscegenation; her racial status in the state of Alabama would be reclassified as "not white." Thus what would lead to Agnew's exoneration would lead to her indictment.

The only evidence that could have easily incriminated Pendley and Agnew on the crime of violating an antimiscegenation law would have been clear evidence that Pendley was white and her child was black. One piece of evidence appears to have overwhelmed any other testimony about Pendley's race; she had signed a petition giving her baby to the state of Alabama. The petition indicated that "the father of said child is a Negro and she cannot provide a normal life for him." The petition thus confirmed the crime of interracial sex that could have led to the conviction of Agnew and Pendley. During the appeals court trial, however, the justices determined that the incriminating petition had been improperly introduced in the lower court. The court ruled a mistrial at the lower level and thus overturned the lower court conviction.

Although this case centered on improper admission of evidence in a lower court, it is revealing that the appeals court ignored Agnew's contention that Pendley was not white. Had the court been forced to consider Pendley's race in order to rule, it would have exposed the precarious nature of antimiscegenation laws in a society that relied on cultural definitions of race. State antimiscegenation laws were formulated to regulate sexual and marital relations between bodies that were clearly racialized white or black. As postwar definitions of race replaced scientific definitions, courts struggled to rule in antimiscegenation cases such as *Agnew v. State of Alabama*.

We should also consider why Vena Mae Pendley and her black lover, Agnew, were set free while Luby Griffith was not. After all, both women were found to have engaged in adulterous relationships with black men. Pendley's signed petition relinquishing parental rights to her mixed-race child confirmed her "crime." No such smoking gun existed in Griffith's case, yet it was she who was convicted and not Pendley. We might speculate that each woman's defense shaped whether she was convicted. Pendley sought to defend her racial status as white. She did not deny the relationship, though she did deny that her child belonged to Agnew. Perhaps Pendley had slightly redeemed herself by giving her child to the state, thereby relinquishing her legal claim over a nonwhite child. Furthermore, in defending her white racial identity, Pendley forced Alabama's appeals court to question race itself. In short, had the court considered Agnew's claim that Pendley was not white, it would have turned this case about adultery and patriarchy into a case about the arbitrary nature of race.

Luby Griffith, on the other hand, was incontestably white, and Nathan Bell was incontestably not white. Griffith's case did not, therefore, call into question the logic of racial classification, and in this way her case was more easily prosecuted even though there was very little evidence. Moreover, in denying her adulterous affair, Griffith sought a voice in a southern court in which she was positioned against the state and her husband. Given the dual function of antimiscegenation laws to regulate race and gender relations, we might speculate that Griffith had less chance of an acquittal than Pendley.[39]

In the wake of the Supreme Court's *Brown v. Board of Education* decision, state supreme courts were faced with a new context for deciding antimiscegenation cases. The Court held that official separation of the races in the realm of public services was unconstitutional. Nonetheless, it was not clear whether this ruling applied to cases of antimiscegenation law. At the heart of the matter was whether marriage was primarily a civil matter that granted rights in the public sphere or whether marriage was fundamentally a private contract. If the former, then it would seem that *Brown* would lead courts to find antimiscegenation laws unconstitutional, for like racial segregation in education, these laws officially enforced racial segregation in marriages. If marriage was primarily a private relationship that does not affect rights in the public sphere, then courts could conclude that *Brown*'s outlawing of official separation of races in the public sphere did not apply to the private relationship of marriage.

The Supreme Court had the opportunity to determine the constitutionality of antimiscegenation laws just six months after *Brown* in the appeal of Linnie Jackson, who was convicted under Alabama's antimiscegenation law. Yet the Court refused to hear this case because, as Rachel Moran argues, it believed that in the wake of its *Brown* decision, it was prudent to avoid such controversial matters. A law clerk for Chief Justice Warren said of the decision to ignore Jackson's claim, "the denial of cert[iorari] was totally prudential, totally based on a high-level political judgment."[40] As Moran shows, the Court was not only fearful of cases involving black/white marriages, for one year after it refused to hear Jackson's appeal, it refused to hear an appeal of Virginia's *Naim v. Naim* case.

Antimiscegenation laws have never been deployed only to regulate interracial sexuality and marriage; they have been used to determine property relations, inheritance, and punishment in cases of adultery. For our purposes, what is significant about the postwar cases is how the context of postwar racial ideology made the defense of state antimiscegenation laws difficult. At a time when biological definitions of racial categories were replaced with cultural definitions of race, and at a time when the nation had just waged a war for democracy and against fascism, it would seem unlikely that antimiscegenation cases could remain intact after the war.

California's supreme court believed that the war made antimiscegenation laws seem un-American. For the California justices, the war was a fight against racism and in support of human rights. In this way, they argued, antimiscegenation laws violated the human right to marriage. Yet they went further than this by arguing that antimiscegenation laws were unconstitutional because such laws relied on spurious racial categories. This challenge to biological definitions of race undermined the legitimacy of antimiscegenation laws.

Most telling for our purposes is how the legal regulation of interracial intimacy illustrates a contentious debate over competing publics. After the war, shifting racial discourse, new ideas about the family and normative sexuality, and the growing significance of civil rights reforms made debating the legitimacy of antimiscegenation laws confusing and potentially explosive. Yet the color line was protected after the war by a consensus that interracial sexuality and marriage were best regulated by local, regional, and state jurisdictions. Tracing the history of antimiscegenation court cases in the ten years after the war exposes how states' rights arguments could be used to save antimiscegenation laws and to protect the color line from criticism that such policies were un-American. At times, protecting a state's right to deploy antimiscegenation laws meant reversing a lower court antimiscegenation conviction. Yet even as such decisions were overturned, state appeals courts successfully navigated the complex historical contexts that threatened to take away their power to regulate intimate social relations.

We can begin to understand the implications of the legal debate over interracial sexuality on American culture in the 1940s and 1950s by placing this debate in dialogue with the cultural representation of interracial intimacy in postwar mass culture. Just as courts limited interracial intimacy's reach to nonfederal realms, postwar popular culture represented interracial sexuality as a private matter of romantic choice, rather than as a meaningful challenge to the color line. In this way, popular culture understood interracial sexuality through a romantic narrative of the nuclear family that managed the connections between interracial sexuality and the growing politics of race reform. I now turn to the romance of interracial sexuality and to the ways in which the narrative strategy of the romance helped contain social understandings of race and sexuality.

Chapter 2

Containing Contradictions

The Cultural Logic of Interracial Intimacy

IN 1934 JOHN STAHL'S remarkable film *Imitation of Life* engaged the politics of interracial intimacy through its exploration of a light-skinned black woman's attempt to pass as white. But in order to do so, Peola (Fredi Washington) had to reject her dark-skinned black mother, Delilah (Louise Beavers). Stahl's adaptation of Fannie Hurst's 1933 novel concludes with Delilah's death, attributed in part to her anguish over Peola's rejection. Peola, by the end of the film, feels guilty for rejecting her mother. Yet the film leaves open the question of Peola's future. Will she now freely pass as white, or will she continue to be confused? The film does not offer narrative closure. Peola is racially ambiguous and confused as a result.

Imitation of Life is also about women's economic independence. Beatrice Pullman (Claudette Colbert) is a single mother who employs Delilah as a live-in domestic. A widower who is looking for employment, Beatrice decides to open a chain of pancake restaurants featuring Delilah's secret recipe. Although Beatrice gets rich and moves from an apartment to a mansion, Delilah never leaves her role as domestic. Beatrice's ideal life, however, is undermined by misdirected love. At the end of the film, Beatrice breaks off her impending engagement to a man because her daughter has romantic feelings for him. In this drama, viewers witness a failed nuclear family, unable to form because of misdirected desires.

Both of these plots are concerned with "unnatural" desires. First, Peola's ability to pass as white suggests a hidden history of interracial sexuality and violence. Because the black actress Fredi Washington plays the role of Peola, audiences are asked to consider race mixing, passing, and the limits of racial categories. The film's lack of narrative closure with regard to

Peola's future avoided containing this history of interracial sex and left audiences to wonder about the meaning of race if a black woman could be "mistaken" for white.

Second, the film presents the unnatural desires of a child toward her mother's fiancé. Thus the film concludes with a mother and daughter left to work out their complex relationship. What is clear, however, is that neither of them needs a man to complete their family. Marriage, in Stahl's film, was not a requirement for family bonding. In this way, the film is remarkable for its narrative ambiguity. The film is able to probe the meaning of racial mixture and of women's economic independence without fixing these issues within the boundaries of the nuclear family. Although the film is not without its racist assumptions—after all, Delilah is a mammy figure throughout the film—it examined the complexities of racial identity in ways that were unavailable just two decades later.

If, in 1934, Stahl's *Imitation* could end without much narrative closure, by 1959 such indecisiveness in matters of race and sex was not possible; the family had emerged as an ideological space that contained the possibilities of women's economic freedom and the politics of interracial sexuality. In 1959 Douglas Sirk remade Stahl's *Imitation of Life*. Sirk's version maintained the theme of the tragic mulatta, while ignoring the drama of women's independence. Yet two production choices severely limited the kind of political message Sirk's film could make about race. First, Sirk cast the white actress Susan Kohner in the role of the mulatta, Sarah Jane. This casting decision showed Sirk's assumption that audiences would feel more sympathy for a white tragic mulatta. Second, Sirk added a new conclusion to the film that answered the audience's questions about Sarah Jane's future after her mother dies. In the conclusion of Sirk's film, the misdirected desires of the white daughter are ignored, and the white couple decides to marry. Sarah Jane is included in this family, suggesting that now that her mother is dead, she can fully pass for white and live a "whole" life. Sirk's narrative choice to conclude his film with the successful formation of the white nuclear family, and Sarah Jane's inclusion in this family, fixed Sarah Jane's racial confusion as white. In doing so, Sirk's film turned the drama of racial passing into a story of white assimilation. The film ignored the legacy of interracial sexual relationships that was central in Stahl's film.

In order to understand the complex politics that shaped the post–World War II transformation of *Imitation of Life*, we need to recognize how the

postwar culture constructed and represented the politics of interracial intimacy. This was a period when a number of leftist cultural workers attempted
to confront racial problems through their art. Yet this was also a moment
when the radical potential of 1930s' popular antifascism was in decline and
the containment culture of the 1950s was ascendant. Most critically for our
purposes is how the politics of interracial sexuality and marriage were ideologically managed within popular culture. Interracial intimacy became a
trope through which American culture contained the possibilities of interracial sexuality through narrative and artistic choices that turned the political
issues of interracial intimacy into private matters of individual romantic
choice and away from questions of civil rights. Such narratives limited the
available representations of black bodies and of sexuality by placing them
outside the spheres of the nation and of the family, and all sexuality was contained to the domestic sphere of the home. In this way, the politics of interracial intimacy were contained to the very limited public of the domestic
sphere, a space that is highly politicized and ideologically contained.[1]

This chapter examines two predominant postwar cultural forms: the comic
book and film. While these forms catered to different audiences and were
often motivated by different political imperatives, they shared an assumption
about the appropriate space of interracial intimacy. Through narrative techniques that placed all matters of sexuality in the domestic sphere, these forms
contained the explosive potential of interracial sexuality. In the case of comic
books, romance narratives frequently played with the possibility of interracial romance. The specter of love across the color line undoubtedly titil-
lated a juvenile readership that was increasingly encountering interracial
experiences in schools, in music, and in films. Yet in the comic formula, interracial romance was a trope for mediating appropriate gender norms between
white bodies. Interracial romance was a cautionary narrative plot not used to
suggest transgressions of the color line as viable alternatives to postwar conformity but instead to show readers what could happen when romance was
misdirected.

Many postwar films also relied on the narrative device of the family
melodrama to contain the possible implications of interracial intimacy.
Films carried a wider range of representational options than comics. Leftist
filmmakers who were cognizant of the need to improve roles for African
Americans made films in which the politics of interracial intimacy were
engaged through the drama of racial passing. While such films conveniently

averted the vexing issue of interracial love, they nevertheless focused on how racially ambiguous bodies would be received within a predominantly white society. Such film representations carried the potential to unravel a tangled history of interracial sexuality and racial violence. Yet like their peers in the comic books industry, filmmakers attempted to contain such explosiveness by achieving narrative closures within the domestic sphere. Such closure relied on making passing characters choose between blackness and white-ness, thereby fixing passing as a drama of monoracial identity. Moreover, casting decisions that placed white actors in the roles of passing characters similarly undermined the transgressive potential of racial ambiguity.

In both the comic narratives and the film narratives explored in this chapter, the family emerges as a trope that contains the subversive potential of interracial intimacy. Although the family is thought of as the bastion of privacy, it is also a space permeated by social ideas about gender, race, and sexuality. As Robert Lee argues, the family stands at the center of debates about nationhood and race.

> *The family is . . . the primary ideological apparatus, the central system of symbols through which the state contains and manages contradictions in the social structure. It is the principal social unit through which the individual can become a national subject, a member of the community through birth, adoption, and marriage. The family is a primary site in which labor power and class relations, gender and sexual relations, ethnic and racial identities are produced and reproduced. It is also the symbolic system that gives meaning to and organizes the closest psychological, economic, and sexual relations among people and within a community.*[2]

Even as some comic books and films contained the range of possibilities for interracial intimacy, these forms came under intense scrutiny from congressional subcommittees determined to manage the spaces of interracial sexuality. For example, the Senate Subcommittee to Investigate Juvenile Delinquency monitored comic books because of their suspected link to childhood crime and delinquency. Led by Senator Estes Kefauver, this subcommittee sought to regulate not only comic book content but also the places where comics could be bought and read. Similarly, the growing influence of the House Un-American Activities Committee severely constrained the kind of radical politics that could be represented in film. As the cultural front of the 1930s, as Michael Denning calls it, came under attack during the

1940s, leftist filmmakers had to limit their films' political content. Thus, as Denning has shown, by the 1950s even the 1940s films' limited representations of interracial intimacy were severely constricted.

This chapter is therefore about how comic book and film producers contained interracial intimacy within the domestic sphere. Yet it is also about how the very representation of interracial intimacy in these forms caused intense concern from the federal government. In this way, cultural representations of interracial intimacy brought to light contested notions of publicness. Even as comic book publishers and film producers contained interracial intimacy to the domestic sphere, these two culture industries were already very public. Thus even a limited representation of interracial intimacy unwittingly made such representations public issues and open to subversive readings. Because of this, the federal government sought to limit the kinds of representations of sexuality produced by comics and films. This effort signified the federal government's attempt to contain mass culture's publicness.

In 1954 the comic book industry was compelled to succumb to the power of Senator Estes Kefauver's Senate Subcommittee to Investigate Juvenile Delinquency by creating and enforcing self-censorship rules called comic codes. Consisting of forty-one regulations stipulating the boundaries of appropriate comic book stories and photos, the codes were constructed so that the comics could, in the end, "teach good citizenship lessons."[3] The codes mirrored governmental regulation of popular culture in the aftermath of World War II. Popular culture was viewed both as a medium through which to present the American case for its superiority to itself and the rest of the world and as a medium that, if placed in the wrong hands, held the potential to undermine the American way. These twin perceptions about mass-mediated popular culture led to governmental regulations of film content and, in 1954, of comic book content.[4]

When pressed to defend themselves in front of the Senate subcommittee, comic book executives argued that comics played an important role in educating youth and new immigrants about American history. As one publisher noted in 1954, "the U.S. Information Service uses comic booklets to explain American ideals to foreigners." Moreover, comics were used by the Atomic Energy Commission to teach readers "what an atom is, how it is split, and what happens when it is split." Perhaps the most powerful argument in the comic book publishers' arsenal was that the comics presented historical narratives that every good citizen ought to know. These stories included, according to one publisher, "historical facts about American Indians; history of 'Old Ironside' (USS *Constitution*); story of immigration to the United States; curious romantic customs; significance of rings and other jewelry in various countries; and marriage customs in other lands."[5]

American Indians, immigrants, war machinery, and romance in foreign lands constituted a complex pastiche of narrative tropes that registered much larger social issues related to race relations at home and the meaning of American empire after World War II. In examining the contest between the House Un-American Activities Committee and the comic book industry in 1954, we must therefore place this debate in a much larger frame than mere censorship. At stake here was who had the power to enter the public realm of mass culture and what kinds of representations were appropriate to the public realm. The politics of interracial intimacy was at the center of this contest over mass culture, as the comic book industry suggested that narratives concerning "romances in foreign lands" could, in the end, train good citizens.

The struggle over monitoring children's culture was an important part of the postwar anti-Communist crusade. The rise of niche programming for teens in music and television led government censors to focus attention on mass-marketed children's culture. Comic books became an important target for these censors because of their popularity among youth and because of their engagement with narratives deemed devious in the context of postwar society's attempt to contain the disruptions caused by World War II. According to John Goldwater's study of the comics industry, in 1954 fifteen national distributors, 1,200 wholesale firms, and 110,000 retail outlets produced one billion comics per years. Readers purchased about $100 million worth of comics annually. Although it is difficult to ascertain precisely how many people read comics and who read comics, a few municipal studies from the postwar decade indicate that comic readers ranged in age from eight to thirty. In New Orleans, researchers found that adults purchased one-quarter to one-third of comics for their own consumption. In Dayton, Ohio, nearly all kids ages eight to fourteen purchased comic books. Among consumers between twenty-one and thirty, 43 percent of men and 5 percent of women purchased comics.[6] It is impossible to know whether adults who purchased comics did so for their own consumption or whether they were providing the comics for children. Comic book advertisers clearly imagined older readers whey they published ads for nursing schools, domestic appliances, and beauty products.

The debate over the comics illustrates the explosive nature of mass culture, sexuality, and race in the postwar years. Senator Kefauver's Senate subcommittee critiqued numerous types of comic books in its 1954 hearings. Especially disconcerting to the subcommittee were those comics that placed the fate of white women in the hands of nonwhite subjects. Through a richly detailed discourse of obscenity and sexual promiscuity, the Kefauver subcommittee targeted all kinds of comics, including the romance variety.[7]

The federal case against the comics relied most heavily on the testimony presented by psychologist Frederic Wertham. A personal friend of the Frankfurt School scholar Theodore Adorno, Wertham was primed to analyze mass-mediated culture with skepticism. Yet Wertham was also acclaimed as a civil rights activist. His LeFarge clinic provided psychological services for African Americans in New York and was celebrated by Ralph Ellison in *Shadow and Act*. Wertham's critique of the comics centered around their presentation of sexually explicit material. According to William Savage Jr.,

> *The doctor's research confirmed the view . . . that stories about Batman and Robin were "psychologically homosexual," pervaded by "a subtle atmosphere of homoeroticism." Indeed, the association of these two crime fighters was "like a wish dream of two homosexuals living together." And only "someone ignorant of the fundamentals of psychiatry and of the psychopathology of sex" would say it wasn't so—a splendid ploy for preempting the layperson's criticism of the critic. As for Wonder Woman, she was the "Lesbian counterpart of Batman," a "frightening image" for boys and a "morbid ideal" for girls.*[8]

Wertham thus constructed the comics as a medium for "deviant" sexuality that would confuse and damage young readers. The Senate Subcommittee to Investigate Juvenile Delinquency, formed in part to regulate public discourse on sexuality, heard testimony from comic book industry representatives, local and civic leaders, and professional psychologists like Wertham. Although the subcommittee claimed that it was not "a subcommittee of blue-nosed censors," its investigation contributed to an extensive set of laws regulating comic book content. Pressured by local civic and community groups, in addition to the Kefauver subcommittee hearings, eighteen states passed laws restricting the magazines. For example, the Louisiana state legislature enacted a law stating,

> *No person shall sell any printed or photographic material which might be detrimental to the morals of minors, such printed or photographic material consisting of any book, comic book, magazine, pamphlet or other printed matter devoted to the*

publication of criminal deeds or stories or to the publication of any obscene, lewd, lascivious, filthy, or sexually indecent print, picture, or other matter.[9]

Louisiana legislators connected comics to the most dangerous form of insubordination whey they argued that comics were "a cause of anxiety to . . . civil and religious life."[10]

In New York, the state that contained the bulk of comic book companies, lawmakers passed the most powerful regulations. Beginning in 1951, the state annually monitored the comics. The legislature accused some publishers of causing crime and, importantly, inciting inappropriate passions.

A small stubborn, willful, irresponsible minority of publishers of so-called "comics," whose brazen disregard for anyone whose sole objective is financial gain without thought of the consequences of their depredations, are responsible for the publishers of all comics. The reading of crime "comics" stimulates sadistic and masochistic attitudes and interferes with the normal development of sexual habits in children and produces abnormal sexual tendencies in adolescents.[11]

The hysteria surrounding juvenile delinquency and its ties to comic books was most powerful at the municipal level. In San Francisco, for example, city leaders argued that "parents, home, God, and spiritual values have too little place in the lives of the self-sufficient young extroverts characterized by comic books." In Canton, Ohio, city leaders censured "literature that advocates the violation of the Ten Commandments."[12] Among the private organizations that supported municipal efforts to censor the comics were the American Legion, the General Federation of Women's Clubs, American Veterans, tne California Congress of Parent Teachers, the National Council of Juvenile Courts, the National Organization for Decent Literature, Safeway Stores, the University of Santa Clara, and the Milwaukee Archdiocesan Confraternity of Christian Mothers.

During the Senate subcommittee's hearing on juvenile delinquency, the comics came under attack for many reasons; they were accused of teaching children to defy their parents and law enforcement and of titillating juvenile readers. Yet what is most important for this discussion is the critique that the comics should be censored because they were sexist and racist. In St. Cloud, Minnesota, for example, city leaders outlawed a large range of crime and romance comics that were accused of presenting "horrors, robberies, murders, assault . . . burglary, kidnapping, rape, theft, voluntary manslaughter, ridicule of law enforcement, parental authority, or person by reason of race, creed or color; or advocates of un-American activities.[13] St. Cloud's city leaders constructed a broad list that equated murder and racial discrimination as damaging to juvenile readers.

In their defense of their medium, comic book publishers suggested that presenting comics that represented interracial intimacy could signify respect for racial difference during a time when race relations were integral to the American image abroad. Hence what for municipal crusaders were dangerous representations that led to delinquent behavior were, for comic book publishers, didactic tools that educated readers about American values. In this reading, comics did not advocate deviance but aired deviance in order to encourage alternative behavior.

The debate over comic book censorship reads as a public performance in which senators and comic book publishers debated questions of citizenship, race, and gender in an abstract way that ignored the existence of racial discrimination and sexism and the problems these realities posed for democracy. The national and municipal debate, because it was so spectacular, ignored consideration of actual racial discrimination, sexism, and inequality in general. In developing the parameters for acceptable comic narratives that could teach good citizenship, the Senate Subcommittee to Investigate Juvenile Delinquency came to a consensus that antiracism and antisexism were values that supported good citizenship. The comic codes were a set of self-censorship guidelines developed by the comic book industry to deflect senators' criticism of their form. The codes are revealing testimony about the values of heterosexuality, marriage, and the nuclear family to postwar notions of good citizenship.

Among the comic codes agreed to in 1954 were those that outlined the parameters for how comic characters could be drawn and what type of information about sex could be presented. This section of the codes prohibited "nudity in any form" in addition to "suggestive and salacious illustrations." The codes upheld the notion that the nuclear family was the only appropriate location for female sexuality. "Divorce," the codes read, "shall not be treated humorously nor [sic] represented as desirable. . . . Illicit sex relations are neither to be hinted at [n]or portrayed. Violent love scenes as well as sexual abnormalities are unacceptable."[14] The codes did not elaborate exactly what comprised "illicit sex relations."

Because of their ambiguity, the codes read not only as a guideline for what could and could not be represented in the pages of comic books but also as an affirmation that publishers of this mass culture shared dominant ideas about the importance of the family and the protection of the young female reader as paramount. The codes referred to above begin to suggest the centrality of monitoring and policing sexuality in postwar America. "Illicit sexuality" and the "lower and baser emotions," which the codes were constructed to prevent, registered the serious anxieties of a society that viewed female sexuality as politically explosive.[15]

When comics received the seal of approval from the comics codes authority, they gained acceptance as popular cultural forms that conformed to postwar norms of gender, race, class, and sexuality. Although the codes upheld the value of respect for all people, especially women, the comic codes allowed for a wide range of comic narratives that would seem to undermine this creed. Especially in those comics that represented interracial romances, or at the very least, the possibility of cross-racial desire, it was quite common to represent people of color as exotic relics of the past, as sexual predators, and as uncivilized others living in foreign and exotic lands. Such exoticization of people of color, according to Ann McClintock and Mary Louise Pratt, has been a staple of the process of imperialism. The limits of the codes, therefore, lay in the contradictions of their vision of democracy and citizenship. While espousing respect for all creeds and for women, the codes, and the much more significant Senate subcommittee policing of mass culture, ignored the racism of comics that posed the (im)possibility of interracial intimacy. In the comics analyzed below, interracial intimacy was cast as an acceptable comic book narrative and representation so long as it appeared as a fleeting specter and not as the concluding moral of the story. Hence interracial intimacy was acceptable so long as it was used as a cautionary trope, intended to shuttle young readers' desires toward "appropriate" sexuality.

Comics rarely represented successful interracial romances, and when they did represent interracial intimacy, they did so in the most fantastic and unrealistic ways. Numerous comics portrayed the possible, though never realized, love affair between a white explorer and an African tribeswoman or between a white woman and a presumed Mexican "tortilla maker." What is telling about all of the narratives discussed below is that they almost always set the place of interracial intimacy outside the United States. When comics did pose the possibility of interracial love within the United States, it was invariably a representation of a relationship between a white man and a Native American woman and always in some unnamed "past." In other words, in order for a comic to represent interracial intimacy within the nation, it would have to do so by "going Native"; that is, by connecting white protagonists to the American landscape through their relationship to Native American princesses. That the comics placed interracial intimacy outside the nation may suggest that one way that Americans reconciled the United States's new role as a global superpower was by writing "global people"—read non-Anglo—outside the nation through the convention of interracial intimacy.[16]

We can only speculate about the uses and meanings readers made of the comics. However, the very popularity of the form invites a close reading of how the comics represented interracial intimacy. The romance comics discussed here present cautionary tales in which a female protagonist has to negotiate an obstacle before she can assume her prescribed role in the nuclear family. Although there were many different kinds of comic book genres produced after World War II, approximately half were of the romance variety. My reading of the comics focuses on the ideological and social importance of stories in which a white female protagonist is both heroine and potential victim of a racial other.

The overwhelming majority of comic book romances present interethnic and interclass marriages as Americanizing. Typical of this convention was a 1954 *Heartthrobs* comic called "My Parents Stood Between Us."[17] In this comic, a young white female leaves her steady and respectable boyfriend for a dance instructor named Freddie Ryan. Freddie is coded Irish through his name and his blazing red hair. Freddie has an uncertain financial future, and the comic focuses on the disapproval voiced by the young woman's parents about their daughter's choice to leave a stable, middle-class boyfriend for Freddie. In a characteristic sudden reversal, the comic shows that Freddie can become the right kind of man by abandoning his dancing job and "cleaning himself up." As the young woman's father explains to Freddie in the concluding frame, "We all make fools out of ourselves at one time or another, Freddie! The important thing is that we realize it—and change our ways! You'll have to prove you've grown up son!" The interethnic and presumably interclass romance can continue because ethnicity and class can be changed. Freddie can become a suitable suitor by quitting his feminizing dance job, wearing respectable clothes, and romancing the right kind of woman. This comic therefore espouses an inclusive notion of romance across difference, so long as those differences can be subsumed into one universal notion of the heterosexual good life and the family.

The comics also focused on working-class women who needed to learn lessons appropriate to the nuclear family. For example, in a 1952 *Confessions of the Lovelorn*, female readers were asked, "Do you expect too much?"[18] Cautioning against demanding too much from potential spouses, the comic advised, "Wise is the gal who realizes the responsibilities of marriage even before the wedding—and happy is the guy who finds such a gal!" In 1949 *Love Story* comics similarly cautioned against women who wanted too much; "How soft and fragile a thing is the human heart—yet it is capable of the most powerful of all emotions . . . love! Toni Livingston invited romance, but only on her own terms, and her heart was as calloused and impenetrable as a dungeon door is unmoved by the fluttering wings of a caged dove."[19]

While comics taught lessons about appropriate gender roles, they also showed protagonists who were discontent with the middle-class conformist society of the postwar years. During a time when strict gender roles severely limited the acceptable possibility for women's participation in the public sphere, the comic books showed women who shirked their domestic imperatives by exploring the outside world. In doing so, the comics presented models of female behavior that were independent and powerful. Moreover, during an era of middle-class suburbanization, the comics presented young, "unmelted" ethnic couples holding on to their working-class and urban ethnic roots. Although it is impossible to know whether audiences made comics popular because of the possibility for imagining subversive identities in postwar America, it is telling that the comics engage issues that postwar historians argue were at the center of social debate; namely, the role of women in society, appropriate sexual behavior, and, to a lesser extent, race relations.[20]

While the comics challenged confining notions of domesticity and at times resisted the postwar imperative for middle-class conformity, they also taught what comic book publishers referred to as good citizenship lessons. These lessons frequently revealed complex representations of nonwhite characters, often in romantic relationship to white protagonists. What concerns us here are the ways that the debate about comic readership in the Senate Subcommittee to Investigate Juvenile Delinquency revealed fissures within the postwar ideologies of gender and class at the expense of casting nonwhite bodies as threats to national security. The specter of interracial intimacy ultimately racialized the shape of postwar discontent over gender and class norms and contributed to a racialized discourse of deviant sexuality. Stories of "marriage customs in other lands" lent themselves to critiques of the nuclear family *and* cast "foreign" bodies as sexually perverse and dangerous to white protagonists. Here I suggest that, to use Toni Morrison's phrase, comics are "playing in the dark." Morrison suggests that at transitional moments in American history, black bodies are employed in the service of an exclusionary whiteness. That is, through the spectral image of blackness, the nation constructs itself as white. In this way, the comics visually represent nonwhite sexuality as a way to comment on social relations of class and gender. Moreover, the discursive placement of the space of interracial intimacy outside of the nation's space and time turned interracial intimacy into fantasy and not reality.

Stories about white women who explored the jungle were a common literary genre in comic books. *Jan of the Jungle, Nyoka Jungle Girl,* and *Tarzan* are just a few of the titles that dealt with jungle romances. According to comic book historian William Savage Jr., people of color entered the jungle adventure comic book as inferior and predatory.

> *All [people of color] required Caucasian intervention on their behalf. Natives were natives, it seemed, and wherever the white hero found them, they could be depended upon to have submitted already to liquor, drugs, Communism, scams of various kinds, and all sorts of criminal activity, either as perpetrators or as victims.* [21]

A 1952 *First Love* comic story called "Savage Love!" offers an extraordinary example of how interracial intimacy could be used to uphold the values of the white nuclear family. A story of a working-class white woman who, just for fun, passes as a "Native" African by posing as a "savage guide" for her future love interest, "Savage Love!" is a complex narrative that employs two forms of interracial intimacy. [22] The first entails a fascination with the working-class white woman's racial passing as a "savage"; the second entails the fears of the predatory sexuality of "real" Africans, as they threaten to attack a white woman. The comic thus airs two versions of interracial intimacy containing both a desire for the exotic and the repulsion of the actual nonwhite body.

The introduction sets the stage for the narrative in the racialized space of the jungle. The reader opens the comic to learn that Janet Grant, the wealthy daughter of a white explorer, is in love with the man her father hired to guide her through the African jungle. Janet opens the narrative by foreshadowing the perils of white heterosexuality in a context of nonwhite sexuality: "The perilous jungles of Africa were paradise to me because I was with the man I loved! Nothing, I thought, could rob me of this ecstasy! Until primitive passions flared and I had to face the torture of Savage Love." Readers are presented with the juxtaposed white heterosexual couple and the dark jungle, a place of "primitive passions." Yet while this comic will show the threat of nonwhite sexuality to white heterosexuality, it ultimately is a cautionary tale about white women who want too much. Janet Grant loses her love interest because she is demanding, relies on her father's wealth, and is not compassionate toward the African "Natives." Interracial intimacy is employed not only to air the possibility of interracial desire and terror but also as a trope through which to discuss "appropriate" gender and class ideologies.

In order to navigate the dangerous terrain of the jungle, Janet and her guide, Jack, hire someone they think is a local guide. The comic shows Janet's shock when she learns that the "African guide is a girl. A beautiful native girl." This "beautiful native" is a blond bombshell who seemingly fools only Janet and Jack into believing she is black. Goldie, as the "native girl" is called, is white skinned with blond hair. She is an expert of the jungle and a threat to Janet's relationship with Jack. As the expedition progresses, Janet is overcome by her jealously of Goldie. She admits that "I, wealthy Janet Grant, was jealous of an ignorant little savage!" Janet's jealously leads her to insist that Goldie be dismissed from the expedition. But Jack refuses because he believes that Goldie, the "savage guide," is the only person capable of fending off the bad Natives. "The natives are beginning to get nasty! Goldie is the only who can control them."

The visual presentation of Goldie and Janet juxtaposes two models of womanhood. Janet is overbearing, uses her wealth to get what she wants, and attempts to control Jack's choices about a guide. Goldie, on the other hand, is idealized as pure and in control. Part of her appeal is her ability to control the "savages" but also to act the savage as well. Goldie therefore assumes the role of the historic Native American princess, yet she does so in such a way as to leave her whiteness unchallenged.[23] Goldie's power over the "savages" makes her attractive to Jack. As the comic continues, Janet is increasingly jealous of Jack and accuses Goldie of attempting to steal her love interest. "You brazen sneaky savage!" she proclaims. "It's all a pack of lies to get rid of me so you can have Jack."

Janet is partially correct; Goldie is living a lie, but her purpose, at least at the outset, is not to steal Jack away. Goldie is only masquerading as a black "savage," and she will soon unmask herself. The climax occurs when, at night, the Natives come after Janet and Goldie intervenes to protect her. "In the blackness of the jungle night" the Natives are held back by Goldie. Having exhibited complete mastery over the "savages"—both because she defended a white woman and because she can pass as black—Goldie reveals her fakery to Jack. "I'm not a native, Jack. . . . My name is Alice Denton! My parents are American missionaries and when I heard about your expedition, I thought it would be fun to pretend to be a native guide." Once revealed as white, and religious as well, Goldie becomes Jack's new love. Goldie is capable of negotiating the jungle and coming out white and, in so doing, exhibiting the kinds of desire and repulsion that Eric Lott has identified at the core of blackface minstrelsy.

"Savage Love!" is a comic that presents interracial intimacy as only a possibility while evading any representation of an interracial romance. Goldie can be desired as an exotic and racial "other," but in order to consummate romance she must be white. By pitting Janet against Goldie as possible mates for Jack, the comic made a statement about what type of woman would fall in love and begin families; it was the woman who may have enjoyed posing as a "savage guide" but who, in the end, did not trade in blackness and chose marriage. The message had relevance in a culture in which unprecedented numbers of white audiences listened to African American musicians. Indeed, the rise of rock and roll necessitated ways of policing racial transgressions among white women. The racial mimicry that formed the basis of "Savage Love!" showed that real romance could only be formed when white women negotiate the color line cleanly.[24]

Exhibiting mastery over people of color was an important act for comic book heroines. Yet experimenting with alternative racial identity could not, in the end, include staying on the wrong side of the color line. In 1945 the comic series *True Stories* included a short story called "Jungle Queen, The True Story of Ursula Graham-Bower." The story focuses on the 1939 expedition of anthropologist Ursula Graham-Bower, who joined an East Indian tribe to fight Japanese soldiers during World War II. In order to undermine the seeming interracial respect between Graham-Bower and the "Naga" tribesmen, the comic presents her as both a mother and master of the tribe. The comic introduces Graham-Bower as a comrade to men of color. "The Naga head-hunters of Northeastern India were strong companions for the pretty Englishwoman Ursula Graham-Bower. But together they held the Jap invaders at bay." Graham-Bower is represented as a mother figure for the Naga. She takes care of Naga children and is seemingly the only nurturing parental figure among the tribe. Graham-Bower's skills as mother are confirmed when the reader learns that the Naga allow Graham-Bower to give Anglo names to their children. In addition to her nurturing role, Graham-Bower is also presented as a military leader, inspiring the Naga to enter battle with the Japanese. When Japanese soldiers approach the home of the Naga, Graham-Bower must convince the tribe to fight. She assumes control and posts "alert savages to guard every trail in the territory." When the Naga capture Japanese soldiers, they bring them to the "white woman." Graham-Bower is maternal to escaped allied men, but to Japanese captives of war she is tough, "This man is a Jap spy! Put him under guard." The story ends with Graham-Bower as the leader of the Naga victory.[25]

Like the fictional Goldie of "Savage Love!" Ursula Graham-Bower becomes a useful representative of white femininity for postwar readers. While Graham-Bower does not engage in a romantic relationship with the Naga tribesmen, the comic nonetheless considers the meaning of interracial bodily closeness at a time when, as Eileen Boris has argued, fears of bodily closeness punctuated the spaces of the World War II home front. Graham-Bower becomes a mother figure that encourages her subjects to fight the enemy. Like Goldie, Graham-Bower commands a level of respect and control over men of color. In this way, the foreign spaces of jungles become spaces of self-realization for white women. The specter of interracial bodily closeness functions as a trope for intraracial heterosexuality.[26]

The jungle was the terrain in which comic book characters negotiated the postwar imperatives of the nuclear family and the desires for alternative roles for women. People of color emerged in these narratives as captors and deviants. Yet the comics did more than narrate white women's roles in the jungle; they also constructed images of nonwhite women as beyond the pale of civilization. Comics utilized historical narratives to imagine the appropriate roles of white women in the nation and to erase nonwhite women from the national landscape. White comic heroines challenged the domestic imperatives of the postwar world by being independent and by threatening to engage in sexual behavior outside the realm of marriage. Ultimately, however, these narratives present motherhood and the family as redemptive entities that "cure" inappropriate behavior. According to the postwar comic, women of color cannot find redemption in the family or in motherhood. Rather, women of color are written out of American time and space because they are represented as too sexual or because they spurn the rewards of the nuclear family. In other words, not all women negotiate the jungle as clearly as Goldie and Graham-Bower. Where Goldie and Graham-Bower successfully master nonwhite subjects, American Indian women and Mexican women were unable to escape their foreign milieu. The comics therefore narrate national inclusion through romantic stories that cast some kinds of women as desirable and worthy of white men and other women as undesirable or unwomanly altogether.

In a 1949 *Women Outlaws* story called "Maverick, Queen of the Bounty Hunters," readers are introduced to an American Indian cowgirl who performs the role of the American Indian princess, popularized by the myth of Pocahontas. The comic begins:

> *Treachery was rampant when the first cattle trails stretched Northward from Texas. With the law unable to cope with the vast number of roving outlaws certain shady characters turned their evil talents to hunting down wanted men to collect the rewards offered for their capture. Naomi Pallette, a voluptuous half-breed dance-hall girl, became known as Maverick Queen of the bounty hunters. For it was she who betrayed more than a score of outlaws to the vultures who would kill any man who put a price on his head!*[27]

The comic introduces Naomi Pallette as a "dance-hall girl" working in a saloon. When she is approached by a few men and asked to help them find a presumed outlaw named Shane Alton, readers learn that Naomi is frequently asked to hunt for outlaws because she has gained fame as a woman whose beauty attracts outlaws. Despite her seeming passivity in front of the men, Naomi also exhibits an aggressive side when harassed by customers in the saloon. When called a "squaw gal" by one of the customers, Naomi protests, "Don't call me a squaw gal or I'll git a full blooded Cheyenne to bring me your scalp. . . . I'll slit your raspin throat." In the eyes of the saloon patrons, Naomi is an exotic beauty and a fierce warrior; she embodies both a Pocahontas mother-goddess image and the image of the dredge squaw who is overly masculine.

In order to lure Shane Alton, Naomi spreads the word around town that she's looking for him because she's "sweet" on him. But just as the reader learns that Naomi will hunt for Shane, a new band of outlaws enters the narrative and kidnaps Naomi. These outlaws also want to find Shane and plan to use Naomi as bait. The comic shows a bound Naomi sitting in an open prairie with her kidnappers hiding behind a large boulder. When Shane arrives to rescue Naomi, the kidnappers spring on him and a struggle ensues. During the struggle, Naomi frees herself and joins the fight on Shane's side. Shane and Naomi make a powerful team. After the outlaws are subdued, readers learn quickly that Shane is not an outlaw but is really a Texas Ranger named Shannon. He is traveling west to join Bill Cody's Wild West Show. Naomi claims that she has always wanted to join the Wild West Show. The comic concludes with Naomi and Shane riding off into the landscape.

Like the mythical image of Pocahontas, Naomi is both a subject in need of rescue and an agent who guarantees Anglo conquest through her loving acceptance of a white man. Yet Shane and Naomi's union is not romantic, and marriage is not the concluding event. Naomi's "half-breed" status precludes her participation in a nuclear family, and hence she is removed from the nation. "Maverick, Queen of the Bounty Hunters" erases Native American women's presence in the 1950s by replicating myths of vanishing Native Americans. While white female comic heroines seem empowered by their independence, women like Naomi Pallette are cast as too independent and somehow unworthy of love.

Mexican women also entered postwar comic narratives as outsiders and threats to "appropriate" heterosexuality. A 1953 *Girls Love Stories* story called "Heartbreak in Mexico" tells the story of Faye, a single white woman who visits Mexico in search of true love. "For many Americans, Mexico is a land of exciting romance, and when I first saw Van Barrett in the tiny village where I'd come to visit my cousin Miriam, I thought that I, too, had found such romance!" Faye believes that Van Barrett is a local Mexican merchant who sells his homemade tortillas to tourists. Yet like Goldie of the "Savage Love!" comic, Van is passing as a Mexican; he is really an Anglo tourist "slumming" in Mexico. Faye's initial interest in Van raises the specter of interracial intimacy, for Faye believes Van is Mexican. Despite her initial trepidation, Faye's cousin encourages her to "make the first move. Just think . . . you could eventually be Mrs. Van Barrett and help him serve tortillas to American sightseers for the rest of your life."[28]

But, alas, there is another woman in Van Barrett's life: a Mexican painter named Felicia. In constructing Felicia as the antithesis of Faye, the comic threatens to undermine the power of a white woman over bodies of color.

Van will choose between Faye and Felicia, who has a "husky voice" and "strange beauty." While at a picnic with Faye, Van confesses that he really wants to court Felicia, and he asks Faye for advice on how to achieve his goals. Later, readers see Van propose to Felicia, but Felicia refuses. Within the span of one comic frame, readers learn that Van is an American and that he really wishes to marry Faye. Both Van and Faye have desired interracial relationships—Van with Felicia and Faye with a Van in brownface—yet both ultimately find their intraracial relationship more powerful. "And soon," Faye explains, "Mexico was dripping behind us . . . and our future lay ahead."

At a time when women were expected to marry a man at a young age and form a nuclear family, this comic showed the route to these dreams was littered with the specter of interracial intimacy. Faye leaves the United States in order to find love and finds the task of forming a nuclear family challenged by a Mexican woman's "strange beauty." That Felicia disavows domesticity makes her undesirable and transforms Faye into an ideal type for Van Barrett. Stories about dangerous women like Felicia discouraged readers from viewing interracial intimacy as a route toward happiness.

The jungle, the Southwest, and Mexico serve as liminal scenes in which white heterosexuality can be achieved. In the comic book jungle, white women were freed from the domestic imperative, and they could be happy with their working-class status. In the Southwest, women were also seen as independent and desirous of a male savior. And in Mexico, women tried to find romance with an exotic racial other, only to learn that the racial other whom they desire is only passing, that intraracial romance is best. Although it was not unique for popular narratives to rely on foreign and historical American spaces, what made the postwar comics discussed above important were their publication during a moment when Americans were confronting the presence of unprecedented numbers of "foreigners" under American military and economic control. Interracial intimacy became a trope for mediating the differences between Americans and outsiders by showing the perilous consequences of their coupling.

Popular films, like mass-mediated comic books, aired interracial narratives in order to represent and mediate social conflicts. Yet while the comics cast nonwhite bodies outside the boundaries of American time and space, the movies were more directly engaged with confronting the politics of race in postwar America. The film industry had a long history by the 1940s of confronting social problems in mature and often complex ways.[29]

Unlike comic books, popular films did not have to rely on formulaic narratives that would appeal to children. Directors confronted social problems related to anti-Semitism, racism, and American attitudes about Native Americans. If the comics represented interracial intimacy in fantastic ways to foreclose the possibility of interracial sexuality, films more directly engaged interracial intimacy in order to comment on how the United States could overcome racism after the war. The films examined here represented interracial intimacy in such a way as to define it as a utopian relationship that could overcome the problematic realities of labor exploitation, imperialist wars, and racist practices.

Beginning in 1948, largely in response to African American demands for recognition, Hollywood producers and writers began to produce explicitly race-conscious films. These productions included a series of 1949 films, such as Stanley Kramer's *Home of the Brave*, Louis du Rochemont's *Lost Boundaries*, Daryl Zanuck's *Pinky*, and Dore Schary's *Intruder in the Dust*, as well as Darryl Zanuck and Joseph Mankiewicz's 1950 film, *No Way Out*. In addition to these race-conscious, social-problem films, Hollywood producers and writers developed a series of films that featured the story of racial passing and intermarriage. Although the following films did not have racial uplift and democracy as their stated purposes, they were nevertheless influenced by the social context of civil rights and the cold war. Such films include King Vidor's *Duel in the Sun* and *Japanese War Bride* and Hollywood musicals such as *South Pacific* and the 1951 version of *Show Boat*.

While there exist important distinctions between the race-conscious films produced by leftist filmmakers and those postwar films made by more mainstream producers, for purposes of this discussion, I want to group them together. While they differ in their vision of racial equality and full democratic participation, they share an assumption about how to represent interracial intimacy through casting decisions to have white actors play racially ambiguous roles and narrative choices to contain all sexuality within the domestic sphere. Furthermore, each of these films shared a central focus on the drama of racial discrimination, with the mulatta as an integral figure.

Lost Boundaries (1949), *Duel in the Sun* (1949), and *Japanese War Bride* (1952) each employed interracial intimacy to illustrate more favorable race relations in the postwar years.[30] Yet even as these films addressed the social problems of racism in the United States, they shared the comic books' practice of containing the possibilities of interracial romance and sexuality.

While they go farther than the comics in representing successful interracial relationships, they espouse a vision of universality that ironically erases material racial differences, even as they make interracial intimacy their focus. For purposes of this discussion, universality signifies a particular kind of claim to sameness and equivalency that renders actual differences mute. By playing on the similarity of all humans, the films discussed here espouse a vision of racial equality that ignored how, both structurally and culturally, people of color did not have full inclusion in society. Interracial intimacy played a particularly important role in this vision of universality because of the ways it conflated romance and attraction with the insignificance of the color line. If people can fall in love across the color line, these films suggest, then the color line is not so significant after all. Yet such a vision of inclusion meant ignoring the problems faced by interracial couples, whose relationships were illegal in many states, and of all people of color in the pre–civil rights movement years. The films used interracial intimacy as a tool to erase racial difference and in so doing undermined minority claims to group rights.[31]

Lost Boundaries, directed by Alfred Werker, starred Beatrice Pearson (Marsha Carter) and Mel Ferrer (Scott Carter) as a light-skinned African American couple who pass for white in a small New Hampshire community called Keenham. Based on a *Reader's Digest* story, "Document of a New Hampshire family," *Lost Boundaries* tests the level of acceptance an all-white New Hampshire community can have for a family that has been passing as white. The film engages a central contradiction of the wartime era; namely, how can a country that discriminates against people of color wage a war to protect democracy? *Lost Boundaries* resolves this contradiction through a utopian story of racial reconciliation in which interracial intimacy is integral. Inspired by postwar understandings of racial difference, the film concludes that race is merely skin deep. Interracial intimacy helped resolve the problematic history of racial terror and sexual abuse by turning the public matter of discrimination into a private deception.

Furthermore, *Lost Boundaries* contains the explosive potential of interracial intimacy through its casting decisions. Producer Du Rochmont and director Werker chose white actors to play the roles of the passing family. This choice seemed to suggest that actual racial passing among blacks was not credible. As Judith Smith reveals, Werker believed that audiences would not believe that actual African Americans passed as white. Hence he believed that casting the part-Cuban Mel Ferrer as Scott Carter would be most believable. Yet such casting decisions also whitened the nature of racial passing, thereby severing its link to a history of interracial sexuality. Instead of serving to examine racial problems in the past and present, *Lost Boundaries* represented interracial intimacy as a route toward white assimilation.[32]

Another 1949 racial passing film that contained the political implications of interracial intimacy was *Duel in the Sun*. *Duel* brought together a stellar cast of actors, including Jennifer Jones, Joseph Cotten, Gregory Peck, Lillian Gish, Lionel Barrymore, and Butterfly McQueen. This postwar western, marketed as the next *Gone with the Wind*, focuses on the attempt of a mixed-race mestizo woman named Pearl Chavez to become "a lady." Directed by King Vidor, *Duel* employed interracial intimacy as a trope to moralize about appropriate gender roles. In placing Pearl in some nineteenth-century moment in southern Texas, Vidor allowed his audience to imagine the possibilities of interracial sexual desire in a fantastic, safely contained context. In *Duel*, like its comic book counterparts, we can see how interracial intimacy allowed filmmakers and audiences to challenge gender and class roles in postwar America in ways that left racial boundaries fixed.

The norms of gender and the family help Vidor contain the explosive potential of interracial intimacy. By constructing *Duel* as a drama of Pearl Chavez's attempt to be a true woman and not, primarily, as a story of interracial intimacy, Vidor safely aired the specter of interracial intimacy without identifying the history of interracial sexuality and violence. In this way, interracial intimacy was only a background, yet structuring, element to the film that made legible Vidor's discussion of gender and domesticity. Becoming a true woman in *Duel* meant negotiating interracial romantic relationships cleanly.

In similar ways, *Japanese War Bride* (1952) employs interracial intimacy within a family melodrama in order to moralize about postwar race relations without invoking the problematic and contradictory history of racialized labor relations and anti-Japanese sentiment. Produced by Joseph Bernhard and directed by King Vidor, *Japanese War Bride* starred Don Taylor as a Korean War veteran (Jim Sterling) and Shirley Yamaguchi (Tae Shimizu) as a Red Cross nurse working in a Veterans Affairs hospital in Japan. *Japanese War Bride* shows an interracial marriage that succeeds in confronting racial prejudice in America. The film uses interracial intimacy in order to sublimate certain contradictions between postwar cultural pluralism and the racism that existed during the war, especially as it shaped the reentrance of the Asian

American subject into the nation. In considering whether Jim Sterling can successfully wed Tae Shimizu, the film tests the possibilities of cultural pluralism, while recasting the racist politics of internment and the exploitation of Japanese American labor as relics of the past. In this way, interracial intimacy serves as a tool for reconciliation and forgetting.[33]

Each of the films' narratives revolves around the potential for the politics of race and sex to be made public. Not unlike most popular forms, these films reveal certain fissures in a cultural moment and offer narrative closure. In this case, these films invoke legacies of racial and sexual violence only to reconcile these issues as problems of the past. Because of this, such films ought to be considered part of the attempt to ideologically contain the politics of interracial intimacy, in this instance through narrative strategies that direct matters of interracial intimacy into stories of family formation. And while the family is undoubtedly a site of all sorts of state regulations, it is socially defined as a site of privacy and hence of separation from public policy.

For the passing family in *Lost Boundaries*, the legacy of racial and sexual violence is revealed and closed off in one profound scene when the doctor's son, Howie, learns that his family is black and has been passing. Howard is shocked to learn of his "true" racial identity, and his response is to run away from Keenham and discover what it is like to live in a black neighborhood. The film shows Howard emerging from a Harlem subway station. Whereas Keenham's residents spend their days in the privacy of their own homes, Harlemites are seen living in public. Brown bodies hang out on porch steps and play in the street. In this context, Howard is a stranger. The world of Harlem is alien to him, not just because his skin is light but also because he does not understand how the good life can exist outside of home and family. He rents a room on Sugar Hill, where we see him uncomfortably lying on his cot.

While in Harlem, Howard intervenes in a fight and is momentarily suspected of committing a crime when the police show up. In a Harlem jail, Howard must come clean to the black Lieutenant Thompson (Canada Lee) about how he just learned he was "a Negro." Upon hearing that Howard has just discovered his "true" racial identity, Lieutenant Thompson comments, "one of *those* cases . . . sometimes they just go screwy." In suggesting that Howard's case is common, Thompson hints at a much longer history of interracial sexuality and of passing. Yet in concluding "sometimes they just go screwy," Thompson contains the drama of interracial sexuality to Howard's own private confusion.

In the most significant dialogue of the film, Howard and Lieutenant Thompson have a heart-to-heart talk about racial identity and passing. Thompson attempts to ease Howard's confusion by appealing to the universal norms of humanity.

THOMPSON: *Whether they're white or whether they're black, people are pretty much the same.*

HOWARD: *Except me, I'm neither white nor black, I'm both.*

THOMPSON: *Howard, you're a Negro. There are plenty other Negroes whose skin is light enough to be mistaken for white—8 million or more. . . . I've been a Negro among Negroes my whole life. . . . Can you honestly blame anyone for trying to cross the boundary into the white man's world? . . . Your father was trying to buy you a happy childhood, free of fear and hatred and prejudice.*

This exchange between Howard and Lieutenant Thompson illuminates the central tension exposed in *Lost Boundaries*. What could have been an invocation of the material realities of race relations and the history of interracial sexuality instead turns into a moment of universality. While Lieutenant Thompson's speech invokes a hidden transcript of interracial sexuality and racial violence, this history is contained by the more pressing issue of getting Howard back to his family.

Lost Boundaries attempts to resolve the contradictions exposed by Howard's adventures in Harlem by reuniting the Carter family in Keenham. In the film's concluding scene, we see the Carters at church in Keenham. The priest delivers a sermon that resolves the racial tension of the film by appealing to universal claims of humanity: "All men are brothers . . . one man is the image of all men." Moreover, during his sermon the priest announces the passage of the Selective Service Act, an act that committed the armed services to recruiting more black soldiers. The sermon has reconciled the Carters and Keenham. The film ends with the narrator telling us that the Carter family's story is based on true events and that "Doc Carter is still our doctor." Yet the true events that the film relates are more complicated than the narrator suggests, for in relating a story of racial passing, the film, unintentionally perhaps, identifies some contradictions in racial formations and U.S. nationalism after World War II. The history of interracial sexuality and racial violence is shot through the film's narrative. Nonetheless, the film attempts to contain this history through the narrative logic of a family melodrama. In other words, it attempts to contain the very public history of racial violence and interracial sexual violence into the presumably private world of a small New England town and the domestic space of the family. What the film actually reveals, however, is the very public nature of family life, for the Carters cannot establish a private life outside of the public discourses of race and interracial intimacy. Scott and Marsha Carter are able to overcome racism because they can pass as white. When passing is no longer an option, the heterosexual family becomes the salve the resolves the Carter's racial confusion.

In a similar way, Pearl Chavez of *Duel in the Sun* is a potentially explosive character who threatens to expose the western history the film purports to represent as a story of racial and sexual violence. Through similar techniques as those employed in *Lost Boundaries*, Pearl Chavez's racial identity is subsumed under a more conventional family melodrama, in which her task is to become a "true" woman. After her father dies, Pearl moves to Paradise Flats, the "Paris of the Pecos," where she will live with her father's first lover, the unmistakably white Laura Bell (Lillian Gish). While at Laura Bell's house, Pearl attempts to learn how to become a true woman, which in this film means becoming a wife. Vidor's film suggests that Pearl's racial otherness precludes her entrance into the category of a lady, for while Pearl knows that she ought to choose Laura Bell's good son, Jesse, she cannot help herself in the presence of Laura Bell's outlaw son, Lewt. Pearl's failed choice leads to her death at the end of the film. In framing Pearl's tragedy as a result of "choice" and not racism, Vidor cleanly negotiates the complex history of interracial intimacy his film invokes.

Japanese War Bride is also invested in a project of containing complicated and contradictory public histories. In this case, the film is concerned with reconciling the postwar politics of cultural pluralism with the seemingly contradictory history of Japanese internment. Interracial intimacy is a narrative trope that allows Vidor to show racial progress while enacting a process of historical amnesia around anti-Japanese violence and dispossession.

The film turns on whether American GI Jim Sterling and Red Cross nurse Tae Shimizu can form a family in the context of Salinas, California. In locating the newlyweds in Salinas, the film engages the question of Japanese labor and Japanese internment during World War II and the contradictory rhetoric of cultural pluralism and internment. As David Palumbo-Liu astutely points out, Vidor's choice to locate his subjects in Salinas underscores the film's attempt to imagine a transnational space that is both Japanese and American. Inhabited by both Asian and white workers, the Salinas landscape resembles Japanese and American spaces. Yet while the film resolves tensions between Asian and American spaces through interracial intimacy, it also reveals the anxieties produced by interracial spaces. The film's interracial intimacy serves to shape understandings of internment as a thing of the past and to make romance a trope for forgetting racist practices toward Japanese Americans. Tae is confronted with racism; yet the film suggests that with time, Jim and Tae can be accepted.

The film's conclusion revolves around two competing plots: first, the assimilation of the biracial baby into the home, and second, the growing anxieties among Anglo farmers that "the Japanese farmers are farming again." After Jim's former girlfriend, Fran, pens a letter accusing Tae of having an affair, Tae flees the family. In a very quick resolution to the film's central tension, Jim goes to the household of former Japanese American internees, the Hasegawas, to find his wife. The Hasegawas help Jim find Tae, and in so doing, Vidor suggests that the Hasegawas are reformed Japanese Americans, willing to aid a white man in finding his Japanese wife. Jim finally locates Tae on a cliff overlooking the Pacific. In this transnational space, Tae contemplates ending her life. As she prepares to jump from the cliff, Jim catches her. In a concluding embrace, Jim represents the utopian fantasy of the film: "We can't give up. I love you." Vidor hopes that romance and love can transform racism into reconciliation. Interracial intimacy is therefore a trope for forgetting certain historical realities—in this case, histories of internment and labor migrations—while constructing new symbols of racial tolerance. Although *Japanese War Bride* resolves the problems of racial difference between Jim and Tae and between Jim's family and Tae, it leaves unresolved the problem of racial labor that causes tensions in the Salinas community. Hence the film suggests that interracial intimacy can substitute for actual racial reconciliation that might lead to structural change.

The cultural forms I examine here and the legal cases I examined in the previous chapter construct interracial intimacy as a discourse through which to ideologically police multiple social relationships, some of which were outside the realm of race relations. For example, the legal regulation of interracial romance allowed white males the ability to regulate transgressions by white women, black men, and white men who failed to use their racial privilege properly. In postwar cultural representations, interracial romances ironically masked telling critiques of racism. Moreover, they avoided illuminating the contradictions between prohibitions on interracial intimacy and postwar democratic rhetoric. Although the cultural forms are not uniform in their use of interracial intimacy, they each contain the explosive potential of interracial romance and sexuality through the narrative of heterosexual, intraracial marriage. In the rare social-problem film such as *Japanese War Bride* or *Lost Boundaries* where interracial intimacy is the subject, the explosive possibilities of interracial romance and sexuality are contained through a universal understanding of racial difference that, ironically, upholds racial categories. The universal understanding of interracial intimacy assumes that interracial intimacy ought to be tolerated because, in the end, all bodies are similar regardless of race. Yet this claim simultaneously elides the material realities of racial difference, thereby containing the problematic histories of racial and sexual violence engendered by consideration of interracial intimacy. These very public visual art forms are fully engaged in an act of privatization in that they contain interracial intimacy to limited visual and narrative spheres.

In the next two chapters, I consider how interracial intimacy figured into African American approaches to civil rights. At the heart of the matter is the question of how the private matter of interracial intimacy figured into the very public matter of civil rights. This consideration begs for a new analysis of how the politics of sexuality and race figured into civil rights struggles broadly.

Chapter 3

Making Marriage Matter

Interracial Intimacy and the Black Public Sphere

IN 1956 THE ATTORNEY GENERAL of Georgia, Eugene Cook, hatched a political strategy to undermine the civil rights movement in his state. Reminiscent of the 1864 ploy to label Lincoln an amalgamationist, Cook attributed to a fictional Howard University professor, Roosevelt Williams, a speech advocating interracial marriage. Williams's speech conflated interracial marriage and civil rights reforms during a time when segregationists were especially uneasy about the implications of desegregation.

> *We demand the abolition of all state laws which forbid intermarriage of the different races. . . . The whole world knows that the white man prefers the Negro woman. The white women have been subjected to persecution and restriction. . . . It is well known that the white woman is dissatisfied with the white man, and they along with us demand the right to win and love the Negro men of their choice, so they can proudly tell the world he is my man . . . a man in every respect. The average Negro man has adopted the attitude that why buy a cow when he can get plenty of mountain butter for nothing. We demand the right for every Negro man or woman to marry the white of his or her choice, if he can find one fit to marry.*[1]

Cook's speech enacted a blackface minstrel performance that piqued segregationists' fantasies and fears that desegregation would lead to racial amalgamation. This fear would become common during the 1950s as southern segregationists accused the NAACP of the twin evils of Communism and amalgamation.[2]

Cook's hoax was part of a larger southern campaign of terror and legal prosecution aimed at civil rights leaders who defended the right to intermarriage. In April 1950, for example, John McCray, an NAACP leader in South Carolina, was indicted by a grand jury in Greenwood County for criminal libel for publishing his defense of Willie Tolbert, a black man who had been convicted, sentenced, and electrocuted for the alleged rape of a local white woman. McCray had ignited furor when he suggested that the rape allegation was completely false and that such allegations were common practices among those intent on undermining civil rights.

The argument that civil rights could only mean amalgamation shaped segregationist responses to any mainstream press's portrayal of the NAACP legal defense lawyer, Thurgood Marshall. In 1955, for example, *Time* published an article about Marshall's legal victory in *Brown*. Furious that *Time* would publicize such an achievement, many readers wrote to the magazine to argue that Marshall's legal prowess was a smokescreen, hiding the NAACP's desire to racially mix with the white race. One reader wrote, "I never thought I would live to see . . . TIME eulogize a man obviously determined to destroy the white race. Miscegenation, NOT integration, is the correct term used in describing the sinister scheme sponsored by the NAACP." Another reader responded, "Your reporting on the whole matter is dishonest. . . . How many of your staff would welcome mulatto grandchildren?"[3]

By the mid-1950s, in the minds of most segregationists, all civil rights gains were conflated with fears of racial intermarriage and sex. This conflation attempted, like the 1864 hoax planned to undermine emancipation, to taint all civil rights gains and to preempt certain civil rights demands. If desegregation could be attached to amalgamation, then the fight against antimiscegenation laws would be especially vexing for civil rights leaders.

Meanwhile, after World War II a burgeoning black public culture began to represent interracial romance, marriage, and sexuality in its own, and often rebellious, way. In a 1946 *Ebony* story titled "Five Million U.S. White Negroes: Century of Race Mixing Erases Meaning of Color Lines," the black journalist Roi Ottley argued that a century of forced and consensual racial intermixture had so blurred the color line that it would, in time, be unrecognizable. Ottley argued that in the wake of World War II, as "scientists today are wary of rigid racial definitions," racism would slowly dissipate as it became more difficult to determine racial identities. Next, Ottley turned his analysis of racial intermixture into advocacy of interracial marriage as a civil rights strategy, for such a practice, he believed, would further confound color lines.[4]

Ottley's advocacy of interracial intimacy as a civil rights strategy offers a telling example of how World War II changed the context for black understandings and representations of interracial intimacy. While the legal and cultural discourses of interracial intimacy attempted to police and ideologically contain the possibilities of crossing the color line, Ottley advocated interracial intimacy as a civil rights strategy in order to undermine racial formations themselves. In so doing, he attempted to make public what the legal and cultural representations discussed earlier attempted to contain—the fact that interracial sex was a reality in American society. Ottley thus rewrote Eugene Cook's narrative of amalgamation, rooting the politics of interracial sex in a long history, rather than in the modern civil rights movement era. This revision of the segregationist narrative of miscegenation—a narrative that ignored the legacy of sexual violence against blacks—focused on the historical fact of interracial sex and the unacknowledged role of white men as sexual aggressors toward black women.

What concerns us here is the very existence of Ottley's argument in a black magazine during a time when advocating interracial intimacy was fraught with all sorts of limits and complexities. Although Ottley's bold advocacy of interracial marriage was not common, postwar black politicians could and did debate the implications of interracial marriage in important ways. Interracial intimacy entered civil rights activities in the 1940s because of the unique status of interracial marriage as a private and public matter. Marriage, in civil rights leaders' views, was a private matter of choice, but one that held numerous public implications. For example, marriage enabled people to make legal claims to inherit wealth and to demand custody of children. Moreover, marriage gave access to other forms of wealth accumulation. Culturally, marriage signified "normal" gender roles and the appropriate sphere of adult sexuality. Advocacy for the right to intermarriage thus meant far more than the right to choose a mate, it meant the right to accumulate social and material capital. Civil rights activists debated among themselves whether the fight for the right to intermarriage was a public matter that ought to fall within the scope of all desegregation struggles or whether intermarriage was primarily a private matter, unrelated to the fight for desegregation of public institutions. This debate would emerge at the very moment that World War II made new forms of black public culture possible.

This chapter explores the contested debate about the meaning of interracial intimacy within black public culture after World War II. Mining

NAACP manuscripts and black newspapers and magazines, this chapter traces a subtle, yet significant, shift in black constructions of interracial intimacy from the early twentieth century to the postwar era. Before the war, black conversations about interracial romance focused on how antimiscegenation laws made black women vulnerable to white male sexual violence. Such an argument attempted to place white men as agents of interracial intimacy and to hold up black women as victims. After World War II, as black civil rights groups earned victories on a national scale, the argument against antimiscegenation laws moved away from the issue of protecting black women. In the postwar era, civil rights leaders challenged antimiscegenation laws as violations of black men's right to choose sexual and romantic partners. This shift from black women to black men as the focus of the attack on antimiscegenation laws had profound implications on the nature of civil rights activism after World War II. The black public-sphere politics of the postwar era frequently ignored black women's issues, which were often confined to the domestic sphere. Public representations of interracial intimacy were thought to rescue the black male body from the weight of historical representations of black male sexuality as perverse, disabled, and dangerous. No analogous argument rescued black women from similar stereotypes. In fact, black women who married white men were less celebrated than black men who married white women and, in some instances, were even scorned as race traitors.

While Roi Ottley argued that interracial marriage would obscure racial boundaries and render them meaningless, black civil rights leaders approached the subject with considerable trepidation and care. Within the NAACP, the postwar years sparked massive attacks on racial inequality in schools, in employment practices, and in housing policies. Yet with these activities came uneasiness within portions of American society in general, and within the civil rights movement in particular, about the role of racial intermarriage and the fight against antimiscegenation laws in civil rights struggles. For segregationists, anxiety over the implications of civil rights reforms was expressed in the statement, "Would you want your daughter to marry a Negro?" Yet even within black communities, interracial marriage and sexuality caused concern. As one *Ebony* reader asked in 1954, "Would you want your daughter to marry a white man?"[5]

In order to understand the contested politics of interracial intimacy within black communities, this chapter traces three developmental moments in the black debate about the implications of interracial marriage. First, it considers the early-twentieth-century argument against antimiscegenation laws that advocated the protection of black women from sexual violence. Next, it considers the shift in focus away from protecting black women to the right of men to choose their partners. Finally, the chapter examines the creation of the black public sphere through black magazine and newspaper publishing. Where the NAACP was reluctant to advocate the abolition of antimiscegenation laws for fear that such advocacy would be labeled amalgamationist, black magazines and newspapers publicized and celebrated black male interracial intimacy with white women.

When civil rights activists of the early twentieth century criticized the growing number of state antimiscegenation laws, they had to develop an argument that would challenge the laws without advocating interracial marriage. The first three decades of the twentieth century witnessed the growth of the Ku Klux Klan and the release of the film *The Birth of a Nation*. During the Jim Crow era, segregation was understood as a necessary means to prevent racial amalgamation. As well, during and after World War I, millions of black people migrated from the rural South to the industrial North in search of higher-paying employment. This migration led to the creation of black communities within urban cities. The black migration also caused concern in the North that urban cities would be places of interracial intimacy. Hence fears of bodily closeness structured northern and southern communities, and this made it especially dangerous to advocate the abolition of antimiscegenation laws in this context.

The attack on antimiscegenation laws had to garner sympathy from an American public that embraced scientific racism. Under scientific racism, mixed-race progeny were understood to be degenerate. Such a thesis led scientists and social reformers to fear that interracial intimacy would lead to "race suicide." Thus, in order to challenge antimiscegenation laws, black civil rights leaders would have to frame their argument in terms that did not invoke fears of amalgamation.

In the early twentieth century, black activists challenged antimiscegenation laws by arguing that such laws left black women vulnerable to the sexual advances and violence of white men. This argument focused on black women as victims and white men as sexual predators. In framing the attack on antimiscegenation laws in such terms, civil rights activists tapped into a narrative of female vulnerability and male aggression that held currency

during the Progressive Era of reform. During the Progressive Era, reformers sought to rescue "fallen women" through a program of redemption that
held women as victims of confidence men. For example, in her analysis of
pregnant single women during the Progressive Era, Regina Kunzel argues
that the evangelical model of reform rested on a narrative of female victims
of confidence men. For black activists during the 1920s and 1930s, arguing
that black women were vulnerable to predatory white men both reoriented
the discourse of miscegenation away from black men and built on the narrative of evangelical reform that suggested female redemption through
admission of male vice. Moreover, the appeal to the protection of black
womanhood sought to restore a gendered order in which black men—and
not white men—were the appropriate patriarchs for black women.

As well, black civil rights activists argued that amalgamation could produce superior racial bodies. This argument challenged the scientific racist
assumption that racial hybridity meant degeneracy and instead pointed to
highly successful scholars and artists who were biracial. Further, activists
attempted to replace scientific understandings of race with a cultural understanding. For example, in 1910 W. E. B. Du Bois published "Racial Intermarriage" in the *Crisis*. Du Bois argued three things: first, that racial
intermarriage and interracial sexuality were instigated most frequently by
white men and women; second, that antimiscegenation laws left black
women vulnerable to sexually predatory white men; and third, that racial
amalgamation had produced superior "stocks" of human beings. Racial
intermarriage, Du Bois wrote, "is about the last of the social problems over
which [black people] are concerned, because they so seldom face it in fact
or in theory." Although Du Bois believed that all marriage was primarily a
matter of private choice, he nevertheless felt compelled to address antimiscegenation laws in the context of civil rights activism. "This brings us to the
crucial question: so far as the present advisability of intermarrying between
white and colored people in the United States is concerned, both races are
practically in complete agreement. Colored folk marry colored folk and
whites marry white, and the exceptions are very few." Yet even though rates
of intermarriage were very low, Du Bois addressed antimiscegenation laws
because, he argued, such laws led to violence against black women.

*The moral reason for opposing laws against intermarriage is the greatest of all: such
laws leave the colored girl absolutely helpless for the lust of white men. It reduces*

colored women in the eyes of the law to the position of dogs. Low as the white girl falls, she can compel her seducer to marry her. If it were proposed to take this last defense from poor working girls, can you not hear the screams of the 'white slave' defenders? . . . We must kill [antimiscegenation laws], not because we are anxious to marry white men's sisters, but because we are determined that white men shall let our sisters alone.[6]

Du Bois's argument anticipated the charge that the attack on antimiscegenation laws lent outright support to intermarriage. Rather, Du Bois argued that black men did not desire intermarriage but only the right to protect black women in the same way that white men could protect white women. In this way, Du Bois's argument identified a contradiction inherent in antimiscegenation laws. Such laws actually sanctioned white male sexual violence against black women because they consigned such behavior to the private sphere.

Perhaps most significant was Du Bois's engagement with contemporary racial theory. Writing during a period of intense concern over racial degeneracy and "race suicide," Du Bois sought to transform the discourse of miscegenation away from biological understandings of race and toward cultural understandings. In "Marrying of Black Folk," a 1910 article in the *Independent*, Du Bois argued,

I believe that in general the best results follow when persons marry in their own social group. . . . I believe that there are human stocks with whom it is physically unwise to intermarry, but to think that these stocks are all colored or that there are no such white stocks is unscientific. . . . I believe that intermarriage between races is apt to unite incompatible personalities, irreconcilable ideals and different grades of cultures.

In this argument, Du Bois agreed that certain forms of intermarriage would be "unwise." Yet he rejected the notion that race was the most salient border crossing. Furthermore, Du Bois conceded that racial intermarriage may "unite incompatible personalities, irreconcilable ideals and different grades of culture." While this argument may seem to uphold scientific racist arguments about racial degeneracy in amalgamation, quite the opposite was true. Du Bois sought to replace a scientific understand of race with a cultural understanding. Although interracial marriage may unite different personalities and ideas, Du Bois argued there was nothing inherent in race that caused problems for racially intermarried couples. Next he argued that while some forms of intermarriage were inadvisable, many racial intermarriages had produced "new gifted, and desirable stocks and individuals, as witness the English nation, the 'Homo Europaeus', the Egyptians, and such men as Robert Browning, Alexander Hamilton, Lew Wallace, Lafcado Hern, Alexander Dumas, Alexander Pushkin, and Frederick Douglass."[7]

Taken as a whole, Du Bois's argument revised the segregationists' narrative of racial intermarriage in three important ways. First, Du Bois argued that antimiscegenation laws should be opposed not because black men sought white women but because such laws harmed black women. Second, Du Bois challenged the assumption that racial intermarriage was a priori harmful because it united incommensurable racial bodies. Rather, he argued that there are many forms of incompatible marriages and that race is merely one cultural trait among many that determine compatibility in marriage. Finally, Du Bois undermined the assumption that amalgamation meant racial degeneracy by holding up the example of the numerous mixed-race people who led exemplary lives. Such an argument located interracial intimacy in history and undermined the narrative of tragic mixed-race bodies.

Du Bois's early-twentieth-century arguments against racial intermarriage would shape the activism of the civil rights organizations he founded—the Niagara Movement and its descendant, the NAACP. On the one hand, the NAACP argued that antimiscegenation laws ought to be opposed because they harmed black women. On the other hand, it argued that interracial marriages were not detrimental and could even be beneficial. In a 1917 protest letter to the Wisconsin senate, for example, the association challenged a proposed state antimiscegenation law. The letter argued that

whenever such laws have been enacted they become a menace to the whole institution of matrimony, leading directly to concubinage, bastardy, and the degradation of the Negro woman. . . . To prohibit such inter-marriage would be publicly to acknowledge that black blood is a physical taint, something no self-respected colored man and woman can be asked to admit. We oppose it for the moral reason that all such laws leave the colored girl absolutely helpless before the lust of the white man, without the power to compel the seducer to marry.[8]

The NAACP appealed to the rights of black women to protect themselves from white men, and it argued that antimiscegenation laws assumed the inferiority of "black blood." Yet the association was careful not to suggest that black people should marry whomever they wanted, for such a claim would feed arguments that civil rights meant intermarriage.

In 1923 a federal antimiscegenation bill was introduced in the U.S. Senate (the "Federal Marriage Bill"). The Federal Marriage Bill would have prevented many forms of intermarriage, with interracial intimacy conflated with the transmission of disease. "No license to marry shall be issued to one who is . . . insane, or an imbecile, pauper, epileptic, feeble-minded, or afflicted with tuberculosis or a venereal disease, or related to each . . . or where the applications are members of different race; that is to say marriage between members of the white and black or of the white and yellow races shall not be valid." The association protested the bill but had to do so very carefully. James Weldon Johnson argued that the association opposed the bill not "because colored people advocate or desire inter-marriage with whites" but because such laws leave black women vulnerable to white men.[9]

The fight against the Federal Marriage Bill took two forms. First, some argued that the marriage bill was unfair because it prevented certain forms of intermarriage and not others. Such an argument did not engage the fundamental presumption that racial intermarriage was degenerative but instead focused on the bill's unfair designation of only some marriages as illegal. For example, Carl Murphy, the editor of the *Afro American*, argued that the Federal Marriage Bill was misguided because it "forbids the intermarriage of the blacks and whites, but has nothing to say of the marriage of blacks and yellows, reds and whites, or reds and blacks."[10]

Others argued, more radically, that the Federal Marriage Bill ignored the real instigators of racial intermarriage—white men and women. For example, Butler Wilson, president of the Boston branch of the NAACP, suggested that anti-intermarriage laws not only prevented people from marrying but also obscured the origin of interracial intimacy: white women's interest in black men. In his protest against the Federal Marriage Bill, Wilson argued that such a law "is not only a source of great danger to colored women, but it would show a distrust of white women by white men who compose the legislature. . . . [It] would be an insult to white women in that the implication will be inescapable that legislation is necessary to prevent white women from marrying colored men and white men from marrying colored women."[11] Wilson's critique of the law went further than the NAACP's by linking a concern for the protection of black women to an analysis of white patriarchal control over white women. He attempted to show how white men, to regulate black and white women's sexuality, used antimiscegenation laws.

Another strategy developed to challenge proposed state and federal antimiscegenation laws prior to World War II was to show how such laws had historically been undermined by cunning interracial couples and, perhaps most significantly, by white men who had the privilege of privacy to protect their sexual indiscretions toward black women. Alice Stone Blackwell, for example, a member of the Boston NAACP, challenged the proposed Massachusetts antimiscegenation law by arguing that such a law could not prevent interracial marriage and sexuality. "A Massachusetts [resident] wishing to contract a mixed marriage could go over the border into any adjoining state and get married and then come back and live in Massachusetts." Most important, however, Blackwell argued that antimiscegenation laws had never been a deterrent to interracial sex. "If it is said that racial intermixture is undesirable, the answer lies in the obvious fact that forbidding intermarriage does not prevent the intermixture. It is precisely in the South where the bar against intermarriage is absolute, that we find the largest number of persons of mixed blood." Blackwell argued that while antimiscegenation laws were publicly justified as tools to prevent racial amalgamation, they in fact did little to deter racial violence against black women. In this way, Blackwell revised the narrative of miscegenation by showing the historical double standard that prevented blacks from marrying whites but sanctioned white sexual violence against black women.[12]

In the 1910s and 1920s, during a period of Progressive Era reforms and large-scale black migration from the South to the North, black civil rights activists attempted to challenge antimiscegenation laws by appealing to black women's sexual vulnerability to white men. Such an argument was strategically formulated to make the discourse of miscegenation about white racial terror and violence and not about black sexual degeneracy. In a context in which black men were regularly murdered for presumed indiscretions toward white women, civil rights activists had to be careful not to appear interested in advocating intermarriage but instead to appear only interested in protecting the virtues of black women.

World War II and its aftermath presented civil rights activists with an entirely new context within which to challenge and debate antimiscegenation laws. While early in the century the NAACP was willing to articulate a critique of antimiscegenation laws as destructive to black women, after the war the association was less willing to publicly challenge antimiscegenation laws because of the especially damaging ways that segregationists conflated civil rights gains with amalgamation. Also, the NAACP legal attack on desegregation after World War II focused civil rights activities on battles that held the most potential for success. In thinking about antimiscegenation laws in the postwar era, the association thus had to define for Americans the difference between desegregation of public institutions and integration of social and cultural institutions. Desegregation, the association argued, entailed the legal fight for access to public institutions such as schools and transportation. Integration, on the other hand, meant creating social friendships and personal relationships with whites. The NAACP suggested that integration would likely be the result of desegregation but that the fight for desegregation was not primarily a fight for integration.

Interracial intimacy as a political issue was especially vexing to the association because it engaged the public, legal institution of marriage and the private, intimate matter of sexual behavior. The struggle against antimiscegenation laws therefore entailed advocacy for desegregation and integration, and this became especially problematic as the association was increasingly labeled amalgamationist. This complexity made interracial intimacy simultaneously troubling and strategic for civil rights activists. It was troubling because of the ways the fight against antimiscegenation laws could easily confirm segregationist arguments; it was strategic because of the ways this fight enabled a critique of the ways racial segregation affected the most private intimate relations. Civil rights activists thus attempted to make the private world of intimacy and sexuality a public rights issue.

In his important 1948 work on American racial attitudes, *An American Dilemma*, Gunnar Myrdal observed that black civil rights activists were reluctant to discuss the issue of racial intermarriage. According to Myrdal, black leaders were unwilling to make the fight against antimiscegenation laws central to their civil rights activism.

> The request [among black civil rights leaders] for intermarriage is easy for the Negro leader to give up. Intermarriage cannot possibly be a practical object of Negro public policy. Independent of the Negroes' wishes, the opportunity for intermarriage is not as favorable a thing as the great majority of the white population dislikes the very idea. As a defense reaction a strong attitude against intermarriage has developed in the Negro people itself.[13]

Myrdal's observation of the reluctance of black civil rights leaders to advocate the abolition of antimiscegenation laws was supported by sociologists Horace Cayton and St. Clair Drake, who argued in their 1945 *Black Metropolis* that black leaders carefully selected their battles for social equality so as not to inspire white protest. Among those things upon which Cayton and Drake found black leaders and segregationists agreed was that social equality should not take the form of "intermarriage, membership in white cliques, churches and social clubs, and visiting and entertaining across the color line."[14] Here Cayton and Drake show that the fight for desegregation did not necessarily mean a push for integration. Civil rights leaders, they argued, did not advocate interracial marriage, though they did oppose antimiscegenation laws.

> Ask a Negro civil leader in Midwest Metropolis whether "his people" want social equality, and he's likely to answer: "If you mean the right to procure goods and services anywhere—yes, absolutely. We don't call that social equality. If you mean the right to rent or buy a house anywhere in the city—why, of course. Is that social equality? If you mean a yearning to visit white people in their homes and to be visited by them—nonsense! But, as for the privilege of doing even that if both white and Negro individuals desire it—why not? This is a free country. Intermarriage? Well, it takes two to get married, and if one of them is white, what right has the law to interfere? But why should Negroes seek to marry white? They have all colors within their own race."[15]

Cayton and Drake observed the delicate balance between advocacy for civil rights, best characterized by desegregation, and the right to be intimate with whomever one chooses. Even as *Black Metropolis* and *American Dilemma* accurately located the complexities of the fight against antimiscegenation laws, however, their argument that no black leaders advocated intermarriage overstated the point. Some civil rights activists recognized the unique position of interracial marriage and sexuality as public and private matters that therefore were integral to civil rights advocacy. The sociologist Oliver Cromwell Cox, for example, argued in his 1948 *Caste, Class, and Race* that interracial marriage could undermine the racist logic of segregation within the public sphere. In this way, Cox marks a shift in black discourse about interracial marriage and sexuality from caution to a utopian claim about the possibilities of interracial sex.

Cox maintained that racial intermarriage could be a route toward economic and social mobility for black people. He suggested that black men had most to gain: "It must not be supposed that it is the white as mere sexual object which is the preoccupation of colored men; it is rather her importance to him as a vehicle in the struggle for economic and cultural position."[16] Cox's analysis anticipated a growing number of arguments within black political and social organizations that equated racial intermarriage with racial uplift and social mobility. Yet this brief example hints at a more significant shift in black arguments against antimiscegenation laws—Cox turned the focus of his analysis away from the issue of protecting black women and toward the issue of black male social mobility. This shift was subtle yet was developed more broadly in the representations of intermarriage in the burgeoning black press. Whereas before the war intellectuals like Du Bois viewed antimiscegenation laws as tangential to civil rights struggles, after the war some intellectuals and public figures like Cox, Roi Ottley, and Harlem's most famous preacher, Father Divine, began to view racial intermarriage as a strategy for civil rights. Hence official NAACP claims that intermarriage was not a goal of civil rights organizing were undermined by a growing black public culture that publicized and celebrated interracial marriage.

After World War II, black civil rights leaders transformed their argument against antimiscegenation laws so that it focused on the right to choose, rather than on the victimization of black women. In the postwar years, cultural understandings of race prompted black intellectuals to suggest that race was not a factor in choosing a romantic partner and that antimiscegenation laws violated people's right to love whomever they chose. For example, although Morehouse president Benjamin Mays had always maintained that civil rights were not about a desire to intermarry, after the war he was able to expand his critique of antimiscegenation laws by arguing that race did not shape his choice of friends.

> *Honestly I cannot say that I prefer Negro companions to that of Jews, Gentiles, Japanese, Chinese or Indian. There are Negroes that I take great delight in being in their company. There are some Negroes whose company I do not cherish. I have white friends, North and South, whose company I appreciate. I have friends in Asia, Europe, and in Africa whose friendship and companionship I appreciate. To me I prefer the companionship of those persons who have something in common with me.*[17]

Mays's statement was reminiscent of Du Bois's cultural argument about incompatible marriages. Yet Mays's argument was located in a society in which cultural arguments about race had replaced scientific arguments. Thus, while Du Bois's argument remained focused on how antimiscegenation laws harmed black women, Mays's argument focused only on the freedom to choose companions.

Similarly, in 1954 Roy Wilkins, then editor of the NAACP's *Crisis* magazine, suggested that fears of racial amalgamation were antiquated in postwar America. Wilkins's argument against the charge that civil rights meant interracial sex was that such a claim was an "old chestnut" that white racists' "fall back on." Fears of miscegenation, according to Wilkins, don't "put the white women in such a good light because it assumes that white women only want to have sexual relationship with black men." Where his prewar peers would have argued that antimiscegenation laws harm black women, Wilkins instead argued that "there is no color nor division in womanhood, which is the pillar and the greatest heritage of mankind."[18] That Wilkins conflated the interests of white and black women reveals the changed atmosphere in which black politicians understood and debated interracial intimacy. For Mays and Wilkins, race was merely cultural. Thus racial intermarriage was not as profound a border crossing as segregationists suggested.

The shift in focus among black intellectuals from the protection of black women to the implications of black men's romances was perhaps most starkly represented in the very public marriage of Harlem preacher Father Divine to a Norwegian woman who became known only as "Mrs. Divine." Father Divine had become Harlem's most boisterous and popular minister during the 1930s when his Peace Mission movement organized an interracial movement for social justice. Much more than a black religious experience, the Peace Mission movement was a political organization engaged in radical racial and class politics. Divine's Peace Mission formed economic collectives and interracial communes. Although Divine's ministry waned after World War II, he sought to expand his congregation after the war by using his interracial marriage to appeal to white and non-American audiences. He consciously attempted to embody his call for an international and interracial congregation through his marriage.

Divine had previously been married to a black woman named Peninnah. When Peninnah died, Divine prophesized that God would reincarnate his wife in an improved and purer version. His Norwegian wife came to represent the improvement on his black wife. His politics of interracial and international intimacy, therefore, rested on an implicit statement about racialized notions of womanhood. In a pamphlet, Divine outlined the evolution of his church through his marriage practices.

> *ANGEL (MOTHER DIVINE)—this Marriage begin* [sic] *international, interracial and truly spiritual in nature, for the purpose of propagating virtue, Holiness, Honesty, Competence and Truth. It symbolizes the Marriage of CHRIST to the church and the Union of GOD and man. MOTHER DIVINE declared of FATHER DIVINE "I KNOW YOU ARE GOD,"—and FATHER DIVINE, in marrying her, married everyone who has that same conviction.*[19]

For Divine, his interracial marriage to his "SPOTLESS VIRGIN BRIDE" was an attempt to bring "AN ABOLITION TO ALL DIVISION AMONG US!" Although Divine's political uses of interracial intimacy were by no means common, they did represent the extreme end of a contentious debate about the implications of interracial marriage on desegregation struggles.[20]

The most significant framing event for postwar representation of interracial intimacy was the 1945 marriage between the head of the NAACP, Walter White, and the white socialite Poppy Cannon. The White/Cannon marriage sparked a torrent of debate within black-run publications. Some maintained that the marriage signified the culmination of World War II civil rights activism. If the representative of the nation's largest civil rights organization can marry a white woman, some argued, then perhaps racism would eventually dissipate. Others argued that the White/Cannon marriage would threaten civil rights gains because it would feed segregationists' arguments that civil rights meant interracial intimacy. Some claimed that the marriage did not have an impact on civil rights in any way, that the marriage was a private matter. Such debates brought to light issues of publicity and privacy within the civil rights organization.

Concurrent with the White/Cannon marriage was the creation of a profitable black magazine industry after World War II that represented the interracial marriage. Led by the self-made John Johnson, the Johnson Publishing Company began to market a series of magazines that would represent black politics and social life. Entering the field of magazine publishing allowed Johnson to shape black aesthetics and politics in unprecedented ways. Fashioned as the black *Life Magazine*, Johnson's *Ebony* played an important role in shaping black tastes and in representing black views on domestic and international politics.

Nowhere was the focus on interracial marriage more pronounced than in the pages of Johnson's *Negro Digest, Ebony, Jet,* and *Tan Confessions* and in the most widely read black newspapers like the *Chicago Defender.* During the period of this study, approximately one in five of Johnson's magazines contained a feature on an interracial romance or marriage.[21] While black magazines and newspapers contained a similar focus on interracial romances after the war, one must read the Johnson magazines with caution. Johnson Publishing was notorious for fabricating interracial stories in order to sell copies. In their autobiographies, published well after the period of this study, Ben Burns and John Johnson each claim that stories about interracialism were suggested by the other. Burns claims that Johnson sought to increase sales with sensational stories of interracial romance and marriage. Johnson, for his part, claims that it was his white editor, Burns, who recommended stories about interracialism in order to represent Johnson Publishing's interracial audience and integrationist philosophy. Further, Johnson states that he ordered Burns to cease publishing such stories in the late 1950s because, he argued, such stories lowered the integrity and quality of his magazines. While there has yet to be a comprehensive study of how Johnson's magazine stories changed after the mid-1950s, a brief survey of the magazines suggests that the frequency of interracialism stories did decline after 1955. This may have more to do with the success of the civil rights movement than with the spat between Burns and Johnson.[22]

What most concerns us is that the most successful black magazines and the more legitimate black newspaper industry spent considerable time publicizing and even celebrating interracial romance and marriage after World War II. Regardless of who ordered their publication, stories about interracial intimacy were a key ingredient of Johnson Publishing's attempt to represent black lives. Because of their role in representing the private and public sides of black life, Johnson's magazines and other black publications were important sites of debate about the implications of interracial intimacy. In order to mimic its major influence, *Life Magazine,* Johnson's magazines engaged aspects of black domesticity and respectability. This meant placing a large focus on famous black families and the courtship practices of influential socialites. At the same time, Johnson's magazines were charged with a mission to infuse their coverage of black life with civil rights politics. Hence the magazines employed well-known activists and writers to publish smart editorials concerning civil rights. Johnson's magazines therefore represent a contradictory space in which middle-class notions of domesticity and the nuclear family collide with civil rights coverage. In the pages of Johnson's magazines, the presumed private space of the home was saturated with the public discourse of civil rights. Regardless of whether it was Johnson or Burns who made the editorial decisions and regardless of whether the stories were fully accurate, coverage of interracial intimacy was a necessary component in the magazines' shaping of fully integrated black private and public lives. In this way, I advocate reading interracial intimacy at the center of Johnson's vision of racial uplift and black respectability and not simply as a ploy to sell subscriptions.

Within the pages of black magazines like *Ebony* and black newspapers like the *Defender* and the *Pittsburgh Courier* arose a contentious debate about the state of black politics and the civil rights movement as reflected in the politics of racial intermarriage. At the core of this debate was whether the private matter of intimacy ought to enter the public realm of civil rights activism. In its December 1946 issue, *Ebony* published "Famous Negroes Who Married Whites Featuring Walter White and Poppy Cannon." This lengthy exposé, containing numerous articles representing African American sociologists and psychologists, offers telling evidence about the changing understandings of interracial intimacy in postwar black culture. The coverage of White's marriage contained an important subtext—White had married a white woman after divorcing his black wife of twenty-seven years. Although White's previous marriage to a black woman was mentioned in the *Ebony* coverage, black women were nearly absent from the entire discussion. This absence was nevertheless an important indication of how debates about interracial intimacy had changed after World War II from a concern over protecting black women to a concern over how black men's interracial romances would affect civil rights. Black women in postwar debates were a structuring absence, a subtext whose voice was largely silenced.

For Walter White, however, marriage to a white woman was not a political act but was a private romantic choice. It would be up to the black press to debate and decide the implications of his marriage. In the *Ebony* exposé, the magazine used the occasion of White's marriage to note an increase in the number of interracial marriages due to "a general lowering of racial barriers in the U.S. The Chicago marriage license bureau reported a record number of 200 marriages last year."[23] Hence, where the NAACP was reluctant to argue that race reform would lead to amalgamation, *Ebony* suggested that lowering "racial barriers" was likely to lead to intermarriage.

Next, the *Ebony* article sought to present a debate about whether the White/Cannon marriage was good for civil rights or whether it posed particular problems. The magazine presented the views of a black editor from the *Norfolk Virginia Journal and Guide*, who argued that the marriage would embarrass the NAACP and imperil its reform efforts. At a time when segregationists were quick to label all civil rights gains as amalgamationist, this editor feared that "the detractors of the association have made much of the charge that its anti-segregation program is in reality a disguise of the Negro's yearning to marry whites. This is a fallacy, of course, but the denial is subjected to a deflating slap when it is recalled that the associations' most vocal official hopped across the race line in matrimony."[24]

The Norfolk editor's argument was a common one. In the *Defender*, C. C. Spaulding similarly maintained that White's marriage was detrimental to black civil rights. According to Spaulding, White had jeopardized desegregation struggles because, as the representative of the nation's largest civil rights organization, he had opened up the organization to racists' claims that desegregation meant social integration and, ultimately, racial amalgamation. What is perhaps most revealing about Spaulding's lengthy critique is the delicacy with which he attempted to negotiate within his analysis the public and private functions of marriage.

Unquestionably, it is the right, the privilege, of every American to live richly and as fully as he chooses—and is able to do under the American system. It is his right and privilege to do those things which do not violate the laws of God nor man, nor infringe upon the prerogatives of others. . . . Therefore, I take no issue with this foremost representative of the Negro people in the exercise of his God-given right to choose his helpmate. It is indeed regrettable that a greater proportion of the American people have not yet been able to reconcile themselves to the justness of this fact when it comes to the Negroes. . . . Walter White is no ordinary man—nor is he an ordinary Negro. He is one who has labored long to bring all Negroes closer to the goals of full citizenship and mutual respect. He has done this through the medium of an organization of the American people and their close support. Forty years of struggle by the NAACP, in turn has brought great rewards to our group, but in doing, has made the association the major target of those bigots who would deprive us of a fair chance in American society. . . . By his recent act, however, Walter White has snatched at the rug of economic, social and political advancement upon which the feet of the Negroes rest, and the fibres of which comprise a great part of his life in weaving. . . . Moreover, he has given credence—if you choose to accept it that way, to the inaccurate charge of the white South that the highest aspiration of Negroes is to invade the white race. While I reject this contention emphatically and completely, I cannot be blind to the manner in which this aspect of the matter has been emblazoned upon the pages of the newspapers of the South.[25]

In this lengthy rant, Spaulding blends together a defense of racial intermarriage as a private choice among free individuals and a pointed critique of White's behavior. According to Spaulding, White's marriage choices were never purely private because they represented the entire civil rights movement.

The editor of the *Oklahoma Black Dispatch* challenged the argument that White had harmed the civil rights movement. In the *Ebony* exposé, this editor contended that White's marriage would benefit black communities because of White's unique status as an ambassador for black people. Specifically, this editor focused on the public nature of White's marriage as an opportunity to influence politics. He argued that White's ability to respect and love across the color line could provide an example for white and black people to follow. Yet this argument was critically engaged with prewar arguments against antimiscegenation laws regarding the protection of black women. "Walter White has shown far greater respect for white womanhood than several of our honored Presidents have shown for black mothers. . . . How can we condemn Walter White, who has become joined in marriage with a white women and at the same time honor Washington, Jefferson and Jackson for their depraved relationship with slave women?"[26] This editor used the White/Cannon marriage as an opportunity to reveal the historic double standard whereby white men's sexual violence was protected by privacy while black men's interracial intimacy was intensely prosecuted. The White/Cannon marriage thus signaled a moment to articulate and bring into the public previously hidden discourses of interracial intimacy.

The *Ebony* exposé next offered black experts' opinions about "why Negro leaders often wed whites." These experts were divided over whether White's marriage represented a civil rights gain. Louis Wirth, a professor of sociology at the University of Chicago, argued that *Ebony* readers should anticipate more interracial romances and marriages among black leaders. Yet he downplayed the role race played in such relationships, instead arguing that what attracted people of all races to black leaders were these leaders' exceptional human qualities. In this way, Wirth advanced the cultural argument that personal traits, of which race was just one example, determined attraction and romantic compatibility. Similarly, Walter Adams, a neuropsychiatrist and psychoanalyst from Chicago, embraced a cultural argument to explain White's marriage. Adams argued that black leaders' interracial intimacy was a result of these leaders' understanding that race was not the most important factor in choosing a romantic partner. "[White's] behavior in marrying 'white' may symbolize his belief that one race is as good as another, and one who preached against prejudice cannot afford to advocate prejudice."[27]

Other experts maintained that racial intermarriage was a flawed route toward civil rights, one that placed too much emphasis on assimilating to white standards of desire and beauty. Kenneth Clark, for example, argued that racial intermarriage signified an attempt among black men to achieve social and economic mobility through their legal relationship to white women. Clark, a psychology professor from the City College of New York and the person whose research would contribute to the Supreme Court's *Brown* decision, argued, "In our culture beauty has been systematically and continuously associated with whiteness and lightness of skin. Thus a successful Negro male tends to demonstrate his success, maybe unconsciously, by seeking a light or white female." Such a view underscored the tensions within black debates over the implications of intermarriage. For Clark, racial intermarriage supported the view that whites were indeed more desirable than blacks. Similarly, F. Ashley Montagu, an anthropologist at Rutgers University, suggested that black men who married white women desired to be white themselves. "Short of becoming white oneself, the next best thing would be to marry a white and be accepted into a white milieu."[28]

Clark and Montagu reformulated an old debate within black communities about the politics of color. Historically, lighter-skinned black people had access to privileges that darker-skinned black people did not. Clark and Montagu argued that Walter White desired the lightest-skinned wife possible because doing so gave him social privileges he would not have otherwise. The black journalist Roi Ottley made a similar argument when he noted that blacks in Harlem had created a "caste based on color," with light-skinned black women "the props of Negro society . . . since they meet more nearly Caucasian standards of beauty, they possess enviable positions in the Negro community, and are much sought after as wives." Yet Ottley noted that even light-skinned black women in Harlem felt competition from white women. "Mulatto women, often enjoying a position in the Negro group far beyond their social and personal worth, view with the fiercest antagonism the competition of white women. To combat the situation, they effectively raise the slogan of race pride."[29]

The debate surrounding the implications of White's marriage reveals the political and ideological differences within black communities about how to represent civil rights and about the meaning of interracial intimacy. The experts and journalists who commented in *Ebony* and in other black publications gave readers conflicting information about whether racial intermarriage would help or harm the cause of civil rights. Some readers responded to the *Ebony* exposé with equally conflicted arguments about whether the White/Cannon marriage was important at all. For example, Clifford Patterson, a reader from New York City, wrote to the editor of *Ebony*, "It is utterly ridiculous to regard two people who are as white as Walter White and Poppy Cannon as anything but white people." In the same issue of the magazine, another reader, identified only as GGL, argued that Poppy Cannon's dedication to civil rights issues made her decision to wed Walter White a natural choice; Cannon behaved like a black civil rights leader. "I am of the opinion that she is just as much colored as Walter White."[30]

In Johnson's magazines and in more legitimate black newspapers, interracial intimacy between black men and white women was publicized and frequently celebrated for its potential to contribute to civil rights reform. Throughout the decade after World War II, Johnson's magazines published dozens of articles about interracial romances and marriages. These stories engaged the politics of interracial intimacy in overt and covert ways. The most obvious manner in which the magazines' representations of interracial marriages participated in postwar politics was in the way that these stories suggested that race relations were improving and that intermarriage and interracial romance were a signal, if not a cause, of these changes. Yet more subtle were the magazines' celebration of a certain kind of intermarriage and interracial romance. The magazines overwhelmingly focused on relationships between black men and white women. While some very famous black women's marriages to white men were the subject of magazine stories, one could read Johnson's magazines and think that interracial intimacy was a civil rights issue only for black men. Finally, interracial romance stories completely revised other public representations of interracial intimacy that attempted to contain the possibilities of crossing the color line to the domestic sphere. In Johnson's magazines, as well as in black newspapers, interracial intimacy was explosive and resisted any clean containment.

Johnson's magazines' coverage of interracial intimacy took three, often rebellious, forms: publicizing "studies" that showed that interracial sexuality produced superior offspring, overemphasizing the popularity of intermarriage, and arguing that desegregation would lead to intermarriage. First, in making the case the interracial sexuality had produced superior human beings, the magazines challenged segregationist arguments about amalgamation and degeneracy. Furthermore, by locating interracial intimacy and mixed-race bodies in history, these articles placed contemporary debates about amalgamation in a much larger historical frame. Such was the goal of a reader who wrote to *Ebony* to claim that biracial progeny were superior. William Kennedy, a reader from Los Angeles, wrote:

> *The world's most beautiful people come from mixed ancestry. Look at Lena Horne, Katharine Dunham, Nina McKinney, Josephine Baker, the late Florence Mills and tens of thousands of others throughout the U.S., France, Central and South America. Race mixing has always been and will always be. It will kill Jim Crow. It will knock out the problem.*[31]

A *Jet* article that featured a more legitimate source—Ernest Pettinger, a geneticist from California—supported Kennedy's optimistic analysis of interracial intimacy. *Jet's* article focused on Pettinger's genetics research showing that mixed-race children were superior to monoracial children. According to the article, "Ever since a dark-skinned African slave woman presented her white lover, Robert Sweet, with a mulatto boy child in Virginia in 1640, students of race have sought an answer to this question: are children of mixed parentage superior to 'pure-blooded' Negroes and whites?" The article argued that the success of famous "mixed" people "is a strong refutation of the phony 'superior white blood' theories."[32]

Johnson's magazines often overstated the growing popularity of interracial marriage after World War II. The U.S. Census Bureau did not track rates of interracial marriage until the 1960 census. In 1960 the census recorded 0.4 percent of Americans (157,000) were married to a person of a different race. Of these marriages, only 51,000 of them, or about 30 percent, involved black/white marriages.[33] It is difficult to measure whether this data represents a marked increase in intermarriage after the war. What seems certain is that Johnson's magazines overstated the preponderance of intermarriage in order to sell magazines and to contribute to a growing fascination about the implications of mixed-race romances and marriages. For example, a 1950 story in *Ebony* claimed that "one of the postwar phenomenon of the American social scene has been the huge increase in mixed marriages." As evidence for this claim, the magazine noted the opening of "Club Miscegenation" in Los Angeles, "Club of Tomorrow" in Detroit, and "Club Internationale" in Washington, D.C. These were social clubs for mixed-race couples that *Ebony* advertised to represent the presumed increasing numbers of mixed-race marriages. Yet such stories overemphasized the numbers of mixed-race marriages and ignored historical evidence of mixed-race social clubs such as the black and tans of the Progressive Era and the mixed-race social clubs that could be found during the Harlem Renaissance.[34]

The same year, *Ebony* published yet another story that played up the prevalence of interracial romances and marriage. This story, titled "Is Mixed Marriage a New Society Fad?: Growing Number of Rebellious Bluebloods Who Wed Negro Mates Rocks Social Register World and Makes Newspaper Headlines," focused on a few examples of white women who married black men. This story was especially concerned with how upper-class whites received and behaved toward black people. Interracial romances and marriages involving upper-class whites signified a special kind of assimilation into mainstream America.

Within the past few years some of the top drawer names of the U.S. elite have shunned the dictates and decorum of New York's Park Avenue to march to the alter with Negro mates and bring down upon their heads the frowns and fury of social arbiters. So evident has become the increase in interracial marriage in high places that some of the smart set sneeringly scoff at the matches as a new but passing society fad.[35]

In the mid-1950s, as school desegregation was a national political issue, Johnson's magazines began to publicize how desegregation had led to increasing number of interracial romances and marriages. Such stories were politically explosive as they fed segregationist arguments against desegregation, and they troubled civil rights activists' attempt to downplay the issue of interracial intimacy in civil rights. Moreover, in the years leading to the *Brown* decision, Johnson's magazines seemed to taunt opponents to desegregation with stories linking civil rights to interracial intimacy. For example, a 1953 *Jet* article titled "Are Mixed Marriages Increasing?" reported that rates of intermarriage were increasing beyond what census takers even knew. "It is estimated by one authority that upwards of 15,000 mixed couples now marry annually in the United States." The story went on to suggest that desegregated colleges were the most important factor in explaining the increase in mixed marriages.[36]

In 1954, the same year as the *Brown* decision, *Ebony*'s article "Interracial College Marriages" measured the success of desegregation in terms of interracial marriages.

> *With more and more Negro students being welcomed into integrated colleges, inter-racial dating is on the increase. Once common in Northern schools located in cosmo-politan cities like New York and Chicago, the practice is rapidly becoming a common occurrence at small colleges which today have a greater Negro enrollment than ever before. Even in Southern cities like Atlanta, liberal students from segregated colleges are getting together at off-the-campus social parties. . . . In traditionally-liberal New England, bi-racial marriages are so common that practically no one questions the right of anyone to marry a person of his choice.*[37]

Although the *Chicago Defender*'s coverage of interracial intimacy was less sensational than Johnson's magazines, it was just as frequent. Much of the *Defender*'s coverage was dedicated to interracial romances between black GIs and European women, a subject that will be examined in the next chapter. The *Defender*'s most consistent contributors of stories about interracial intimacy were Earl Conrad and Lillian Smith, the latter the author of the 1944 *Strange Fruit*. Conrad's and Smith's contributions to the postwar black public sphere illustrate the convergence of liberal politics and the politics of interracial intimacy.

In the January 19, 1946, national edition of the *Defender*, Earl Conrad reported a story titled "It Happened in Norfolk: White Dixie Pastor to Marry Negro Girl." Conrad's story, which was one of the only stories to appear in the *Defender* about a white male/black female romance, detailed the marriage of the Reverend Frank White, thirty-one, who was the pastor of the Unitarian Church of Norfolk, Virginia, to Anne Anderson, twenty-three, a black woman from Norfolk. Conrad reports that the newlyweds planned to translate the interracial message of their marriage into "work at once in the organization of a national interracial church." White told Conrad, "It is important that we not only talk about the new world, but that we should also be the new world. We must express in our daily lives the ideas which we profess." White's argument linked his romance and marriage to a politics of interracial cooperation. White attempted to convince *Defender* readers that marriage was not just a private relationship but also a public act that affected politics in the public sphere. In making this argument, White appealed to a culturalist argument about difference that downplayed the significance of race. In doing so, White revealed the limitations of cultural arguments about race, as his defense of interracial intimacy teetered on the verge of a color blindness that erased the historical legacy of racism.

> *Marriage is not an individual matter, it's a social matter. If it were a private affair there would not be witnesses to marriage and no public weddings. Marriage is a group matter, it is a matter of people, of society, of public welfare. No two individuals stand alone apart from the rest of society and it is faltering nonsense to hide any longer behind outdated, apologetic notions. People marry, not colors; human beings, universal in spirit and body, marry and the marriage of a man and a woman can never stand outside or apart from the destiny of humanity.*[38]

Two weeks after Conrad's article on Rev. White's marriage, Conrad responded to a reader who disliked the tone of White's defense of interracial marriage. The reader thought that interracial marriage was not a grand achievement but a personal matter that detracted from the "real" politics of civil rights. The reader disliked White's assumption that he had transformed race relations in any meaningful way. Conrad responded by defending White's analysis of marriage as a public act. Yet, like White, Conrad embraced a culturalist understanding of racial difference to such an extreme that the historical particularities of racism were secondary to the social good of integration.

> *When we fight for our rights in our industry, education, and the arts, what makes you think the Negro people do not have the right to fight also for social equality? And if social equality is achieved, what is wrong with people in love marrying if their faith in each other can transcend the barriers that have been created by three centuries of fascist-segregation-slavery-feudal rule? . . . If you want progress, you have to take the path of integration, and as I see it, this is going to lead to happier social relations between the groups. . . . This is not a question of color; it is an issue of*

human begins, of people's rights, of a man's right to love a woman, of the right of people everywhere to seek understanding with other people.[39]

In this example, two white male liberals supported the right to intermarriage within a black newspaper.

Lillian Smith was also interested in a different aspect of intermarriage than the one predominantly published in black magazines and newspapers. Responding to a growing critique that only black men's intermarriages were the subject of celebration, she wanted to know whether black women had as much to gain through intermarriage as black men. Such a question was crucial to the discussion of intermarriage yet nearly completely absent. Smith's article in the *Defender* argued that while black women did not profit from intermarriage in similar ways as black men, they nevertheless challenged the color line. Moreover, Smith argued that if black women increasingly intermarried, the subject of black men's intermarriages would cease to be newsworthy, and all intermarriages would become private issues. Smith's story failed to recognize that it was the very publicity of intermarriage that made it rich political terrain.

In developing her analysis of black women's roles in intermarriage, Smith noted,

Usually the Negro men who have married white wives have been prominent in Negro affairs, and a great deal of publicity has been given their choice. But very often, a Negro woman may be married to a middle class white man who, because he continues to work and make a living in the white economic world, seeks to avoid newspaper headlining of his marriage for fear of financial retaliation. . . . It is not as much of an economic risk for it to be widely known that a Negro man has chosen white women as the converse.[40]

Nevertheless, Smith argued that black women did intermarry and that this fact ought to reduce the amount of coverage given to black men's intermarriages. "As intelligence seeps through all the segments of the population that Negro women, too, have chosen many white husbands, there will be less and less resistance to intermarriage. And more truly than ever marriage will be a really private affair."[41] Smith's argument correctly understood the gendered logic of magazine and newspaper coverage of interracial intimacy. Black men's interracial marriages received far more coverage than black women's. Yet Smith misunderstood marriage as only a private relationship, and this moved her critique of interracial intimacy away from the issue of black women's exclusion from the postwar black public sphere.

Letters to the editors of black newspapers and magazines exposed the tensions inherent in publicity about interracial romances and marriages. Black men's interracial romances and marriages with white women received most of the attention. This led many black women to argue that the politics of interracial intimacy were exclusionary. Many women wrote to the magazines and newspapers to claim that intermarriage was not a civil rights victory; it was, rather, simply a marriage. More critically, some women developed an analysis of the link between racial uplift and patriarchy that revealed how the politics of interracial intimacy excluded women.

In 1950 Nannie H. Burroughs, president of the Women's Auxiliary of the National Baptist Convention, criticized interracial romance and marriages in *Ebony* as an "escape into the white race." Challenging *Ebony*'s overwhelmingly favorable coverage of interracial intimacy, Burroughs lamented what she believed were the racist implications of interracial marriage. "Crossing the line is not the solution but holding the line and educating the mind is the answer." Burroughs argued that black people had lost faith in the beauty of blackness and that intermarriage signified the desire among black men to be white.[42]

In the *Defender*, editors asked readers, "Is it true that Negro women harbor deep resentment to interracial romances?" Readers' responses to this question revealed criticism of interracial romances and marriages, while affirming the private nature of intimacy. Readers did not oppose interracial marriage, as such, but instead opposed the notion that interracial marriage was a public issue that ought to affect civil rights. In this way, readers shifted the focus away from arguments about the publicity of intermarriage and toward the privacy of intimate matters.[43]

For example, Edith Alexander, executive director of the Chicago Mayor's Committee on Unity, argued, "I feel, like Mrs. Roosevelt, that marriage is a personal affair and the choice is up to the individuals. On the other hand, I don't feel a person should marry anyone just because he or she happens to be Negro or white." Alexander understood marriage as a private choice, and in this way she attempted to disassociate the politics of interracial intimacy from the politics of civil rights. An anonymous writer argued, "If an interracial marriage comes about from the normal reasons of proximity and compatibility, I'm in favor of it. I object, however, to the feeling some Negro men have that white women are species totally different and more desirable than Negro women." This reader understood that the politics of interracial intimacy was a male discourse that ignored the historical legacy of sexual violence toward black women and excluded black women from civil rights issues. In placing the white female body as the ultimate symbol of black male upward mobility, the discourse of interracial intimacy implied that black women were incapable of engendering feelings of belonging and respect for black men.

In 1953 *Jet* explicitly linked the gender bias within the politics of interracial intimacy. In an article titled "Are Negroes More Amorous Than Whites?" *Jet* suggested that intermarriage revealed contradictions in how black men and black women were positioned within civil rights discussions. Black men, the article argued, were currently in vogue. "Just as many believe that Latin and Frenchmen are the world's greatest lovers, it is common belief that Negro men by some quirk of nature—are gifted with qualities that make them more amorous." Yet the article hinted that black women were less praiseworthy of black men's romantic abilities. "Strangely enough, Negro women—who have a closer relationship with Negro men than any other females of the species— contradict this longtime notion. Whereas white women often spread tales about Negro proficiency in love, conversations among Negro women invariably seem to get around to the declaration that Negro men are lousy lovers."[44]

In posing white women and black women as arbiters of black male desirability, this *Jet* article underscored the tensions within the logic of interracial intimacy. All publicity of interracial romances and marriages called into question the relative desirability of the excluded party. Nonetheless, given that black women had historically experienced interracial sexuality as violence, it made sense that black women would not embrace interracial intimacy as a civil rights issue. Furthermore, celebrating black male/white female interracial romances and marriages threatened to exoticize such relationships. The *Jet* article suggested, "Sociologists point out that the testimony as to Negro male talents as a Lothario comes from white women who are seeking outlets in doing something 'exotic' and in deliberately seeking out colored romantic partners are demonstrating a form of discrimination in reverse."[45]

From the founding of the NAACP in 1910 to the postwar discussion of racial intermarriage in black magazines and newspapers, a slow change had taken place. In the prewar society, defending racial intermarriage focused on protecting black women. W.E.B. Du Bois and James Weldon Johnson, for example, suggested that black women were left vulnerable to the desires of white men if black women were unable to compel white men to marry them. Moreover, they argued that antimiscegenation laws encouraged illegitimacy in black families. This argument invoked the rights of black men to protect black women in the same ways that white men were allowed to protect white women.

After World War II, however, changes within the NAACP and within the nation altered the ways black activists positioned interracial intimacy within civil rights issues. The growth of the NAACP into a massive political force during the 1940s catapulted its civil rights activism to the public stage. In doing so, the association would have to carefully negotiate the role its attack on antimiscegenation laws would play in its struggle. Yet the NAACP was not the only public representative of black people. The growing black magazine industry and the continuing work of black newspapers played a significant role in publicizing and mediating discussions of interracial intimacy. The black public sphere was congested terrain after World War II that marked the collision of divergent understandings of the role of intermarriage in civil rights politics. Most significantly, however, was the failure of the postwar mainstream popular culture and legal cases to contain the politically explosive matter of interracial romance and marriage.

In 1954, the year that the Supreme Court made its landmark *Brown* ruling, Benjamin Mays, then president of Morehouse College, wrote to the Southern Advertising and Publishing Company to protest an article that claimed that the NAACP's goal was first and foremost racial intermarriage. Seeking to detach the role of intermarriage from the issue of desegregation, Mays claimed, "The thing that disturbs me is that it is intermarriage we have objected to all along. . . . I don't agree with you that the abolition of segregation means intermarriage. It has not happened in Boson, New York, and Chicago."[46]

Mays's insistence that intermarriage was not the goal of desegregation was not universally shared within civil rights coalitions. Even Walter White contested Mays's claim. In 1958 White published an article in *U.S. News and World Report* in which he argued that desegregation would lead to a rise in intermarriage. Such an argument was politically charged both within black society and within American society in general. White argued, "When human beings get to know each other and to respect each other, friendships develop and some of those friendships develop into love and into marriage."[47] Because White was the representative of the nation's largest civil rights organization, this argument likely incensed segregationists and some civil rights activists alike. White had publicly articulated what many feared was the likely consequence of desegregation.

Perhaps no other example illustrates the public nature of interracial romance and marriage than the case of black GI romances during and after World War II. As black GIs represented the U.S. military in postwar Europe and Japan, their intimate practices entered into national and international political spheres. Such publicity allowed GI interracial intimacy to become a political lightning rod for critique and optimism. Yet as we compare black/white interracial intimacy in Europe to black/Asian interracial intimacy in Japan and Korea, we begin to see the limitations of interracial intimacy as a public-sphere issue.

Chapter 4

At Home and Abroad

Black Soldiers and the Spaces of Interracial Intimacy

Two black soldiers sitting on the dock at Brest at the end of the First World War spoke of what they would do when they were shipped home. One said that he would take a lesson from the French, who had no race feelings and drew no color line. On arriving in their home town he would buy a white suit, white tie, white straw hat, and white shoes. "An I goin' put 'em on an 'den I's goin' invite some w'ite gal to jine me an' wid her on my arm I'z gwine wolk slow down de street bound fur de ice-cream parlor. Whut does you aim to do w'en you gits back?" His companion replied, "I 'spects to act diffe'ent frum you, an' yet, in a way, similar. I'm goin' get me a black suit, black from haid to foot, and black shoes, an I'm gwine walk slow down de street, jes' behin' you—bound fur de cemetery!"[1]

BLACK PARTICIPATION in the U.S. military during the First World War, as this folktale reveals, was punctuated by tensions over civil rights and the specter of interracial sex. The war inspired one black serviceman to believe he had earned the "right" to marry a white woman. Yet the other serviceman's prediction that an interracial romance would lead to his friend's death illustrates the limits of this "rights" approach. Interracial intimacy was therefore a contested issue that illuminated certain contradictions centered on black participation in the nation.

Military engagements always bring to the fore issues of social and cultural differences within and without the nation. Thus the military often finds itself mediating not only international geopolitical tensions but also tensions within its forces and between its forces and foreign civilians. During and after World War II, fears of interracial intimacy within the military and between servicemen and civilians threatened to blur racial and national boundaries.

Yet unlike the First World War, during World War II a growing civil rights movement, in addition to the rhetoric of antiracism that justified the war, made policing interracial intimacy more difficult. The U.S. military thus attempted to mediate and contain the explosive potential of wartime mobilization, especially as it influenced interracial dating, romance, and marriage. In this way, the project of containment was central to the military's war effort.

If black soldiers at the end of World War I knew that interracial romances were taboo and dangerous in the United States, black soldiers fighting in World War II could not be as certain. Court rulings after the war such as *Perez* and *Brown* indicated that civil rights reforms were leading to desegregation of many social institutions. Yet as we saw in the first two chapters, interracial intimacy continued to represent the limits of postwar civil rights reforms. Through various legal and discursive forms of containment, the postwar society attempted to limit the possibilities of interracial intimacy. Hence, while the returning black GI may have expected his service to translate to increasing tolerance of his intimate choices, in reality he would have learned that the civil rights implications of his service would not be fully realized. What concerns me here are the ways that black GI interracial intimacy signified the most public form of black activism centered on interracial intimacy and marriage. As soldiers, black GIs represented black communities and the nation. Their intimate choices were thus uniquely positioned to represent the struggle for expanded civil rights at home and in the military and to undermine the nation's attempts to contain the civil rights implications of World War II.

While there is a rich body of work on black participation in World War II, few studies have focused on romance and sexuality as a significant component of black military service. Some studies have argued that black soldiers' interracial romances exposed contradictions between the goals of fighting for democracy and the practices of racial segregation. While this is surely true, more important here is the issue of how black soldiers and black communities at home understood the role of interracial romance and marriage as civil rights issues. Black GI interracial intimacy, at least in Europe, challenged white military officials' and soldiers' abilities to control white female and black male sexuality abroad. Further, because GI interracial intimacy took place in the context of a military occupation, such intimate matters became central to civil rights organizing.[2]

At the same time, black GI interracial intimacy revealed all sorts of divisions within black understandings of civil rights. As magazines and newspapers celebrated and publicized black/European romances, they simultaneously derided black/Asian romances. Such disparate representations of interracial intimacy in Europe and Asia suggest the limits of interracial intimacy as civil rights. The public sphere was a racialized space that privileged whiteness. Therefore, employing interracial intimacy as a strategy to enter the public sphere meant limiting interracial intimacy to black/white romances and sexuality. Yet this also limited for whom interracial intimacy could become a strategy for advancing civil rights. Nonwhite women were nearly absent from black representations of GI interracial intimacy, and because of this, understandings of what constituted a civil right for black people became a gendered discourse that privileged black men over black women.

The international and interracial environment of military service helped black male soldiers imagine new understandings of civil rights focused around ideas of desirability and personal intimacy. The power of interracial intimacy to shape black soldiers' civil rights activism can be understood in terms of the contentious struggle between black GIs and the NAACP, on the one hand, and the Departments of State and War, on the other, over the implications of and right to intermarriage. This chapter places two contending discourses in dialogue: the military's desire to contain the possibilities inherent in black participation in the war while still promoting antiracism as the motive for its involvement in the war and the NAACP's and black magazine and newspaper editors' desire to use the black GI as a new symbol of American citizenship and as a champion of black masculinity. This contest over the meaning of interracial romance and marriage abroad went to the very core of what activities could be considered within the sphere of civil rights.

In order to understand the complex matter of GI interracial intimacy after World War II, it is important to examine the racial politics shaping the war itself. The Second World War was justified as a fight against fascism and Nazi racism. These motives made practices of racial discrimination within the nation contradictory and, for a time, un-American.[3] On the eve of the United States's entry into the war, the military had to balance the need to present a front of racial equality and democracy to the outside world with the need to ensure that wartime social relations would not disrupt the home front hegemony—which depended on well-defined racial and gender boundaries—the military was created to enforce.

Interracial romances during and after the war between black GIs and European and Asian women raised troubling concerns for the War Department. Prohibiting black GI interracial intimacy would contradict the stated goals of the United States's participation in the war, and it would invite black protest at home. Yet permitting GI interracial intimacy—especially marriage—meant sanctioning a relationship that was illegal in most southern states and taboo nearly everywhere on the home front. The War Department responded to black GI interracial intimacy by tolerating it as long as it could be contained abroad; it made interracial marriage very difficult, and it made war bride migration to the United States nearly impossible for black GIs' spouses.[4]

A military training film produced during the war illustrates the military's attempt to mediate the desire to be looked upon as committed to equality while ensuring that the war would not drastically alter race relations at home. In December 1943 the popular American actor Burgess Meredith narrated an hour-long film called *Welcome to Britain*. Intended for newly arrived servicemen, the film cautioned white GIs to expect, and to tolerate, unfamiliar race relations in England. Meredith plays a white soldier who has just arrived in England. The soldier experiences British culture and base life. In the most telling sequence, Meredith, an Englishwoman, and a black GI are seated in the same compartment on a train. During idle conversation, the British woman and the black GI realize that they both come from cities named Birmingham. At this moment, Meredith interrupts the narrative by addressing the audience, here defined as white servicemen, directly.

> *Now look men, you heard that conversation; that's not unusual here, it's the sort of thing that happens quite a lot. Now let's be frank about it. There are colored soldiers as well as white here and there are less social restrictions in this country. . . . You heard an Englishwoman asking a colored boy to tea. She was polite about it and he was polite about it. Now . . . look; that might not happen at home but the . . . point is, we're not at home, and the point is too, if we bring a lot of prejudices here what are we going to do about 'em?*[5]

Welcome to Britain attempted to prepare white GIs for social relations between white women and black men, and it asked them to suspend their prejudice at least while in England. Yet the film revealed the tensions inherent in the military's treatment of black/white romances in Europe. The film advocated toleration of, without lending support to, interracial romances. Such treatment of black/white romances suggests the tenuousness of interracial intimacy within the military. Black/white relationships abroad were grudgingly tolerated so long as they did not undermine race relations at home.

Military officials feared the implications of black service abroad because it threatened to make the privacy of intimacy a public and political matter. For example, according to Nat Brandt, in 1942 Dwight D. Eisenhower, then commanding general of the European Theater of Operations, "confided to a Hollywood actress . . . that he was worried about black troops because they were running off with English girls. He believed in blacks having equal rights, but said those rights should be 'modified when it concerned women and liquor.'"[6] Eisenhower sought to disassociate the public discourse of equal rights from the supposedly private sphere of "women and liquor." For him, negotiating the public discourse of rights and the private discourse of intimacy was vitally important to maintaining the appearance of equality. For example, he wrote to the War Department about the military deployment in England:

> *Here we have a very thickly populated country that is devoid of racial consciousness. They know nothing at all about the conventions and habits of polite society that have been developed in the U.S. in order to preserve a segregation in social activity without making the matter of official or public notice. To most English people, including the village girls—even those of perfectly fine character—the Negro soldier is just another man, rather fascinating because he is unique in their experience, a jolly good fellow and with money to spend. Our own white soldiers, seeing a girl walk down the street with a Negro, frequently see themselves as protectors of the weaker sex and believe it necessary to intervene to the extent of using force, to let her know what she's doing.*[7]

Eisenhower's letter is extraordinary because of its acknowledgment of how the supposedly private politics of racial segregation can be enacted outside of the public sphere. Black GIs threatened to unmask the "segregation in social activity" as a public and very political issue whey they entered legal marriages across the color line. Thus, while military leaders like Eisenhower never legally prohibited interracial romances and marriages, they made such relationships difficult and, at times, impossible.

Many black GIs complained that the military prohibited their marriages to foreign women. For example, in 1945 the military attempted to restrict where black soldiers could socialize outside of European military bases. According to an article published in the *Defender*, "African American soldiers in the 226th Engineers Regiment in Italy have been restricted to a bivouac area. . . . The order to all intents and purposes obviously has as its objective the complete isolation of the Negro soldiers from the Italian populace— particularly Italian women."[8]

In addition to policing the spaces of foreign military bases, the military made obtaining a marriage license for an interracial couple nearly impossible. The process of gaining a marriage certificate and eventually a travel visa for a war bride sent couples down a cumbersome path. A 1942 regulation required personnel on duty in a foreign country to "notify their commanding officers of their intention to marry at least two months in advance. . . . A commanding officer who had to approve a marriage application was required to write the civil or ecclesiastic authority who was to conduct the marriage and to interview the potential bride."[9] However, officers frequently denied certificates to interracial couples because of fears that these marriages would undermine state antimiscegenation laws in the United States. For example, although Howard Peterson, the assistant secretary of war, indicated that his department's marriage regulations "applied without regard to race, creed, or national origin," he recognized that interracial marriages could not be approved if the black GI was a legal resident of a state that had an antimiscegenation law. Thus the color-blind policy regulating marriages abroad was undermined by racist policies at home. In this way, the foreign spaces of World War II service were never free from domestic race relations. Peterson admitted, "Personnel were advised, however, that the laws of certain states did not recognize the legality of marriages between members of different races, and that certain races were ineligible for admission into the United States for permanent residence, under the present immigration law."[10]

Were an interracial couple fortunate enough to have a sympathetic commanding officer, they still could not be guaranteed that their marriage would proceed without obstacles. During the lengthy process of requesting permission, many black GIs were relocated to other foreign bases or even back to a southern base in the United States. Furthermore, getting married did not guarantee that the war bride could live in the United States. A war bride had to apply for a visa to enter the United States, a process that required her to obtain her husband's sworn affidavit of support, "indicating the amount of his salary, bank deposits, insurance, and other financial resources."[11] War brides of black GIs often found that their marriage licenses or travel visas never arrived or that the War Department handled them inappropriately by misplacing them. In the words of one member of the War Department who handled war bride visas, "such [interracial] marriages are considered to be against the best interests of the parties concerned and of the service."[12]

Black servicemen and their fiancées' letters to the NAACP document the difficulties interracial couples had in obtaining permission to marry. For example, Robert Carter, the legal assistant secretary of the NAACP, received a letter documenting the case of a black GI named Reginald Carter who had been stationed in Italy before being restationed in the United States. Prior to his return home, Calder was denied permission from his commanding officer to marry Marie Gagliarbie, his Italian girlfriend. Calder sought to go around his commanding officer by having Gagliarbie travel to the United States, where the couple would marry and raise their child. In his report to the national office of the NAACP, Carter urged the association to help Calder, "because although the girl's name is quite unpronounceable, even for him, he is quite certain that he is very much in love."[13]

Sergeant William T. Malone was denied the right to marry his German fiancée because, according to his commanding officer, his interracial marriage signified his lack of maturity. In his letter to the NAACP, Malone, then living in San Antonio, Texas, indicated that he was denied permission to marry his fiancée because he was deemed "not mature enough at this time to properly consider all the problems that would devolve on this proposed marriage."[14] In rejecting Malone's marriage request, the commanding officer undoubtedly thought that Malone had not considered the implication of antimiscegenation laws on his marriage. Yet such a statement also reveals how military policy relied on domestic race relations as a means to contain the explosive potential of international relations.

Other letters collected by the NAACP reveal black GIs' frustrations with military prohibitions on interracial marriages. For example, Corporal Ceophas J. Randal, stationed in France, wrote to his mother that he was unable to marry his French girlfriend because his commanding officer claimed that antimiscegenation laws in the United States prevented him from granting the corporal permission to marry. Undeterred by the military's denial, Randal sought his mother's assistance in researching antimiscegenation laws in the United States. He asked his mother to "get certificate of legal document showing that it is or is not legal for mixed couples to live there [in our home state]. . . . If it is not legal for mixed couples to live there, let me know what you can find out about living elsewhere. Say California, or wherever it is legal."[15]

While black GIs like Randal had their interracial marriage engagements terminated due to the military's desire to protect the integrity of state antimiscegenation laws, other black GIs had their engagements terminated because they were restationed during the engagement. For example, Milton Alberts complained to the NAACP that he was restationed because he had fallen in love with Adeheid Borsda, a German civilian. Shortly after his engagement, Alberts was punitively relocated to Eglen Field, Florida, a base located in the Deep South, where interracial marriages were legally prohibited. In its letter to the adviser of the secretary of defense, the NAACP indicated, "Alberts is understandably concerned about the problems which may result from his living with a white wife in a state where such would be unlawful. He is not desirous of violating the state's segregation statute and yet is anxious to complete his marital plans and properly provide for his wife's living accommodations in this country."[16] Eglen Field was also the destination for relocated black corporal Elmer Turner, whose engagement to a white British woman was terminated due to Florida's antimiscegenation statute.

The military used its ability to relocate soldiers without cause as a means to regulate interracial romances and marriages. For example, John McMorris was not allowed to return to France to marry his girlfriend after he had been on a three-month furlough. Instead of allowing McMorris to return to his station in France, the military assigned him to a domestic base in the South. "I was preparing to be married to my fiancée in France, but was sent back to the U.S." McMorris knew that, once in the South, it would be nearly impossible to return to France because "the people here don't want me to carry out this marriage." According to McMorris, "The War Department has broken its contract with me and separated me from my child and intended wife. She is still waiting my return."[17]

Another indication of the military's de facto prohibition of interracial marriages were the letters that white fiancées sent to the NAACP requesting assistance. These letters illustrate the military's discriminatory handling of requests for permission to marry across the color line. They also show the scorn many European women felt from their neighbors as a result of their interracial romances. Europe was not the haven of racial tolerance that the military feared. Mothers of mixed-race children often suffered racial intolerance and sought to relocate to the United States to avoid local scorn. In 1946, for example, Gianna Del Prede wrote to the director of the NAACP that during the postwar occupation of Gruno, Italy, she had met a black soldier who, "with much grace and ability succeeded in making me his completely, and I brought a little girl into the world." Del Prede's black GI fiancé had abandoned her because, she speculated, he knew that the military would never allow the relationship to continue. Furthermore, Del Prede complained to the NAACP that she was "despised by everyone because of the child." She sought the association's assistance in helping to end the military's prohibition on interracial marriage and in helping her to raise her abandoned child.[18]

Maisto Iola related a similar story in her letter to the NAACP. Iola met and fell in love with Aaron Amos, a black GI, during the U.S. occupation of Gruno, Italy. Amos and Iola had a child. But when the occupation ended, Amos left the country and abandoned Iola and their child. Iola faced contempt from her neighbors over her biracial baby. "I can't take a step out of the house without being condemned by the people of Gruno." Like Gianna Del Prede, Maisto Iola sought the NAACP's assistance with finding the father of her child and with assisting her with travel to the United States.

Just as black soldiers were told they could not marry across the color line because of antimiscegenation laws in the United States, some white European fiancées were similarly prevented from traveling to the United States because of such laws. For example, Hildegard Lousie Kaiser was living in Nuremberg, Germany, when she fell in love with Walter Woods, a black GI who participated in the postwar occupation of Germany. When Woods's service in Europe came to an end, he and Kaiser sought a marriage license and travel visa so that she could join him in the States. When she went to Woods's commanding officer, she was told, " 'You can't marry a Negro.' " Unmoved by the officer's denial she "told him 'oh, yes I can, for he is an American citizen like you and if a white American citizen can marry a German why should a Negro not marry me?' When the officer saw that he'd not changed my mind, he told me I might get into trouble for colored and white people in American would be bad to me if I'm married with a Negro."[19]

In a similar letter to the NAACP, Marie Draux of France complained that a commanding officer had prevented her marriage to a black GI. She sought advice from the NAACP about where in the United States she could live with her fiancé without breaking the law. Apparently, Draux had been told that antimiscegenation laws precluded her marriage plans, for she asked the NAACP, "Is marriage between a colored man and a white woman forbidden in certain American states? Could you tell me if such a marriage in the state of California would have any validity? In Los Angeles, for example?"[20]

Letters from European fiancées and girlfriends of black GIs like Marie Draux illustrate the difficult barriers established by a U.S. military eager to appear tolerant of racial diversity.

In 1949 *Ebony* published an article that illuminated the military's attempt to regulate interracial intimacy. The article related the plight of Mona Janise, a Welsh citizen who dated black GIs until the U.S. military prevented interracial parties in her town.

> *We had dancing in the Pavilion five nights a week and when the black Americans arrived, there were girls who danced with them and socialized with them just as we would if they had been white. We all had fun, but when the white Americans arrived, they were so appalled at us it was unbelievable, and the coloured were stopped from participating in many things, including not visiting certain hotels. Talk about sin in the Garden of Eden, we thought we had done something wrong but didn't know what. Those were the first and last blacks to be in our town.*[21]

Underlying the War Department's concern over interracial romances in Europe was the assumption that race relations in Europe were better than in the United States and that this disparity would highlight American racism. Although European racial attitudes were often as toxic as those in the United States, black GIs found that the integrated spaces of Europe seemed less oppressive than their segregated military unit. Furthermore, British citizens, to take one example, living near U.S. military bases often subverted the military's attempts at racial segregation by seeking interracial social activities. According to Graham Smith, many British civilians were openly hostile to the idea of segregation. "Everywhere, it was reported, pubs were displaying signs reading 'For British people and coloured Americans only.' Similarly, bus conductresses in all parts of the country were said to be telling blacks not to give up their seats to whites as 'they were in America, no?' "[22]

In addition to such outright defiance of American racial attitudes, British civilians seemed to celebrate black participation in the Allied effort and, in complex ways, to celebrate black GIs by promoting stereotypical understandings of black male sexuality. In this way, British civilians and black GIs used each other to attack U.S. military hegemony. The black GI used British civilians' fascination with black culture and black bodies as a way to contest the military's segregationist practices. The British civilian who embraced racial integration similarly sought to undermine the authority of the American military over British spaces. This is not to argue that black GIs and British women did not, at times, fall in love. Rather, the point is that the politics of interracial intimacy, for black GIs and for British civilians, was targeted by the U.S. military, and such politics caused considerable concern for the War Department.

A 1944 popular British song cited by Graham Smith exemplifies the celebratory tone of British understandings of black participation in the military and the related fear of interracial intimacy on the part of the U.S. military. Written by Elton Box, Sonny Cox, and Lewis Ilda, "Choc'late Soldier from the USA" played on racial stereotypes of "mammies" and "Sammies" in order to compliment black GIs' participation in the military.

> *Choc'late drop, always fast asleep*
> *Dozin' in his cozy bed.*
> *Choc'late drop, has got no time for sleep,*
> *He's riding in a jeep instead;*
>
> *They used to call him Lazybones in Harlem,*
> *Lazy good for nothin' all the day;*
> *But now they're mighty proud of him in Harlem*
> *CHOC'LATE SOLDIER FROM THE USA.*
> *They used to call him just a choc'late dreamer*
> *Until the day he heard the bugle play;*
> *They made a coloured Doughboy out of the dreamer,*
> *CHOC'LATE SOLDIER FROM THE USA.*
>
> *Never in the schoolroom always in the poolroom*
> *For a nickel or a dime he's croon.*
> *His idea of Heaven was seven come eleven*
> *And dancin' ev'ry evening 'neath the yellow Harlem moon,*
> *He used to get a scolding from his mammy*
> *But now you'll hear his mammy proudly say,*
> *He's somewhere over there for Uncle Sammy,*
> *CHOC'LATE SOLDIER FROM THE USA.*[23]

The song's contradictory celebration of black GIs and its deployment of racist plantation iconography underscores the complexities of British attitudes toward black GIs. More important for our purposes is how British representations of black military service caused concern for a U.S. military that was keen on containing the racial implications of black military service.

As the war ended, the military struggled to find ways to address the issue of interracial marriage that would not threaten its desire to maintain the status quo in matters of interracial intimacy. Yet the military would have been unwise to prohibit all interracial marriages, because this would have undermined the pretext of democracy and equality driving the war effort. Instead, the military created a racial front; it publicly committed to race-neutral policies while in practice denying many interracial marriages. By the time the war was over, however, developments on the home front threatened to undermine the military's policy of preventing interracial marriages. The growing civil rights movement made the military's practices of segregation more contentious. Most important, on the home front the NAACP and black magazine editors and newspaper publishers began to publicize GI interracial intimacy in ways that linked such intimate matters to the public discourse of civil rights reform.

Though the U.S. military worked to contain the possibilities and implications of black military service, at home the NAACP and black magazines and newspapers turned black GI interracial intimacy into a civil rights matter. While the NAACP was reluctant to make the politics of interracial marriage central to it civil rights mission at home, it was more than willing to advocate black GIs' right to intermarriage abroad. The issue of black GI interracial intimacy was more strategic and safer than the issue of antimiscegenation laws at home. First, because black soldiers served in a triumphant war against racism and fascism, civil rights violations against them appeared even more contradictory to the United States's stated principles of democracy. Second, soldiers' unique status as representatives of the nation made it difficult for segregationists to challenge their civil rights, as such a challenge would have called into question the segregationists' patriotism. Thus, when civil rights leaders called for a "double victory" against racism abroad and at home, the black GIs' intimate relationships entered civil rights politics. For some black GIs, their role in the military made available a civil rights politics focused on their romances and intimate choices. Because of their unique status, black GIs, more than any group of black civil rights leaders, brought the politics of interracial intimacy to the public sphere.

Just as the black public-sphere politics described in the preceding chapter revealed divergent strategies for representing interracial romance and marriage, so, too, did the matter of GI interracial intimacy inspire different forms of activism within black communities. While the NAACP was loath to advocate the abolition of antimiscegenation laws at home, it was willing to advocate the right to intermarriage abroad. The association protested the de facto prohibition against GI racial intermarriage after the war in ways it had not previously done for U.S. citizens living at home. Because soldiers had the capability to wage antiracist struggles on domestic and international fronts, the association trumpeted their right to serve and, ultimately, their right to have their romantic and intimate choices acknowledged and respected.

For example, in 1945, as the war was ending and soldiers were being deployed around the world in occupational forces, the NAACP wrote to James Forrestal, the secretary of the navy, to express its growing concern that, unlike their white counterparts, black GIs were denied permission to marry their European girlfriends. "This Association has recently received several communications from American Negro servicemen and several from fiancées of Negro servicemen in France, Italy, England and other places reporting that American Army officers have refused permission to those individuals to marry."[24] The association sought to protect soldiers' right to marry whomever they chose. It was especially interested in using the soldiers' patriotism to advocate their rights.

While the NAACP was willing to champion the right of black soldiers to marry across the color line, it continued to subsume the politics of interracial intimacy to other desegregation struggles. Advocating soldiers' rights to intermarriage could invite unwanted criticism of leaders of the association who were engaged in interracial romances and marriages themselves. Yet if the association was cautious about publicizing its advocacy of the right to intermarriage, black magazine and newspaper editors were eager to celebrate and publicize black soldiers' interracial intimacy. Such coverage would focus on the black GIs' newfound status as the most desirable men in the European theater of operations.

While European citizens may have emphasized stereotypes of black male sexuality, black magazines and newspapers focused on stereotypes of European and, later, Asian women. While reporting on black GIs' interracial romances and marriages presented challenges to antimiscegenation laws at home, the black press also revised dominant narratives of black male sexuality as dangerous and threatening. For example, *Ebony* was just one year old in 1946 when it published a poem attributed to an anonymous German poet. Although authored by a German, the poem was clearly engaged in black politics and civil rights; the poem is both a record of European females' desires for black men and of the U.S. military's unfair prohibitions on interracial marriage. Titled "Madel, Liebst De Einen Schwarzen Amerikaner" (Little Girl, If You Love a Black American), the poem emphasized the significant impact black GIs had on European women.

Little girl, if you love a black American
Little girl, just love him always
When he is with you in the evening

Little girl, if you kiss a black American
Little girl, just kiss him always
Because it is only for a short time

And when he goes back to America
Little girl, don't wait for your happiness
Because he is not coming back.[25]

The poem's placement in *Ebony* invited a number of readings. As a catalog of some white women's desires for black men and as a record of unfair treatment of soldiers and their fiancées by the military, the poem intervened in the politics of interracial intimacy as it was constructed by the military and by racists in the United States who understood black male sexuality as undesirable. Yet the poem entered the political arena of interracial intimacy by focusing on black men's sexuality as liberating. Black women might have wondered how black male soldiers' interracial romances could help black women achieve civil rights. Nonetheless, during the ten years after World War II, black magazines and newspapers would publicize and celebrate the black male soldiers' interracial romances as a significant civil rights victory. Black women would have to enter this discourse through letters to editors and in readers' comments sections of newspapers and magazines.

During the ten years after the war, black magazines and newspapers paid special attention to black GI interracial romance in Europe and, toward the end of the decade, in Asia. This coverage represented interracial romances in three significant ways. First, this coverage illuminated the contradictory position of the black GI in a segregated war to end racism. If black soldiers could die to protect American democracy and to end Nazi racism, then why, some asked, could not black soldiers marry whomever they chose? Especially important in this regard were stories focused on black/German romances, for such relationships challenged Nazi and American racism. Second, black representations of GI interracial intimacy focused on European women's desires for black male physicality and culture. Such coverage attempted to contest American attitudes concerning black male undesirability by suggesting that European women, who signified refinement and taste, actively sought black men over white men. Finally, black magazines and newspapers focused on the plight of Europe's biracial babies. These stories illuminated how racist military politics had led to a rise of illegitimate children. In doing so, these stories attempted to show how American racism had prevented, for black men, the formation of nuclear families.

Black magazines and newspapers documented a shift in German attitudes toward black GIs from 1945 to the mid-1950s. At the beginning of this period, black newspapers reported that racism was evident in German racial attitudes toward black GIs. In 1945, for example, Edward Toles, a reporter for the *Defender*, published an article comparing Soviet racial attitudes to German and American racial attitudes. The *Defender* article detailed the experience of Gregor Ratto, a black doorman in Berlin. When "George," as he was called, attempted to get a marriage license to marry his German fiancée, German officials refused his request. After living together without "the benefit of clergy," George was awaiting a license from Soviet officials who assured him that there were "not bans on interracial marriage in the Soviet Government."[26] This article targeted Nazi and American racism and upheld the Soviet Union as a counterexample. In doing so, the article engaged American foreign policy makers' concerns that adverse race relations at home would lend support to the Soviet Union, thereby undermining the American mission in the postwar era.[27]

A year later, *Ebony* documented a change in German racial attitudes. In 1946 *Ebony* published "Germany Meets the Negro Soldier," an article in which the anonymous author suggested the number of interracial romances in postwar Germany was growing. "Many German girls between 18 and 26 have a steady Negro boy friend. . . . Many find their colored GI friends good companions and sometimes fall in love."[28] The location of such romances in Germany was significant, for in the politics of "double victory," Germany signified an important battlefield. If black GIs could end racism in Germany, then surely they could end racism in the United States. Hence romances between black GIs and German women were accorded special status.

By 1951, *Ebony* reported that German women's interests in black men had grown stronger each year after the war. In "Wanted: Negro Husbands and Wives: Germans Forget Aryan Doctrine, Seek Colored Mates in America," the *Ebony* article argued that when German women dated black men, they abandoned their beliefs about Aryan supremacy. In this way, interracial intimacy was directly linked to a politics of antiracism. "In the postwar era these Germans got to know Negroes for the first time and they were impressed with what many call the warm hearts of the colored GIs who did not come as conquerors but as friendly victors." One German woman, the article reported, after marrying a black GI, wanted to work for "equalization of the races socially."[29]

In 1952 *Jet* published a similar story about German women's interests in black men. "Why German Women Want Negro Husbands" illustrated the new context of race relations in postwar Germany. The article stated, "At no other time in world history have so many white women ever sought Negro husbands. . . . U.S. Negro publications are getting sacksfull of mail from fraulines [*sic*] who beg the editors to 'find me a Negro husband.' "[30] This story considered the presumed increasing numbers of German women who sought black GIs as a positive indication of increasing race relations. At the core of the article was the subtle argument that when white women had the opportunity to get to know black men, whites' racial attitudes diminished. *Jet's* coverage advocated a politics of integration in ways that were quite distinct from the NAACP's project of desegregation.

In addition to those stories that focused on black GI/German romances and marriages as strategic in the fight against racism at home and abroad were those stories that presented black male/European romances and marriages as evidence of the newfound status of black male desirability in the postwar era. These stories presented black men as capable of winning the hearts and minds of European women. In this way, black participation in the military contributed to civil rights struggles by recuperating black male sexuality from the historical weight of racist stereotypes. In black representations of GI interracial intimacy, black men were cast as desirable, intelligent, and highly sought after.

For example, when describing why British women sought black GI boyfriends, a 1946 *Ebony* article focused on black men's ability to dance as the main reason why they were more successful at attracting women than their white counterparts.

> *In the scramble for girl friends, the average Negro GI had one advantage over his white Army brother: he knew how to jitterbug. English girls love to dance. Result was that they flocked to dances given by Negro units, were thrilled by jitterbug experts and hot music. Many an English girl found a Negro beau at such dances, dated him regularly thereafter.*[31]

This kind of story contributed to a growing discourse about black interracial intimacy that posited black men as more attractive than white men. In 1945 the *Defender* published an article about a "tan yank" who had a difficult time bringing his Australian wife home to the United States. The article suggested that the military obstacles were due to white GIs' jealousy. "Speaking generally for the most of her country's women, [the Australian bride] Norma said the brown Yanks were more popular at the centers probably because they were more fun and much better dancers. Jealousy was the obvious root of any discrimination that arose between mixed servicemen, she thought."[32]

By 1954, *Tan Confessions* was able to summarize the previous decade's dramatic changes in white attitudes toward black GIs. In explaining "What Europe's Women Think of Negro Men," *Tan Confessions* sensationalized black GI interracial intimacy in ways that invited comparisons between American and European women's treatment of black men.

> *The impact of the Negro male on Europe's female population has been profound and prolific. In certain sophisticated circles in France and Italy, Negro lovers have become quite fashionable. Unofficial opinion surveys have revealed that among certain groups of European women, Negro men are considered more desirable. French women especially, pride themselves on their great feeling for colors—in fabrics, in art, and in human beings. Their too curly and kinky hair is appreciated as having highly attractive qualities that the French envy. Many a Negro GI during the last war was startled, while making love to a French girl, to see her rub her hands over his hair.*[33]

Similarly, *Jet*'s article "How Europe's Women Make Love" positioned black men as expert judges of European women's sexual behaviors. The article publicized black male/white female sexuality as the consequence of black military service.

> *Europeans themselves differ in their country-to-country attitudes toward sex. The French, for example, except for a few prostitutes and "loose" girls, are far more con-servative than most Americans realize. German women, on the other hand, are deeply—and almost morbidly—passionate. They can fall in love with a man they simply pass on the street, and without any other words, go any place he suggests with him. English people have, on the surface, a rather mundane, business-like attitude toward intimacy between the sheets—"bit of sport, y'know, necessary and all that." Swedish women are phenomenally famed for their split personalities; on the surface, they are correct, even prim; underneath, especially away from home, they are the wildest women to be found any place on the Continent.*[34]

Perhaps PFC Louis Farrell summarized the politics of interracial intimacy for black GIs in Europe best when he wrote from Nuremberg, Germany, "As for these German Frauleins, they give a soldier comfort. They make you feel as if you are wanted, not as if you are something that nobody should asso-ciate with." Farrell's letter registered how, for black GIs, Europe amplified their awareness of racism within the United States and how interracial intimacy registered a new experience across the color line.[35]

In addition to their focus on how interracial intimacy contributed to the "double victory" against racism and on how it recuperated representations of black male desirability, black magazines and newspapers presented stories about illegitimate children in order to further criticize the military's racist policies. Newspapers and magazines focused on the number of illegitimate children produced by military policies preventing interracial marriage. Such articles used the problem of GI interracial intimacy as a medium through which to discuss how racism, for black men, made building nuclear families formidable. During a historical era when all normative sexuality was sup-posed to be contained within the nuclear family, black magazines and news-papers illuminated how racism excluded black men from the cultural capital associated with forming nuclear families. For example, in focusing on Europe's "Brown Babies," a 1947 *Defender* article reported, "An untold num-ber of babies of American Negro GIs and Italian girls have been abandoned to death and starvation by their mothers, the spokesperson of a newly formed committee here to aid the homeless children told the *Defender* this week."[36]

Concern for the orphans produced by GI interracial intimacy was no doubt engendered partly by the harsh conditions a mixed-race child had to endure in Europe. As European women's letters to the NAACP illustrate, white women could be ostracized from their communities if they had a mixed-race child. Moreover, throughout Europe, "brown babies" were placed in orphanages without adequate care. Yet in protesting the treatment of Europe's "brown babies," the black press engaged discourses of the family and of motherhood that had historically been used to exclude black people. In publicizing the plight of "brown babies," the press claimed black people's right to form nuclear families and to receive the cultural capital associated with it. In this way, GI interracial intimacy and the protection of mixed-race children helped the black press rewrite popular narratives about black bodies and the impossibility of black families that gained currency in postwar popular culture and court cases.

The politics of interracial intimacy centered on interracial romances and marriages that challenged dominant representations of interracial intimacy. As has been noted in the first chapter, what concerned segregationists during the 1940s was the specter of black male/white female sexuality. Furthermore, although some states developed antimiscegenation laws that prohibited marriages between different groups of color, every law prohibited black/white sexuality. Therefore, certain kinds of interracial intimacy did not carry much weight as civil rights issues. The NAACP and black magazines and newspapers considered black male/white female sexuality as a symbol of racial progress, while ignoring and at times disregarding other forms of interracial romance and sexuality, such as those between black men and nonwhite women and between black women and white men. We can begin to see the limited possibilities of interracial intimacy as civil rights when we compare black magazine and newspaper representations of black/European relationships to representations of black/Asian relationships. While the former were celebrated for what they indicated about racial progress, the latter were less celebrated and often upheld racist stereotypes about Asian women. Furthermore, black women's criticism of black discourses of interracial intimacy reveals telling evidence about the complexities and limits of interracial sexuality as a civil rights matter.

Black military service in Japan raised all sorts of contradictions for black communities. Within some black activist communities in the United States, the war against Japan was seen as a race war against all nonwhite people. Because of this, some black leaders suggested that the black struggle against racism meant refusing to serve in Japan. For example, the historian John Morton Blum argues that some black soldiers viewed Japan as an ally because Japan seemed to be fighting against the forces of white domination in Asia.

> *In Asia the Japanese claimed to be fighting against the domination of white European colonialism, not the least as it weighed upon the corrupt government of China. Germany's Western European enemies had huge imperial holdings within which they subjugated brown and black men to white rule. The battle for freedom, as the Allies fought it, did not promise freedom for dark people.*[37]

Such an internationalist view of black/Japanese alliances led some black leaders to advocate ignoring the United States's calls for black participation in the war in Asia. Yet the majority of black soldiers willingly served in the military forces in Japan.

The racist nature of U.S. involvement in Japan influenced the politics of interracial intimacy. While U.S. policy makers framed the American war against fascism in Europe as a struggle to rescue innocent victims, the same policy makers framed the American war against Japan in terms of Japanese racial violence. As Thomas Englehardt argues, whereas Europeans were seen as victims of Nazi oppression, Asians were seen as inherently evil because of their racial difference.[38] Because the United States viewed Europeans as worthy victims during World War II and because of American fears of interracial sexuality between black men and white women, the U.S. military struggled to police European women's romances and marriages by creating various obstacles to such relationships. Japanese citizens, on the other hand, were viewed as suspect and sinister.

Black politics of interracial intimacy relied on challenging military and U.S. restrictions on blacks' freedom to choose romantic partners. Yet this politics also relied on a sexual politics that valued black male/white female romances and marriages as the most powerful political statement. Black male/Japanese female sexuality lacked the political power of black/white interracial intimacy because, within the United States, amalgamation and race suicide were firmly rooted within the black/white racial binary. Often confirming the dominant sexualized racism of American society, black magazine and newspaper editors altered the politics of black/Japanese inter-racial intimacy so that it confirmed black men's status as deserving patri-archs, not their desirability.

Just as black military service in Europe led to interracial romances and marriages with civilians, so, too, did service in Japan lead to interracial romances and marriages between black GIs and Japanese women. While black magazines and newspapers cast European women as expert judges of black male desirability, these same magazines cast Japanese women as sex-ually expert, docile, and cunning. In this way, black representations of inter-racial intimacy in Japan deployed American stereotypes about Asian female sexuality. Such stereotypes conferred a sort of assimilation for black GIs as deserving patriarchs of "legendary" Asian female docility. While the politics of interracial intimacy in Europe posited white women as the appropriate judges of black masculine desirability, the same politics in Japan posited Japanese women as engendering black patriarchy. Coverage of black/Japanese romances was thus represented either through a narrative of vice or a nar-rative of female submissiveness and male patriarchy.

In 1951, for example, when Japanese citizens accused black GIs of the rape of Japanese women, *Ebony* published a reader's letter denying such claims by arguing that Japan was a sexually promiscuous culture. Therefore, this reader suggested, it was unlikely that Japanese women had been raped. According to Private Frank Topsail, "If you will check on the birth rate in Japan, you will find that most of the girls of Japan are very sexually over-trained. The birth rate is one of the highest in the world. . . . I really cannot believe most of those rape cases, if so, are on the soldiers' part."[39] A similar argument concerning Japanese women's sexuality was presented in *Jet* when the magazine asked, "Is Vice Menacing Our GIs?" The article argued that black GIs were being duped into fathering children. "In Japan, for example, where Negro GIs reportedly have fathered one-third of an estimated 200,000 illegitimate babies, police and citizens alike have long accepted open prosti-tution. Rarely do police bother to make volunteer arrests among the 80,000 prostitutes in Japanese brothels."[40]

When vice was not the primary subject of black press coverage of black/Japanese interracial intimacy, Asian women's docility became the focus. This coverage engaged the politics of interracial intimacy by conferring to black men the "right" to be the recipients of Asian female submissiveness. In 1950, for example, the *Defender* published an article written by Ethel

Payne, director of the Army Service Club in Yokohama, Japan. The article suggested that Japanese women's docility was similar to the ways Japanese civilians treated the Japanese emperor.

> *Ever since the first foot soldier poured off the landing barges in August, 1943, tramp-ing their way into a scared and subdued Nippon, "Chocolate Joe" has set up his own method of bringing democracy to the son's of Heaven's 800,000 subjects. . . . Their hungry, ragged populace found him a good deal more "soft to the touch," kinder and more generous than his pale-faced fellow crusader in arms. It didn't take the Japanese long to get over the shock of seeing for the first time black and tan faces in the uniforms of the American soldiers. . . . Consequently, Jap Joe and Suziko San, already disciplined by a thousand years of emperor worship and iron military con-trol, recognized authority and bowed to it.*[41]

In 1950 the *Defender* reported, "The Average Japanese woman is described as consistently loyal, affectionate, and devoted to the male of her choice. Many of the Japanese girls will apparently make worthy wives for American boys."[42] Similarly, in 1952 *Ebony* reported in "The Truth about Japanese War Brides" that Asian female sexuality was "legendary." In presenting black GIs' Asian girlfriends, *Ebony* called into comparison Asian women and black women. The article seemed to imply that Asian women's docility was a welcome change from black women's aggressiveness.

> *Negro soldiers learn to admire the legendary qualities of attractive Nippon women. . . . Many legends have grown up during the years about these dainty girls but perhaps one Negro GI best summed up the feelings regarding Japanese women when he said: "Many try to find a girl on Seventh Avenue that is as kind and sweet and appreciative as these little mooses. They appreciate the least little thing you do for them."*[43]

Black GIs' letters mirrored stories about docile Asian women and the sta-tus such docility conferred on black men. Bruce Smith, for example, wrote in *Jet* about his experiences as a black GI who married a Japanese woman named Sayoko. He commented that he liked "whey my wife waits on me hand and foot, gives me a massage when I come home from work, washes my back in hot water and turns down the bed so I can take a nap before din-ner."[44] Similarly, PFC Richard Barnes wrote to *Tan Confessions*, "I have been in Korea and Japan 13 months now and I think the people of the Orient are wonderful people, especially the women. They care a lot about our boys and that makes me feel good."[45]

The politics of GI interracial intimacy privileged European women over all nonwhite women. Yet even within black magazines and newspapers, the tensions caused by black women's exclusion from interracial intimacy coverage were evident. Concurrent with the publicity and celebration of black GI interracial intimacy were more subtle articles about some black women's intermarriages and the problems black male interracial intimacy caused for black women. Although black women were largely excluded from newspaper and magazine representations of interracial intimacy, black women's voices can be heard in their protest letters to these black publications. This protest attempted to contest the publicity accorded black men's interracial intimacy. Interracial intimacy, such women argued, was a private matter, not a civil rights act.

Magazine and newspaper coverage of black women's relationships to the politics of interracial romance and marriage was complex and often conflicted. On the one hand, black publications documented black women's dissatisfaction with the politics of interracial intimacy. This critique challenged how magazines and newspapers represented interracial romance and marriage as public issues related to civil rights. Some black women argued that the politics of interracial intimacy ultimately threatened black women's ability to find suitable romantic partners. Black magazines and newspapers, however, also attempted to strategically position black women within the politics of interracial intimacy by arguing that black women were highly prized by some outstanding white men, including those among the European aristocracy. Yet this coverage of black women's participation in the politics of interracial intimacy was never as celebratory as the coverage of black men's interracial intimacy, suggesting that the public-sphere politics of interracial romance and marriage were confined to black men.

In 1946 a Chicago reader named Carolyn Morrison challenged *Ebony*'s coverage of interracial intimacy as a public-sphere political issue. She wrote, "For the life of me I can't see why you must stress so strongly that a Negro man has a white wife. So what. That man didn't do anything outstanding."[46] Beatrice Woodson also wrote to *Ebony* to challenge the magazine's favorable coverage of interracial intimacy. She called the magazine's coverage "outrageous and shameful," because it condoned "miscegenation between Negroes and whites." For Woodson, magazine coverage of interracial intimacy hindered the fight for civil rights. "*Ebony*'s continuous and ceaseless harping upon the men of our race and their white wives will result only in placing more obstacles in the way of our progress."[47]

In 1947 three women wrote to *Ebony* to criticize its focus on black GIs and German women. They argued that such coverage fed segregationists' arguments and that it exposed black men's infidelity. Dorothy Jones, of New York City, wrote, "Your seven-page spread in October *Ebony* titled 'Germany meets the Negro Soldier' left me more than slightly cold and very confused as to what I and other Negroes mean by racial equality. These pictures seem to uphold the timeworn contention of the bigoted enemies of our race who reiterate that all the Negro means by social equality is associated with white women." Edna Banks was similarly concerned that *Ebony*'s coverage would cause some readers to think that blacks actively seek white women. "Those were the pictures of the German women and our colored GIs. You made it appear as if the Negro were searching for association, or as if it were a great honor to be seen with one whose skin is a little lighter than ours." Finally, Ella Penman suggested German women were devious and that published accounts of GI interracial intimacy were damaging to black women. "Your display of our boys (perhaps some Negro working girl's husband over here) flopping around in the arms of those buxom German girls is certainly no credit to the Negro Americans. They entertain them in such a seductive manner, one arm around them, and, no doubt, a knife in their backs."[48] Similarly, *Jet* documented black women's critiques of interracial intimacy when it reported that black women viewed European women as "primarily predatory . . . [as women who] may make passes at [black women's] sweathearts."[49]

Concurrent with some black women's responses to interracial marriages and romances was the publication of a few stories that illuminated the problems interracial intimacy caused for black women. These articles suggested that as black men increasingly desired marriages and romances with white females, black women were finding it difficult to find suitable male partners. In 1947, for example, *Ebony* claimed that "800,000 Negro girls will never get to the altar." Although the magazine never provided evidence for this figure, it nevertheless is telling evidence of the complexities of interracial intimacy. The magazine suggested that black men's increasing interracial marriages and romances were to blame for the rising numbers of unwed black women.

In 1951 Pamela Allen, a reader from Columbus, Ohio, echoed *Ebony*'s concern about unwed black females when she wrote to *Ebony* that racial intermarriage "creates a problem for Negro women. What will happen to our future? Statistics show that there are more women then men who are eligible for marriage. So every time we lose a man to a women of another race, it means one more Negro woman will be husbandless." Most revealing about Allen's letter is its assumption that black women did not enter interracial marriages. In this way, her letter revealed the gendered logic of interracial intimacy; the politics of interracial marriage and romance extended rights only to black men.[50]

In response to black women's critiques of magazine and newspaper coverage of black male interracial intimacy, Johnson's magazines attempted to strategically position black women within the politics of interracial intimacy. The magazines tried to use some black women's interracial romances and marriages to argue that black women were highly prized by some rather wealthy white men. At times, black magazines suggested that black female interracial intimacy was an indication of civil rights progress. Yet such arguments were infrequent and ignored how antimiscegenation laws had never prohibited white male sexual violence against black women. In 1952 *Jet* explored the issue of black female interracial intimacy in "Negro Women with White Husbands." The author attempted to posit black women's interracial romances and marriages as politically fortuitous.

> *Consistently, propaganda has led the public to believe that mixed marriages are those involving white women only. Actually, this is untrue for today there are hundreds of white men who cross the color line annually to legally marry the Negro women they love. Most of these marriages are on high intellectual levels. Symbolic perhaps of a new social trend, the increasing number of white men marrying Negro women is another indication that the traditional laws against race mixing are a thing of the past. . . . The crossing of color lines which resulted in several marriages of white men to Negro women, seemed to begin a new trend shortly after the close of the war.[51]*

Yet the overwhelming majority of black newspaper and magazine coverage posited black women as desirable only to a certain class of white men. Black women's interracial intimacy, the magazines assumed, could function as politics provided the white man involved was wealthy or famous. In 1953, for example, *Ebony* published "Darlings of Royalty: Negro Women Win

Hearts of Men of Noble Blood in Europe." The article posited black women as the objects of European desire.

> *Not alone Oriental potentates, but the royalty of Europe has long paid suit to beautiful Negro women. Each social season on the continent some other colored charmer from America seems to turn up in Paris, Rome, or the Riviera to turn the heads of dukes and counts, princes and lords. The romantic doings of these darlings of royalty are becoming more and more legendary in high places.*[52]

Black women were inserted within the politics of interracial intimacy through articles that showed that some wealthy white men valued black women. Yet this analysis was unable to fully realize interracial intimacy as a civil rights gain for black women because the legacy of antimiscegenation legislation had always sanctioned white male/black female sexuality, so long as such relationships did not lead to marriage. Therefore, publicizing black women's interracial romances and marriages did not challenge the dominant racial paradigm in similar ways as did black male/white female interracial intimacy. Ultimately, Johnson's magazines were unable to imagine a meaningful place for black women within the politics of interracial intimacy. While Johnson's magazines publicized and celebrated black men's interracial romances and marriages at home and abroad, they failed to integrate black women into the civil rights implications of interracial intimacy.

Black soldiers' interracial marriages and romances posed problems for the military. Interracial intimacy threatened to undermine antimiscegenation laws in the United States. Crossing the color line made it difficult for the military to define the boundaries between its soldiers and foreign civilians. And finally, interracial intimacy caused tensions within the military between white GIs and black GIs. Because of these issues, the military carefully regulated interracial intimacy and marriage by policing the spaces of military bases, by preventing interracial marriages, and by creating barriers to war bride migrations. Yet the military's regulation of interracial intimacy exposed the limits of its democratic and antiracist rhetoric. Interracial romance and marriage thus became an important axis of civil rights politics at home.

Black soldiers' interracial intimacy also raised contradictions within black public-sphere politics. Interracial romance and marriage were considered a civil rights victory when black men and white women were involved but not when Asian women or black women were involved. In this way, the politics of interracial intimacy was based on publicizing that which mainstream America sought to make private, but only as it affected black men. Moreover, this politics rested on white women's ability to judge and guarantee black men's desirability. Because of the ways the politics of interracial intimacy upheld dominant ideas of race and gender, it was unable to achieve the kind of uplift that would affect all people. As we will see in the next chapter, the limits of the politics of interracial intimacy were its rootedness in static notions of racial belonging and gendered understandings of racial progress. For some black writers who, for various reasons, felt excluded by the black public-sphere politics of interracial intimacy, examining the public and private sides of black sexuality was integral to any model of black racial uplift.

Chapter 5

From the Outside Looking In

The Limits of Interracial Intimacy

A FTER WORLD WAR II, American culture was divided over whether interracial intimacy was primarily a private or public matter. Postwar mainstream popular culture and courts relegated interracial intimacy to the nonnational spheres of the home and the state or region. As a result, the full political implications of these relationships would not be realized. As a consequence of this positioning of interracial intimacy, black activists attempted to publicize and, at times, celebrate interracial romance and marriage, because doing so pushed certain civil rights questions into the public realm, where they could be dealt with through public policy. Interracial intimacy was a highly political issue whether it was considered a private or public matter; yet the space in which it was positioned mattered greatly in terms of what kinds of politics it could achieve. For example, if located within the private sphere, the implications of interracial romantic and marital relations could be contained. In this way, the private sphere was a space seen to be immune from the sorts of public policies that comprised civil rights activity. Moreover, if located within a public sphere, interracial intimacy was subject to public policy reforms.

Of course, the boundary separating public and private spheres has shifted throughout history. While making public that which was ideologically contained to privacy could expand definitions of rights, it also carried certain limits. The politics of interracial intimacy could contribute to civil rights activism through a discourse that accorded black bodies value, but it also overdetermined the black body as an object of civil rights discourse. In order for interracial intimacy to become entwined with the civil rights movement, the "right" kind of black bodies would have to be involved. In privileging the intimate relationships of only a few black bodies, the politics of interracial intimacy too often obscured the complexities of racial belonging.

Racial belonging represents the ways that race functions as a system of identity and of identification. Group identities, especially those affiliated around race, can be strategic to political struggles. Yet they may also be burdensome when they demand uniformity and uncomplicated ways of belonging to a racial group. Political philosopher Paul Gilroy has argued that black intellectuals have historically challenged simplistic notions of biological kinship through discursive strategies that transform temporalities and spatial logics. For example, Gilroy argues that the concept of diaspora has helped black intellectuals such as Phyllis Wheatley, Olaudah Equiano, and Richard Wright to position the historical and material legacies of slavery at the center of modernity, while at the same time avoiding the binding forces of historical modes of belonging. As Gilroy writes, "We will see that the idea of movement can provide an alternative to the sedentary poetics of either soil or blood. Both communicative technology and older patterns of itinerancy ignored by the human sciences can be used to articulate placeless imaginings of identity as well as new bases for solidarity and synchronized action."[1] Such a positioning operates by blending past and present and by challenging biological notions of kinship that support modernity's fragmented conception of identity. Through an act of what George Lipsitz has called "counter-memory," some black intellectuals have lived within and against race by invoking hidden histories in their politics of the present.[2]

The post–World War II era was no exception to a long history of black authors writing within and against the color line. Important for our purposes are those writers who employed narratives of interracial intimacy as a means to engage in the kind of diasporic imagining Gilroy identifies. For Gilroy, a diasporic identity involves a pan-African conception of self that links the historical legacy of slavery to the project of modernity. Although some postwar writers' fiction, such as Richard Wright's, would employ a pan-Africanist worldview, more common after World War II was a diasporic identity that emerged through a politics of interracial intimacy. Because, as I have already described, much of the World War II era raised a fear of bodily closeness between blacks and whites in particular, interracial intimacy was a trope that could reveal significant contradictions in the postwar era. Specifically, the trope of interracial intimacy brought together disparate temporalities and spaces by invoking the legacy of racial and sexual violence during slavery and by showing how the international politics of U.S. imperialism seeped into the presumed contained spaces of the nuclear family and the home.

There were a burgeoning number of black and white writers who took on interracial intimacy as a theme in their postwar literature. White writers such as Marjorie Sinclair, Clifton Cuthbert, and William Faulkner each explored interracial intimacy. The black writer Frank Yerby published three postwar romances in which interracial intimacy was a subtext.[3] Yet the most critical usages of interracial intimacy emerged from writers who, for various reasons, felt excluded by postwar notions of racial community. At times becoming expatriates and at other times exploring how gender and sexuality were integral to racial identities, William Gardner Smith, Ann Petry, and Chester Himes each used interracial intimacy to explore the contradictions of racial belonging in postwar America. These writers would shatter the spatial binaries that structured postwar conversations and debate about the meaning of interracial intimacy. Smith, Petry, and Himes wrote against nationalist renderings *and* black popular representations of interracial intimacy. These authors sought to reorient the politics of interracial intimacy away from a public/private binary and toward a historical materialist analysis of how racial and sexual ideologies had rendered the legacy of racial and sexual violence invisible. Furthermore, they attempted to complicate black representations of racial belonging by trying to imagine racial and political identities outside the bonds of racial kinship.

For these writers, interracial intimacy was a useful trope through which to explore the historical legacies of racial violence and the contradictions present in postwar America. In particular, these writers revealed the contradictions between wartime rhetorics of democracy and antiracism and postwar practices of racial discrimination. They also challenged liberal optimists who viewed interracial intimacy as racial uplift by focusing on how, historically, interracial intimacy had provided support to race relations during slavery and Jim Crow. Finally, these writers challenged the notion of racial uplift itself by using the trope of interracial intimacy to undermine simplistic notions of racial belonging and community.

William Gardner Smith is not regarded as one of postwar America's most distinguished black writers. Indeed, his fiction lacked the sophistication and elegance of many of his peers. Yet Smith's exploration of the theme of interracial intimacy in his first novel, *Last of the Conquerors,* is an important intervention into postwar racial and sexual politics. In this novel about the romantic relationship between a black GI and a German woman, Smith brought to literature the politics of interracial intimacy that had so profoundly shaped black public culture after the war. Like many black writers, however, Smith's experiences with racism in the United States led him to look beyond the national borders of his homeland to find a space of refuge. In the mid-1950s Smith joined the growing community of black expatriates living in Europe.[4]

Smith grew up in South Philadelphia, where he experienced both the safe haven of a thriving black community and the dangers of crossing the color line. As a young man, Smith was severely beaten by a gang of white men when they mistook for a white woman his light-skinned black girlfriend.[5] Such an experience was profoundly important in shaping Smith's later politics of interracial intimacy. While still in high school, Smith began working as a reporter in the Philadelphia branch of the *Pittsburgh Courier*, one of the nation's largest black newspapers and the paper responsible for coining the "double victory" campaign. In 1945 Smith was drafted into the military and was stationed with an occupation force in Germany. The war had ended, and Smith worked in a unit dedicated to rebuilding Germany. While in Europe, Smith encountered a receptive German populace willing, and at times eager, to socialize with black GIs.

Upon ending his military service, Smith published *Last of the Conquerors* (1948). The epigraph of the novel is a long passage from a *Pittsburgh Courier* article detailing the desire of one black GI to return to Germany once his service was over. The story juxtaposes two competing images; the Statue of Liberty and the specter of interracial intimacy in Europe.

> *The Marine Robin pulled slowly into the harbor and the Negro GIs, crowded on the fore-deck, could see clearly the lights of New York City. It was night. On the left, the Statue of Liberty blazed her welcome home to the men who had waved goodbye to her that day, so long ago, when they had sailed for the first time across the "big pond." But the men, standing crowded together on the ship, did not wave back. . . . "Someday," a soldier said softly on this, the day of his homecoming, "someday, I'm going back to Germany."[6]*

It is significant that Smith begins his novel with the newspaper article, for in doing so he explicitly tied his novel to the politics of interracial intimacy that shaped contemporary black public culture. Moreover, written with a reporter's tone, *Conqueror*'s realism attempts to render visible certain hidden and forgotten histories. At the core of Private Hayes Dawkins's military experience is the inescapable feeling that interracial intimacy confers a sort of assimilation and freedom to black GIs. Furthermore, through his interracial romance with a German civilian, Dawkins begins to recognize the contradictory rhetoric of American democracy. As one of the black GIs with whom Dawkins serves remarks, "I'll always remember the iron of my going away to Germany to find democracy."[7]

Just as his South Philadelphia neighborhood was a space of refuge amid a larger racist society, Hayes Dawkins learns that the military is also a safe haven of sorts. Military service allowed Dawkins to escape the United States and interact with white Europeans for whom race was not the primary register of affiliation. While documenting his developing relationship with a white German woman, Dawkins shows how black military service engendered a new consciousness for many black men. The paradox of American racism and military service encouraged black GIs to imagine alternatives to life in the United States. Dawkins must navigate a U.S. military determined to prevent interracial intimacy. This means avoiding the military police who were constantly on the lookout for victims of venereal disease and for black/white romances.

By the end of the novel, Dawkins's interracial romance must come to an end when he is released from military service and must return to the United States. Although he resolves to return to Germany after the war, he knows this is logistically and emotionally difficult. Dawkins is torn between his sense of racial belonging at home and his new, expanded identity in Europe. The novel concludes without clean closure. As Dawkins leaves his base in Germany, another soldier asks him if he's heading home. When Dawkins responds in the affirmative, the soldier concludes the novel by saying, "Tough." Dawkins's immediate future is uncertain, as he disdains American racism yet feels some cleavage toward his black community in Philadelphia.

While *Conquerors* details a rather predictable story about an interracial romance—indeed, many critics claimed that Smith had merely developed a narrative already established in the black press—it was an important medium through which Smith began to realize the limits of racial belonging. Military service in Europe exposed Smith to new opportunities and a new sense of freedom. Europe lacked the difficulties of South Philly and helped Smith imagine new possibilities for his life. Smith would move to Paris after the war, where he lived and worked as a writer until he moved again to Ghana in 1964, where he became editor-in-chief of Ghana television. Two years later, Smith was ousted from Ghana after a political coup overthrew Ghana's ruling party. Smith lived in Paris until he died of cancer in 1974. Smith understood his traveling lifestyle as an important aspect of his racial identity.

> *I am a roving expatriate. . . . I have wandered from place to place, from country to country. . . . I still have no idea where I shall eventually strike roots. . . . This rootlessness has its inconveniences, but it has an advantage too: It gives a certain perspective. . . . I sailed to Europe for a vacation. This stretched into months, then years.*[8]

Military service expanded Smith's worldview and convinced him that he could belong outside of the United States. For Ann Petry, the complexities of racial belonging were made clear through her childhood in the mostly white community of a New England town. Petry's was one of the few black families living in the town of Saybrook, Connecticut, in the early twentieth century. Furthermore, as the child of a pharmacist father, Petry benefited from a middle-class upbringing in which many of the hardships faced by urban black families were unknown. Petry followed in the footsteps of her father when she trained as a pharmacist. She later moved to Harlem, where, for the first time, she witnessed the hardships and possibilities facing working-class black communities. She joined the NAACP, an organization driven in large part by the kind of middle-class interracial politics that undoubtedly shaped her family's experiences in Saybrook. Petry began writing for the association's *Crisis* and *Opportunity* magazines, in addition to writing for the Negro Theater Project in Harlem.[9]

Petry was keenly aware of the differences within black communities that were revealed most starkly when she compared Saybrook to Harlem. Yet she was also aware of how the politics of racial uplift were different for men and women. Petry received a Houghton Mifflin scholarship to complete her first novel, *The Street*, a text that would become the first novel by a black female author to sell two million copies.

The Street is a naturalist examination of the public and private spaces that shape the experiences of a black single mother named Lutie Johnson. The novel examines definitions of publicness and privacy as a way to reveal how black women's labor is rendered visible and invisible. In this way, Petry's novel is a commentary on how postwar racial and sexual politics make privacy and publicness fortuitous to some and burdensome to others. For Lutie Johnson, that which ought to be private (her home and family life) is made public, while that which ought to receive recognition in the public sphere (her labor as mother, civil service worker, and blues singer) is rendered invisible. For Petry, interracial intimacy is the trope through which she is able to explore Lutie's spatial disruptions.

Lutie Johnson is a single mother who works a civil service job in order to create a private home-life for herself and her son, Bub. She embraces the American ideology of hard work and independence, best characterized by her utilization of Benjamin Franklin's self-improvement philosophy. Using Franklin's blueprint, Lutie plans to work diligently so that she can pull herself and her son up by her bootstraps, with the ultimate goal of someday providing a private home-space similar to those in which she worked as a domestic. Lutie figures that if Franklin can be successful through a well-ordered plan of hard work and self-reliance, then she can, too. Yet Petry shows that the American credo of rugged individualism and free-market capitalism poses all sorts of barriers to black upward mobility. Not the least of these barriers are the ways that black women's economic and reproductive labor are rendered invisible by a capitalist system that rewards most profitably the labor of white men and gives private cover to the their exploitation of nonwhite labor.

Lutie's difficulties stem in part from her inability to create a private sphere in which she and Bub can live comfortably and can be fully human outside the gaze of the rest of society. Lutie seeks the kind of privacy afforded to her previous employers, the Chandlers, a wealthy white family for whom Lutie worked as a domestic. While working for the Chandlers, Lutie becomes keenly aware of the privileged status of privacy and the lack of privacy afforded working-class blacks. Lutie must work as a domestic away from her own family because her husband, Jim, cannot find steady employment. Hence Lutie must take care of a white family as a live-in domestic so that her own black family can survive. The Chandlers live on an unnamed street; it is simply a "private road" where the family's chaotic life of alcoholism and depression are protected from the public gaze. In the Chandler household, Lutie is given her own bedroom and bathroom, a spatial bonanza she is unable to have in her real home.

For Petry, the public sphere is a place where people have relative levels of access based on their race, gender, and class. Yet Petry is also concerned with showing how the private sphere is a privilege for some and a burden for others. While the Chandlers' home is a safe haven for the owners, it is also a space of abstracted labor, for within the Chandler household, Lutie takes care of the youngest child, Henry, in addition to cooking and cleaning the house. Although her labor allows the elder Chandlers to live a lifestyle of leisure, her work is ignored and her presence understood through the trope of interracial intimacy. The Chandlers' friends and extended family continually remark about Lutie's beauty and the threat she poses to the Chandlers' marriage. As one the Chandlers' friends remarks, "Sure she's a wonderful cook. But I wouldn't have any good-looking colored wench in my house. Not with John. You know they're always making passes at men. Especially white men."[10] In this way, Lutie's contribution to the Chandler family and her sacrifice away from her own family are disregarded because of the ways that her productive labor is denied through the sexualization of her body. She was regarded as an object of desire that labored in a household, rather than the person whose labor enabled the Chandlers' private life. Lutie realizes that her labor is viewed through a historically produced prism of interracial intimacy.

> *Queer how that was always cropping up. Here she was highly respectable, married, mother of a small boy, and in spite of all that, knowing all that, these people took one look at her and immediately got that now-I-wonder look. Apparently it was an automatic reaction of white people—if a girl was colored and fairly young, why, it stood to reason she had to be a prostitute. If not that—at least sleeping with her would be just a simple matter, for all one had to do was make the request. In fact, white men wouldn't even have to do the asking because the girl would ask them on sight.*[11]

Petry shows that where there is one person's privacy, there is another person laboring to create that privacy. Similarly, Petry shows that publicness, when enforced, is intrusive both in the ways it precludes privacy and in the ways it invites state regulation. Lutie Johnson cannot find a suitable space of privacy, for in Harlem the public gaze is constantly focused on the private sphere. She ultimately winds up renting a small apartment that was "like living in a tent."[12] In addition to being a watched space, Lutie's new home is also a site of production and consumption, as the first floor is occupied by a brothel.

Publicness and privacy are each oppressive in Petry's formulation because of the ways they are regulated through white patriarchal forces. In *The Street*, Lutie cannot get ahead because at every turn she realizes that Junto, a white man, owns her apartment building, the brothel, the local bar, and the nightclub where Lutie will seek employment as a singer. The *Oxford English Dictionary* defines "junto" as "a body of men who have joined or combined for a common purpose, especially of a political character; a self-elected committee or council; a clique, faction or cabal; a club or coterie."[13] Although Junto is just one man, he functions as a cabal that controls the means of production in black Harlem. He controls the spaces of pleasure and entertainment through his ownership of the bar and the nightclub and controls the spaces of black intimacy through his ownership of apartment buildings and a brothel. As Lutie comes to realize, "If they [blacks in Harlem] wanted to sleep, they paid him [Junto]; if they wanted to drink, they paid him; if they wanted to dance, they paid him, and never even knew it."[14] Junto's control over the economic and social life of Harlem allows him to determine with whom Lutie will be intimate and, more important, from whom Lutie will earn a living.

The novel climaxes when Lutie, unable to find a higher-paying job, learns that Bub has been arrested for stealing letters from the street's mailboxes. Unable to pay for Bub's bail, Lutie turns to Junto for financial assistance. Even before Lutie meets Junto in person, she begins to have hallucinations that Junto is everywhere around her. She begins to realize that Junto is not just a man but also a signification of a larger historical network of oppressive power in her life. Junto's control over the public and private spheres of Lutie's life invokes the legacy of slavery and sexualized racism upon which it rested. When Lutie learns that, in order to receive the money she desires to free her son, she only has to "be nice" to Junto, she begins to remember the constant prodding of her grandmother about the predatory nature of white men.

Here Petry inserts a materialist analysis of the historical legacy of slavery. Such a discussion punctuates the public and the private in important ways. Although Lutie's grandmother has died, the stories she shared during Lutie's childhood operate as a moral compass that competes with Franklin's credo of economic individualism.

You couldn't be brought up by someone like Granny without absorbing a lot of nonsense that would spring at you out of nowhere, so to speak, and when you least expected it. All those tales about things that people sensed before they actually

happened. Tales that had been handed down and down and down until, if you
tried to trace them back you'd end up God knows where—probably Africa. And
Granny had them all at the tip of her tongue.[15]

Granny's wisdom derives from the production of a counternarrative about
black women's value. Her tales caution young black women to be ever wary
of white men and to resist stories of black female depravity. For example,
when Lutie overhears the Chandlers' friends discuss instances of black maids'
sexual advances toward married white men, she remembers her grandmother's stories that had been

said over and over, just like a clock ticking. . . . "Lutie, baby, don't you never let no
white man put his hands on you. They ain't never willin' to let a black woman alone.
Seems like they all got an itch and a urge to sleep with 'em. Don't you never let any
of 'em touch you." Something that was said so often and with such gravity it had
become a part of you, just like breathing, and you would have preferred crawling in
bed with a rattlesnake to getting in bed with a white man.[16]

Her grandmother's stories, encoded in tales and in blues songs, orient the
politics of interracial intimacy in a different time and space than post–World
War II era Harlem. For Lutie Johnson, the fact that "there was always the
implacable figure of a white man blocking the way, so that it was impossible
to escape" illuminated how the legacy of slavery was integral to the politics of
interracial intimacy.[17] This connection is made explicit when, after hearing a
white male talent agent offer to help her if she sleeps with him, Lutie connects interracial intimacy to slave labor relations.

It was a pity he [the talent agent] hadn't lived back in the days of slavery, so he
could have raided the slave quarters for a likely wench any hour of the day or night.
This is the superior race, she said to herself, take a good long look at him; black, oily
hair; slack, gross body; grease spots on his vest; wrinkled shirt collar; cigar ashes on
his suit; small pig eyes engulfed in the fat of his face.[18]

The time and space of the plantation South during slavery and the urban
North after World War II collide in the climax of *The Street* when Lutie meets
Junto. Lutie rejects Junto's offer, and she turns her anger toward Boots Smith,

the black man who arranged the encounter with Junto. In a rage, Lutie kills Boots. *The Street* concludes with Lutie fleeing Harlem and leaving her son in juvenile detention, where "he'll be better off without you."[19] Although *The Street* reveals the material legacy of sexual violence, it also reveals the processes through which black women's productive labor is obscured and forgotten. Such recognition suggests that black women could not be left out of the politics of interracial intimacy after World War II and that their inclusion would have led to different conclusions than the ones developed by those who celebrated interracial intimacy as a civil rights victory. *The Street*'s final paragraph hints at how the ugliness of the past, including the racial and sexual violence of slavery, gets forgotten. "The snow fell softly on the street. It muffled sound. . . . And it could have been any street in the city, for the snow laid a delicate film over the sidewalk, over the brick of the tired, old buildings; gently obscuring the grime and the garbage and the ugliness."[20]

If Harlem was the scene of Petry's first exploration of how interracial intimacy concealed certain economic relationships, her second examination of interracial intimacy was set in a space more directly controlled by white capitalists. *The Narrows* is about a black neighborhood (called the Narrows) in Saybrook, Connecticut, in which numerous contradictions are contained. In addition to middle-class business owners like the mortuary director F. K. Jackson and the Woman's Christian Temperance Union member Abbie Crunch, there are seedy bars such as the Last Chance Saloon and brothels such as China's place. Furthermore, productive spaces such as bars double as homes and spaces of privacy, while private spaces such as houses double as rental apartments. In this way, the spaces of publicness and privacy are completely merged.

The Narrows is also a site of contradiction between the black ghetto— many white residents call it "niggertown"—and a space of ethnic white assimilation. Some Italian and Irish immigrants continue to call the Narrows home. Although the Narrows is an ideologically contained space, it cannot be separated from the white town in which it is located. Many of the Narrow's black residents work in white mansions in Saybrook as domestics and in so doing turn homemaking into productive labor. Furthermore, the largest factory in Saybrook, the Treadway Munitions Plant, invades the space of the Narrows, as the lunchtime whistle marks time in the black neighborhood.

The most striking contradictions within the Narrows are revealed through the illicit affair between the heiress to the Treadway Munitions fortune,

Camilo Sheffield, and Link Williams, a black World War II veteran who works and lives at the Last Chance Saloon. By exploring the romantic relationship between Link and Camilo, Petry is able to show how a long historical legacy of interracial intimacy and sexual violence shaped post–World War II responses to interracial romances. Furthermore, Petry's careful exploration of the black and white characters in a New England town uses the narrative of interracial intimacy to focus on the postwar contradictions between the imperatives of domesticity and the enforced publicness of black life. The novel also exposes the United States's paradoxical commitment to containment and imperialist expansion. Finally, interracial intimacy allows Petry to reveal how the taboo against it signifies an attempt to regulate and contain black freedom through a spatial politics that offers safe havens to producers and exploits the private spaces of workers' lives.

The central character of *The Narrows* is Link Williams. Link is literally and figuratively the "link" between the historical legacy of slavery and the future of postwar race relations. Petry explodes the temporality of the postwar era through a detailed discussion of Link's troubled relationship to notions of racial belonging. Link attempts to imagine a form of belonging that, as Paul Gilroy suggests, extends beyond the boundaries of the skin.[21] Because he is an adopted orphan, his is an identity uprooted from the biological kinships of race. Petry never reveals information about Link's biological parents, leaving the reader to assume that many adults function as parental figures. Link's guardians are middle-class Abbie Crunch, F. K. Jackson, and Bill Hod, the owner of the Last Chance Saloon. Link's status as an orphan means that a community larger than his biological family raises him. Yet it also means that his connection to "The Race" is tenuous. Petry thus examines postwar racial politics through the trope of belonging and interracial intimacy.

Throughout the novel, Link struggles with static notions of racial belonging, often revealing the absurdities of racial community. The education of Link Williams was comprised of a pastiche of competing philosophies of racial uplift. For example, Link's adoptive mother, Abbie, teaches him that working-class blacks are dirty and lack a good work ethnic. Abbie is a social reformer who embraces the "bootstraps" theory of racial uplift. To her, poverty and dirt signify individual flaws. Bill Hod, on the other hand, teaches Link about black history and the importance of black militancy. While Abbie told Link that "black was ugly, evil, dirty, to be avoided," Bill taught Link that "black could be other things too."[22]

"The Race" becomes burdensome to Link because he cannot reconcile its singularity with the complexities of his upbringing. Link tells the men who work at the Last Chance that he cannot figure out how to serve "The Race."

> Link told about The Race, and how he was responsible for all other members of The Race even though he did not know them; and how he couldn't do it any more, it sort of paralyzed him because he never knew whether he was doing something because he, Link wanted to do it; or whether he did something because of the undesirable color of his skin, and that meant he had no control over what he did—it just happened.[23]

Petry explores the limits of Link's dislocation from "The Race" by seeing if Link can forge an identity that allows him to consider the white heiress Camilo Sheffield as part of his extended community. Petry suggests that though Link disavows simplistic notions of racial belonging, ultimately he cannot escape the historical legacy of slavery and racial violence. Though he tries to escape from the black voices that contributed to his upbringing, Link learns that when placed in the context of Saybrook, the Narrows loses its complexity, and blackness becomes most salient. Link and Camilo first meet when a man who is disfigured and has a disability chases Camilo toward Link. Camilo is lured to the Narrows by the local newspaper's coverage of the black neighborhood as a place of vice and forbidden pleasures. When Link rescues Camilo, he does not know that she is white. The dense fog that frequently blurs boundaries in the Narrows obscures her blond hair and white skin. Furthermore, Link does not know that Camilo is married and the heiress to the Treadway fortune. Camilo's whiteness allows her to "walk as though she owned the world" and to protect her private identity. For her, the Narrows is a safe haven, where she can realize forbidden desires. In the Narrows, Link says to himself, "All Cats Be Grey."[24]

It is through the interracial romance that Petry is able to explore the collision of temporalities and spaces in the postwar era. Camilo is the heiress to a munitions factory that made weapons for World War II, while Link was a soldier in the war. In this way, Petry shows the uneven relationship to the means of production. Camilo represents a capitalist owner, while Link is merely a worker. Yet this labor relationship is obscured through the romantic relationship, suggesting that romance, like labor under capitalism, fetishizes—both literally and figuratively—commodities such that the laborer who produced the commodity is abstracted and erased.[25] Similarly, Petry frequently locates interracial intimacy in a larger stream of imperialist expansion. Interracial sexuality, she suggests, is an integral way of understanding and naturalizing race war in the Pacific. The space of Link's first encounter with sex is at an interracial brothel called China's place, where the Asian madam caters to the Narrow's black residents. Further, as a teenager, Link worked as a personal assistant for Mr. Valkill, a wealthy and respected resident of Saybrook. Mr. Valkill asked Link to wear a woman's kimono because Mr. Valkill "liked little boys." In the Narrows, orientalist fantasies collide with antiblack racist stereotypes to create an erotically charged space.

Link cannot escape the legacy of slavery, despite his attempt to do so in his relationship with Camilo. He cannot avoid feeling that Camilo is buying and selling him whenever she uses her racial and class privileges to acquire food, hotels, service, and Link. When Link realizes that Camilo has paid the staff of a fancy restaurant to give them a private dining room and outstanding service, Link begins to recognize his role in a longer history of sexual violence.

> Two [tickets] on the aisle provided by the lady. Dinner afterwards. Private dining room reserved by the lady. Meal obviously paid for by the lady. Plantation buck. How many generations back? Oh, possibly four. Jump four generations and he shows up as a kept man. Objective about race? Hell, no. Nobody was. Not in the USA.[26]

Link's invocation of slavery suggests that his relationship with Camilo cannot engender Link's hope for the kind of identity outside of racial belonging. When Link realizes that Camilo has lied about her identity and is married, he terminates the relationship. Camilo ultimately responds by accusing Link of rape. When her claims are largely ignored—after all, a white woman would not be in the Narrows unless she knew somebody there—Camilo's mother hires two thugs to kidnap Link and force him to confess. Furthermore, the Sheffields convince the local newspaper to run stories detailing vice and corruption in the Narrows so that public opinion will turn against Link. Link recognizes that he will ultimately be convicted of raping Camilo because of the newspaper coverage of black violence and because of a historical legacy of slavery that shapes white people's understanding of black men. One-quarter of the explanation for his abduction by the Sheffield goons, Link reasons, was the media construction of black vice. "The other three quarters reaches back to that Dutch man of warre that landed in

Jamestown in 1610."²⁷ Camilo's husband ultimately kills Link when Link refuses to admit he raped Camilo.

Petry's narrative of the rise and fall of Link Williams poses the promise and ultimately demise of complex forms of racial belonging. Although an orphan and a child of many, Link's blackness connects him to a historical way of belonging that shapes his existence. For Petry, interracial intimacy functioned to obscure political and economic machinations that maintained certain forms of power by conferring privacy to some and enforcing publicity on others. Furthermore, interracial intimacy was a trope that allowed Petry to connect the centrality of slavery to modernity in general and to the World War II era specifically.

If Petry's middle-class upbringing in a white New England town revealed certain contradictions, it was Chester Himes's status as an industrial working-class man that shaped his exposure to postwar paradoxes. A study of Chester Himes reveals a number of contradictions. He was an industrial laborer and a fiction writer. His two autobiographies detail a life during which he was at times bisexual and defensively heterosexual. He disparaged organized political movements yet developed friendships with civil rights and cultural workers like Richard Wright, Ralph Ellison, James Baldwin, Walter White, Thurgood Marshall, E. Franklin Frazier, C.L.R. James, George Padmore, and a very young Malcolm X. He reached the peak of his popularity by writing about two Harlem police officers while living in exile in Europe.

The contradictory position of Himes in the context of organized movements and in the context of group identities underscores his cosmopolitanism. Himes, in perhaps even more successful ways than Richard Wright, embodied and exposed the contradictions inherent in modernist notions of kinship and identity. For Paul Gilroy, cosmopolitanism signifies an identity characterized by cultural and geographic fluidity that privileges hybrid "routes" over territorial roots.²⁸ For Richard Wright, whom Gilroy touts as the most significant postwar cosmopolitan writer, cosmopolitanism relied on a geopolitical and temporal analysis that pieced together disparate elements and sediments of black Atlantic cultures. Himes's cosmopolitanism, on the other hand, was less transnational and pan-Africanist then Wright's yet, like Wright's, was highly attuned to the geopolitics of space. For Himes, cosmopolitanism meant collapsing the discourses of public and private spheres that were integral to racial and sexual ideologies. His fiction therefore conflates the spaces of the home, the factory, and the public in order to show the performativity of identity in different spaces. Second, Himes's cosmopolitanism reoriented the temporality of the postwar era away from cultural pluralism and toward the legacy of miscegenation. The discourse of miscegenation allowed Himes to insert the legacy of racial and sexual violence into the 1940s' rhetoric of American triumphalism and culturalist understandings of race. Most important, however, the metaphor of miscegenation allowed Himes to understand how class and property relations were obscured through the conventions of heterosexual and interracial desire. Taken together, these spatial and temporal strategies enabled Himes to trouble the categories of racial belonging that were especially prominent during the era of cultural pluralism and heterosexual liberalism.

Toward the end of his life, Chester Himes attempted to shape the ways that scholars would remember his fiction when he wrote, "You will conclude if you read [my fiction] that BLACK PROTEST and BLACK HETERO-SEXUALITY are my two chief obsessions."[29] Himes's fiction indeed bridged protest fiction, black political struggle after World War II, and concerns over sexuality. But while Himes's reminiscence about his literature seems unambiguous, his life and fiction reveal a more complex story about the constraints placed on black protest literature in the 1940s and 1950s and the very meaning of sexuality to the civil rights movement. Writing during a period of shifting understandings of both race and sexuality, Himes targeted his protest at postwar ideas of race and sex as they found representation in white and black communities and in doing so challenged the limits of black protest fiction.

Himes's novels were intensely personal and represented his own experiences growing up during the Depression and World War II. Moreover, despite his proclamation that black heterosexuality was the focus of his fiction, Himes's pre–World War II writing expressed his own ambivalent sexuality in a society in which ideas of normative and obscene behavior were undergoing dramatic change. Born in 1909 in Jefferson City, Missouri, Himes spent the first two decades of his life moving across the country as his father, a mechanical professor at black colleges, changed jobs frequently. At a time when black families migrated North, the Himeses migrated vertically and horizontally throughout the entire country in search of steady employment. Himes's mother was a piano teacher who, according to Himes, had light skin. In his autobiographical novel, *The Third Generation*, Himes remembers his mother as someone who constantly considered differences between light-complexioned and dark-complexioned blacks. In the novel, the character based on his mother has a strong hatred of her husband because he is darker skinned. This skin consciousness would later shape Himes's understanding of the color line in American society and the color line *within* the color line. In this way, Himes explored how the color-conscious society and culture of postwar America shaped even the interior beliefs within black families about black value.

Himes's cosmopolitanism emerged through his family's experience with migrant labor and through his personal ambivalence over his sexuality. The family spent time in Cleveland, then in Cheraw, Mississippi, then in Augusta, Georgia, then in St. Louis, then in Pine Bluff, Arkansas, and then back to Cleveland. All of this migratory experience had an impact on Himes's sense of geographical placelessness. Ultimately, Himes attended high school in Cleveland and enrolled in Ohio State University. Himes was educated as a young child by his mother. He and his brother, Joseph, who would become a famous sociologist at Berkeley, excelled in high school. Although Chester was an excellent student, he was nonetheless a rebel. While in Cleveland, he frequented pool halls and participated in illegal activities, including car theft and guns sales. In 1928 Himes was caught selling stolen guns to black steelworkers in Youngstown and Warren, Ohio. Shortly after this incident, Himes was convicted of armed jewelry theft in a wealthy Cleveland suburb. He was sentenced to twenty to twenty-five years in prison and served eight years in the Ohio State Penitentiary.

During his time in prison, Himes wrote his first novel, *Yesterday Will Make You Cry* (1988), which portrayed the bleakness of prison life, including a prison fire that killed several inmates. Significantly, it also portrayed the homosexual relationship between two white inmates (all of the main characters in this novel are white). Himes's description of the homosexual relationship between Jimmy and Rico in *Yesterday* was based on Himes's intimate relationship with a black inmate from Georgia Himes called Prince Rico. According to Himes's biographers Ed Margolies and Michael Fabre, Rico and Himes "read aloud to one another, wrote a play together, [and] worked on an opera together."[30] Moreover, in his autobiography Himes called his relationship with Rico the most fulfilling he had during his life.[31] Himes and Rico ended their intimate relationship when Himes left prison, although they visited each other a number of times in San Francisco during World War II. Yet even after the completion of *Yesterday* and while still in

prison, Himes wrote a story targeted for *Esquire* about a homosexual prison
relationship that prison censors would not allow him to submit.

Upon leaving prison, and now married to a black woman named Jean
Lucinda Johnson, Himes continued to write stories about homosexual relationships in prison, including a homoerotic play called *Idle Hours* dealing
with two convicts. Critics have assumed that Himes's bisexuality was just
a response to the homosocial world of prison. Margolies and Fabre have
argued that the relationship with Rico was a response to the "upside down
world of prison." Yet such an analysis assumes heteronormativity during a
time when scholars such as George Chauncey, John Howard, and Siobahn
Somerville tell us that sexual identities were undergoing significant transformation. Himes's prison fiction emerged during a historical period when
gender was not as tightly connected to sexual practice as it would become
after the war.[32] Himes's manuscript underwent multiple changes until it was
published twenty years later as *Cast the First Stone* (1953), a diluted version
of *Yesterday* in which the homosexual relationship was transformed into a
homosocial friendship.

Himes's family and critics disliked the novel, especially the (now diluted)
homosexual plot. Himes conveyed his dismay over its critical reception to
his friend and financial backer Carl Van Vechten when he wrote that for *Cast
the First Stone*, "the homo-sexual story seems to have killed it."[33] In a letter
that Himes wrote to his friend Richard Wright shortly before migrating per-
manently to Europe in 1953, Himes suggested that critics could not imagine
a hybrid and complex black masculinity. Such critics viewed *Cast the First
Stone*—even though it was considerably diluted from the original version—
as a perverse work from a black male writer.

> I suppose you received the copy of CAST THE FIRST STONE. I must say it has been
> very thoroughly stoned in the press here. It could be that it is a very vulgar, sordid,
> and incompetent book, as most of the critics contend; but if I take their word for it I
> just may as well give up writing, because I'm doing just about the best I can do with
> these themes I choose. And the themes are not always a matter of choice; I am stuck
> with having to write about what I know about, and prison happens to be (along
> with being a Negro) one of the subjects on which I am an authority.[34]

If Himes's first novel was radically transformed because of the ways it
undermined contemporary understandings of protest fiction and black

masculinity, the rest of Himes's postwar American novels were similarly challenged for the ways they fell outside of normative understandings of belonging and protest. Himes responded to the narrow expectations for black protest fiction by challenging such expectations head-on and showing their perversity. Among these expectations were black fiction's presumed compulsory heterosexuality and authentic racial belonging.

While working in numerous industrial factories during the war, Himes attempted to join in African American organizations working for civil rights. Yet he disdained these organizations' invocations of racial purity and authentic black experience. The NAACP and the Urban League, Himes argued, could only advocate one notion of black identity and thus ignored the complexities of black life. But more important, Himes thought that middle-class black intellectuals were incapable of understanding the complex lives of people who lived outside and between the binaries that shaped race and sex. Significantly, Himes chose to chastise these groups for the importance they placed on interracial social and romantic relationships. In 1944, for example, he went to a party in New York attended by Luther Granger, Ralph Bunche, Walter White, Adam Clayton Powell, and E. Franklin Frazier. Despite the political potential of such a meeting, Himes dismissed it and parties like it as "primarily springboards to interracial sexual liaisons."[35] In making this critique, Himes located his disdain of black politics in the history of miscegenation. In doing so, he was able to criticize the presumed racial purity of black political affiliations. After all, if such affiliations were merely "springboards to interracial liaisons," then "The Race" was not so pure after all. Moreover, by reading black civil rights organizations through the discourse of interracial intimacy, Himes also critiqued the heteronormative discourse of civil rights activism that confined normative black masculinity to heterosexuality.

Himes began to understand the racialized nature of working-class life in the United States just as he became a writer. He met Langston Hughes in Cleveland in the late 1930s, and the two became friends. Despite the growing popularity of Himes's writing, he nonetheless continued to have to find work in industries other than writing. In 1937 he worked as a ditch digger. He also worked as a historian for the Works Progress Administration (WPA) in Cleveland. In 1941 Himes moved to Los Angeles, where he encountered new forms of racism in wartime plants and a level of racism that was previously unknown to him. Southern migrant whites interacted with Mexican

Americans, Filipinos, and African Americans in manufacturing plants. To Himes, the boundaries between whites and everyone else were more powerful in Los Angeles than anywhere. Because of this, Himes believed that "Los Angeles hurt me racially as much as any city I have ever known."[36]

In his first postwar novel, *If He Hollers Let Him Go* (1945), Himes illuminates the highly racial and sexual context of World War II manufacturing plants. Himes told his publisher that *Hollers* was originally conceived as a "mystery in which white people are being killed seemingly at random everywhere in LA."[37] However, rather than choosing this narrative, Himes wrote a story about a black worker, Bob Jones, who had gained some level of success by becoming the leader of a team of black workers at the Atlas shipyard. *Hollers* presents wartime racism as emerging on a day-to-day basis not only within the nexus of work relations but also through the nexus of heterosexual and interracial relationships. In this way, *Hollers* conflates the presumed private sphere of sexuality with the public spaces of wartime Los Angeles. Such a conflation exposed how, for black workers, privacy was an elusive sphere because of the ways racism shaped all spaces. Furthermore, *Hollers* is concerned with the performative nature of identity for whites and blacks. Racial and sexual identification, in *Hollers*, fixes identity such that it ceases to be an act of self-making but instead is proscribed and limiting.

The central drama of *Hollers* occurs when Madge, a white female subordinate, undermines Bob's status as leader at the shipyard by refusing to work with "a Nigger." Bob responds to Madge with a fury, calling her a "cracker bitch," and is demoted for his indiscretion. This drama presents the workplace as a queer space where traditional gender roles, labor hierarchies, and spatial spheres are inverted. Madge's racist response gives her power over a male; it represents insubordination in terms of labor hierarchies; and it transports the public ideology of racism into the privacy of the factory. Furthermore, Madge's refusal to work with Bob invokes the legacy of miscegenation in ways that punctures the optimism of wartime manufacturing with the historical legacies of racial and sexual violence.

Madge's relationship with Bob underscores the performative nature of racial and sexual identities, as each character cannot help but to act in the most stereotyped way. Madge performs her race and gender whenever she is in the presence of black male workers. In exposing this racial play, Himes destabilizes the link between race and biology by showing that race can be put on and taken off. He also reveals the lie of miscegenation: the presumption that black men were the sexual aggressors in all interracial sexual relationships. As Bob approaches Madge at the opening of the novel, he notices that Madge's look changes from passiveness to active fright. She pretended to be "a naked virgin and I was King Kong. . . . I was used to white women doing all sorts of things to tease or annoy the coloured men so I hadn't given it a second thought before."[38]

Himes's analysis of the performative nature of racial and sexual identities considered how different spaces and contexts shaped such performances. At one point Bob offers a ride to two white servicemen on leave. In the car, Bob and the servicemen enjoy pleasant conversation. At this point Bob "began wondering when white people started getting white—or rather, when they started losing it. And how it was you could take two white guys from the same place—one would carry his whiteness like a loaded stick, ready to bop everybody else in the head with it; and the other would just simply be white as if he didn't have anything to do with it and let it go at that."[39] Significantly, the servicemen's whiteness turned into a stick as soon as the three turned their conversation to a black woman. When the servicemen see the black woman on the sidewalk, the conversation stopped, and the tensions of race emerged. Here Himes again invokes the legacy of miscegenation, in this case by identifying the real and yet hidden legacy of white male sexual violence toward black women.

The miscegenation theme continues throughout the novel as a way for Himes to trouble notions of public and private and to situate the postwar world of work in the time and space of interracial sexual violence. After his on-the-job encounter with Madge, Bob goes to a black-owned bar in which every male patron's attention is on a single white woman who is probably underage. Bob watches in anger the ways that the white woman performs her whiteness by both transgressing and reaffirming racial boundaries. "She got that frisky white woman feeling of being wanted by every Negro man in the joint." Such a paradox leads Bob to consider the performative nature of racial belonging:

> *All she's got to do now, I thought, is start performing. She could get everybody in the joint into trouble, even me just sitting there buying a drink. She was probably under-age anyway; and if she was she could get the hotel closed, the liquor license*

revoked, probably get the manager in jail. She could take those two black chums flirting with her outside and get them thirty years apiece in San Quentin; in Alabama she could get them hung. A little tramp—but she was white.[40]

Here whiteness functions as a performance that, once produced, triggers larger state apparatuses of control. Bob is thus fearful not simply of white people but of the ways they can invoke their whiteness to enact racial violence. Considering Madge, Bob thinks,

It wasn't that Madge was white; it was the way she used it. She had a sign in front of her as big as CIVIC CENTER—keep away, Niggers, I'm White! And without having to say one word she could keep all the white men in the world feeling they had to protect her from black rapists. That made her doubly dangerous because she thought about Negro men . . . she wanted them to run after her. She expected it, demanded it as her due. I could imagine her teasing them with her body, showing her bare thighs and breasts. Then having them lynched for looking.[41]

Hollers's conclusion portrays a confused Bob, resolved to return to his African American girlfriend, Alice, and ready to apologize to Madge for calling her a "cracker bitch." When he goes to the shipyard to restore his life, he accidentally enters a room in the ship in which Madge is sleeping. Madge awakens to find Bob, and she invites him to join her in bed. Bob refuses and begins to flee the room, but Madge blocks the exit and locks the door. As Bob tries to negotiate his escape, he hears workers outside of the door trying to enter. Realizing that Bob is not going to accept her offer, Madge begins to scream rape. When workers finally enter the room, they apprehend and beat Bob. The novel ends with Bob being convicted of rape. But realizing that the rape accusation is false, the judge sentences Bob to military service.

In the span of a brief conclusion, the terror of racial and sexual violence collapses the private space of the bedroom, the workplace, and the transnational space of the military. Such a convergence allows Himes to trouble the very presumption that sexuality exists in the presumed private sphere of the home. Moreover, Himes connects the problem of racism on the job with much larger issues of colonialism abroad (earlier in the novel, Bob comments on the racist and arbitrary policy of Japanese internment). The combination of war and slavery, of democracy and miscegenation, asked readers to abandon simple "blueprints of black writing," to paraphrase Wright, and to situate racial terror at the center of modernity.

Furthermore, while the miscegenation critique allowed Himes to challenge race and sex purity, it also allowed him to imagine a politics of hybridity that resulted from such interracial intimacy. Such hybridity reoriented the time and space of the nation in the global migrations of laborers throughout the world. In Himes's next novel, *Lonely Crusade* (1947), for example, the black protagonist, union organizer Lee Gordon, describes wartime Los Angeles as a cosmopolitan space where the legacies of racialized labor migration converge to produce a space in which no singular notion of belonging is dominant.

> *Southern dialect mingled with the melodious lilt of Spanish. Here and there came a loud Negro laugh. Pushing and running. Laughing and cursing. Giving and taking. The white and the Black and the in-between. War workers homeward bound. Full of their self importance. Fighting on the their front. Owning the street and the air above the street and recognizing no authority but their own patriotism. Like no other workers on earth.*[42]

Despite Lee's hope that Los Angeles's transnational space can register new affiliations and solidarities that are not structured around singular and static notions of identity, he ultimately finds that such a possibility is foreclosed by the ways that workers embrace notions of solidarity rooted in race and sexuality.

Lonely Crusade describes Lee Gordon's attempt to organize workers at the Comstock Aircraft Corporation in Los Angeles during World War II. Lee is the first black union organizer at the factory, and the Communist leaders of the local admit that they need him to organize the black workforce. In this way, Lee is expected to represent his race by becoming a good role model for unionized black workers. Yet during Lee's attempt to organize black workers, he learns that the black working class is not a singular entity. Some are Communists, while others are vehemently anti-Communist. Thus Himes poses Lee's difficulty in forming the union in terms of the impossibility of constructing a singular notion of the black working class.

Furthermore, just as the union oversimplifies its notion of the "black community," it similarly oversimplifies its notion of the working class. Lee quickly realizes that the problem with organizing black workers is that race divides the working class, as union meetings are segregated and that, but for himself, there are no black workers in leadership positions in the union. As Lee talks to black aircraft workers, he realizes that fears of racial violence from white workers punctuate every discussion about the union. At a party organized by Communist union activists, Lee interrupts one person's call to raise funds for anticolonial struggles around the world by asking why a collection has not been taken up among Communists to solve "the Negro question." He is told, "The Negro problem is indivisible from the problem of the masses. You have no special problem."[43] Although this is a vast over-simplification and even a distortion of Communist views on "the Negro question," Himes uses it to show how Lee increasingly learns that appeals to class solidarity erase race in ways similar to how appeals to racial solidarity erase class. Furthermore, Lee recognizes that the problem with the union is that it confines its activism to a limited understanding of work, without viewing antiracism as a key strategy. Thus Lee ultimately fails to organize black workers and forms the conclusion that "the union can't give the Negro worker equality . . . you can not have equality in the plant and inequality on the street."[44]

Just as in *Hollers*, racial terror and disillusionment in *Lonely Crusade* ultimately emerge out of interracial heterosexual relationships. Black Communists are marked as much by their complicity with white bosses as by their marriages to "blond bombshells." And white women are complicit in the gender and race system that creates tensions at work. Jackie Forks is a white woman who is known for recruiting black workers to the Communist Party through her interracial romances, and Lee Gordon becomes her project. Lee falls in love with Jackie, leaving his black wife, only to eventually learn that racial hierarchies override gender hierarchies; Jackie ultimately betrays Lee by assisting the police in locating him for a crime he has not committed.

As Lee increasingly believes that the union cannot offer black workers hope and as he consequently feels less able to support his wife, Jackie temporarily becomes a redemptive entity in his life. Lee is attracted to Jackie because with her, he feels empowered, and he believes this empowerment comes from interracial sex. Jackie "could be a woman with breasts and limbs and flesh, and not always a condescending counselor like his wife. And to him, a Negro, she could be more than just a woman—a white woman enshrined in the fatal allure of the forbidden, and veiled in the mystery surrounding white women as seen by some young Negro men." After kissing Jackie, Lee "experienced a sense of having gained something."[45] Jackie thus offers something to Lee that he believes his black wife cannot. Jackie can give Lee his masculinity—though it is only illusory—because through interracial sex, Lee can perform a normative gender role rooted in ideas about the white female body. As Himes writes:

> *She could give him this illusion of manhood even while denying that he possesses it, for to her he was the recipient of her grace. . . . So with Jackie he had these moments that rightfully belonged to Ruth [his wife]. It could have been wonderful with Ruth, for she had all that Jackie feigned. But he could never be for her what Jackie could make of him for her own design.*[46]

But Himes shows that this manhood is only transient, for Jackie can easily deny Lee's manhood, even as she can create it. Although Lee's desire for a white woman seemingly affirms his masculinity, it must eventually lead to his subordination; under the (il)logic of racialized heterosexuality, black men ought to desire white women, but white women ought to maintain the color line.

Just as Lee makes choices that ultimately undermine his union drive, the black Communists in *Lonely Crusade* are marked by their interracial sexual liaisons and are unable to effect change because of them. Among the most notorious of black Communists is Luther McGregor, who wants to help Lee organize black workers with the ultimate goal of recruiting Lee to communism. Lee is immediately skeptical about Luther because he believes that Luther's "buxom blond" wife signals a flaw in Luther's commitment to black politics. Himes—as narrator—writes that Luther's hatred of white men led a psychologist to suggest that Luther ought to possess a white woman to "overcome the fixation of racial inferiority."[47] Himes delves deeper into Luther's interracial marriage,

> *How deep within this homicidal mania, and seemingly unrelated, was a desire to possess a delicate, fragile, sensitive, highly cultured blond white woman, bred centuries of aristocracy—not rape her, possess her. Possess her body and soul; her breasts to feel the emotion of his hands; her mouth to seek the communion of his lips; her whiteness to blend with his blackness in a symphony of sex; rejecting all that had come before and would come after.*[48]

Luther's desire for the white female body, Himes suggests, is part of a larger "homicidal mania." In order to reject racial hierarchies "that had come before and would come after," Luther covets interracial heterosexuality.

But this choice distances Communists from the workers. Interracial sex thus places the black bourgeoisie and black Communists—from the perspective of black workers—in the same position. Himes suggests that black Communists and intellectuals in the civil rights movement had been made ineffective by their acceptance of white standards of beauty and desire.

Chester Himes's own relationships with black women were always contentious. Although we know very little about Himes's first wife, Jean Lucinda Johnson, in letters to Van Vechten Himes wrote that she had left him in part because she could not accept his depictions of black women and his protagonists' desires for white women. "As a matter of fact, even the writing of *Lonely Crusade* caused great emotional upheavals in my life as my wife protested bitterly the treatment of the Negro wife." After Himes and Johnson separated, Himes wrote to Van Vechten that "Jean couldn't bear the things I wrote nor the processes of my thoughts which caused me to write them and I couldn't change."[49]

Himes's complex critique of postwar society led to his alienation from many black civil rights activities. In a 1952 letter to Richard Wright, Himes suggested that the postwar era was an especially bleak moment for writing about issues of racism. "The fact is the truth now is as bitter as it has ever been—only no one wants to discuss it—in fact we over here are practically being dared to discuss it."[50] If *Yesterday Will Make You Cry* was "killed" because of the homosexual plot, his postwar fiction would face a somewhat similar fate because it exploited contradictions in postwar understandings of sexuality and race and angered black civil rights activists. By 1953, Himes was distraught that he had not reached the level of acclaim he hoped for. A year before his permanent move to Europe, he wrote to Van Vechten:

As I look back now I find that much of my retardation as a writer has been due to a subconscious (and conscious and deliberate) desire to escape my past. . . . It brought a lot of confusion to my own mind added to which was a great deal of pressure of a thousand kinds being exerted by friends and relatives and loved ones who were half ashamed of what I wrote, forgetting that it was what I wrote that made me what I was.[51]

Himes described his alienation from black politics and from the world of publishing in a lecture he gave at the University of Chicago in 1948 called "Dilemma of the Negro Novelist in the U.S.A." Himes argued that publishers could not understand black rage over racism and critiques of white privilege as anything but psychosis on the part of a defeated group. Publishers, he argued, sought only to publish black writers who wrote protest fiction that did not challenge the privileges of whiteness. Publishers assumed that

> *the honest Negro writer is psychotic, that his evaluations are based on personal experiences which are in no way typical of his race. This publisher does not realize that his own reasoning is self-contradictory; that any American Negro's racial experience, be they psychotic or not, are typical of all Negroes' racial experiences for the simple reason that the source is not the Negro but oppression.*[52]

Himes's disdain for critics was no doubt driven by some especially harsh reviews. *Hollers* was called "unpleasant" by an anonymous *Kirkus Reviews* author, who claimed that Himes was a "poor man's Richard Wright."[53] The *St. Louis Dispatch* called *Hollers* "a Savage Novel."[54] Of his second novel, critics were far more scathing. James Baldwin wrote about *Lonely Crusade* that "much of the rage [exhibited in *Hollers*] is gone and with it the impact, and the book is written in what is probably the most uninteresting and awkward prose I have read in recent years."[55] An anonymous *Ebony* reviewer wrote that it was "a virulent, malicious book full of rancor and venom . . . an invidious, shocking, incendiary work."[56] The Communist publication the *New Masses* wrote the most scathing review of Himes's *Lonely Crusade*. The reviewer, Lloyd Brown, wrote,

> *I cannot recall ever having read a worse book on the Negro theme. . . . The self hate and shameless abasement of Chester Himes, who panders to every depraved element of white chauvinism, is based upon his complete acceptance of white ruling-class ideas. . . . Let Chester Himes go his miserable way, but let him go alone on his lonely crusade, accompanied only by the ghost of Uncle Tom and the nameless wretched slave who betrayed Nat Turner and his people.*[57]

Himes's novels suggested that some civil rights leaders had internalized white standards of behavior and desire. This, in addition to his critique of the black bourgeoisie, led Himes to believe that his genre of protest fiction would be vigorously attacked by black critics.[58]

> *If this novelist, because he has prepared an honest and revealing work on Negro life anticipates the support and encouragement of middle-class Negro people, he is*

doomed to disappointment. He must be prepared for the hatred and antagonism of many of his own people, for attacks from his leaders, the clergy, and the press; he must be ready to have his name reviled at every level, intellectual or otherwise.

Himes concluded, "Negroes will themselves oppress other Negroes, given the opportunity, in as vile a manner as anyone else."[59]

In the end, Himes's cosmopolitanism failed to realize the humanity of all people because of the fixity of gender within his analysis. He was unable to fully consider the plight of black women, and his misogyny cannot be written off, as some of his biographers do, as confusion over his relationship with his mother. Yet I suggest that Himes, while a complex and contradictory figure, represents one among many black writers of the 1940s who attempted to engage in class politics by focusing on the categories of race and sex and by engaging in a politics of remembering racial and sexual violence. Himes hoped, perhaps, that illuminating how laboring bodies were assigned racial and gendered meanings would reveal each worker's relationship to the modes of production. While such a strategy ultimately fell short, it nevertheless ought to help us complicate our notions of group identities and belonging.

For William Gardner Smith, Anne Petry, and Chester Himes, the postwar era was a period of painful adjustments. Smith had to contend with the possibilities and failures that came about through his participating in the U.S. military. Petry witnessed a flourishing civil rights movement that seemed to exclude black women from important aspects of its racial uplift politics. Himes faced a society unwilling to consider his analysis of black sexuality and unforgiving of his anger. For these writers, confronting the postwar politics of interracial intimacy by casting it in a larger historical and spatial realm allowed them to imagine alternative visions of racial uplift and belonging. It is in these writers' larger conceptions of humanity and belonging that we might find a broader and more inclusive politics of intimacy than the kind waged in the immediate post–World War II era.

Conclusion

Strom Thurmond's Legacy

IN 1948 THE FIERY DIXIECRAT presidential candidate Strom Thurmond gave a public address in which he said, "All the bayonets of the Army cannot force the Negro into our homes."[1] Thurmond's segregationist platform linked the issue of desegregation to the privacy of the home and hinted that desegregation would necessarily lead to interracial households. The audience that day witnessed a public figure whose star as a defender of the southern way of life was on the rise; what they did not know was that at age twenty-two, Thurmond had engaged in an illicit encounter with Carrie Butler, a fifteen-year-old African American who worked as a domestic in his house. We do not and cannot know the nature of this relationship, though we do know that today the law defines such sexual relationships as statutory rape. What may be most striking is that during his years as a defender of the southern way and an opponent of race mixing, Thurmond was able to hide the fact of his mixed-race daughter. This example not only illustrates the ironies of segregationists' arguments in the 1940s but also shows how the "right to privacy" accorded white men like Thurmond enabled him to shape his image in public. In this way, Thurmond could enter the public sphere because he was accorded the privilege of keeping his intimate affairs private.

What was Carrie Butler's relationship to privacy and the public sphere? For Butler, privacy was not a right afforded to her but instead functioned to enforce her silence. Her reproductive and productive labor were rendered invisible by the privileged status of her white employer's right to privacy. The rights to privacy accorded whiteness enabled white southerners to ignore multiple forms of labor in their own households. It also allowed them to violate black women's bodies without recognizing the unthinkable consequences on black women in the public sphere. We should therefore examine how the violation of black women's rights to privacy functions to enable the kinds of freedom regularly given white men.

The posthumous revelation of the existence of Thurmond's daughter, Essie Mae Washington-Williams, contributes to this book's central argument: at the center of the politics of interracial intimacy were contested understandings of public and private spheres. *Romance and Rights* began with the example of Paul Robeson's performance in the first interracial production of *Othello* in the United States. The political uses of the play, I argued, illustrate how interracial intimacy could serve as a site of converging interests. Foreign policy makers, civil rights leaders, and mainstream Americans all used interracial intimacy as a means to support larger political issues. Interracial intimacy could signify racial toleration and civil rights progress; it could signify the limits of civil rights reforms; and it could signify, for segregationists, a serious threat to the political future of the United States.

Romance and Rights has attempted to understand the various debates about interracial intimacy in terms of a more fundamental dispute over Americans' notions of public and private spheres and the appropriate "place" of intimate matters. The ideological project of containment after World War II sought to place all sexual matters within the private sphere. This placement, as women's historians have argued, sought to limit women's opportunities in the public sphere by attempting to contain normative femininity in the domestic sphere. Further, the postwar emphasis on the home as the only appropriate space of female sexuality reasserted patriarchal relations in the wake of women's wartime participation in the industrial workforce.[2]

Yet interracial intimacy involves more than sexual matters; it simultaneously engages American racial attitudes and policies. The civil rights movement thrust race relations into the public sphere as activists and policy makers advocated race reforms at the level of public policy. In this way, as civil rights leaders sought to earn a voice within the public sphere, the "private" issue of intimacy became public. Interracial intimacy became a civil rights issue because of the ways that interracial romance and sexuality were at the core of race relations in America and because World War II activism and military service made new forms of intimate relations possible.

The debate I have identified in this book focused on attempts to contain interracial intimacy to the private sphere and on efforts to make public and to celebrate interracial intimacy as a civil rights victory. Postwar anti-miscegenation court cases and mainstream American culture sought to undermine the political implications of interracial intimacy by regarding it as a state issue, and not a federal one, or by representing interracial intimacy as a domestic-sphere, and therefore apolitical, issue. Black magazine publishers such as John Johnson, on the other hand, realized the central role of interracial intimacy to the civil rights struggle. Johnson's magazines, therefore, publicized certain cases of interracial intimacy in order to make public that which postwar society attempted to contain. Doing so helped undermine racist politics in the United States, but it also contributed to an important discourse about black value. Interracial intimacy seemed to confer desirability on certain black bodies that had historically been constructed as dangerous and undesirable.

Yet the politics of interracial intimacy, as it was deployed within the black public sphere, was a reactive politics located squarely within the logic of postwar race formations. While interracial intimacy could engender a new discourse of black male value and desirability, it did so by advancing simplistic definitions of black racial belonging. Only certain types of blackness could profit from the politics of interracial intimacy. In the final chapter, I identified a critique of the politics of interracial intimacy that focused on the historical legacies of interracial sexuality and racism. William Gardner Smith, Ann Petry, and Chester Himes sought to complicate notions of racial belonging and to place the politics of interracial intimacy in a frame that extended before the postwar era. Doing so allowed them to see the limitations of the postwar politics of racial belonging and to imagine alternative ways of racial kinship and being.

This study concludes in 1954 not because the politics of interracial intimacy waned but because the nature of the civil rights struggle changed and the forces of political and ideological containment began to win out. This was the year of the Supreme Court's landmark *Brown* decision. In the wake of this ruling, the NAACP began to advance its legal fight against segregation. Because of this, the politics of interracial intimacy took a backseat to the more successful legal struggle for desegregation. Furthermore, the Supreme Court was unwilling to consider the constitutionality of state antimiscegenation laws, fearing that such a case would be politically explosive.[3]

By 1954, the House Un-American Activities Committee's anti-Communist crusade was growing in focus and fierceness. This was the year when the comic book industry succumbed to congressional committees like Senator Kefauver's, and the range of politically oriented films was severely limited. The creation of comic codes limited the range of artistic and narrative choices available to comic book writers and artists. Furthermore, the Communist Control Act of 1954 codified rules for weeding out Communists from American culture. The Popular Front, by the mid-1950s, had been contained, and it was politically and personally dangerous to challenge American cultural norms in the postwar era. In 1954 Chester Himes lost hope that the United States could radically change its racial politics; this was the year that he became an expatriate living in France.[4]

The politics of interracial intimacy endured but in less visible ways. It emerged in debates about rock and roll music and in the underground subcultures of pin-up magazines and pornography.[5] In the late 1950s the politics of interracial intimacy emerged in debates about television. In 1956, for example, the *Nat "King" Cole Show* aired on NBC without national advertising. Cole was the first black performer to host his own network variety show. Despite the show's promise, however, it never gained the advertising sponsorship necessary to continue on television. In part, advertisers feared southern protesters, who disliked white female participation in the show's audience. As Cole would tell *Ebony*,

> *For 13 months I was the Jackie Robinson of television. I was the pioneer, the test case, the Negro first. . . . On my show rode the hopes and fears and dreams of millions of people. . . . Once a week for 64 consecutive weeks I went to bat for these people. I sacrificed and drove myself. I plowed part of my salary back into the show. I turned down $500,000 in dates in order to be on the scene. I did everything I could to make the show a success. And what happened? After a trailblazing year that shattered all the old bugaboos about Negroes on TV, I found myself standing there with the bat on my shoulder. The men who dictate what Americans see and hear didn't want to play ball.*[6]

For black male artists and entertainers, the politics of interracial intimacy played a powerful role in determining their duration on stage.

In the mid-1960s the sexual revolution, coupled with the civil rights and black nationalist movements, brought the politics of interracial intimacy into public view yet again. Black nationalist leaders like Stokley Carmichael and Eldridge Cleaver made interracial sexuality central to their understanding of rights. As black nationalists linked the politics of interracial intimacy to their understandings of racial uplift, the same complexities and limits that shaped this discourse in the 1940s and 1950s emerged. As Michelle Wallace argues in *Black Macho and the Myth the Superwoman*, black nationalists' understandings of racial uplift was overly invested in notions of black men's progress, much to the detriment of black women. Wallace argues that the politics of black freedom in the 1960s and 1970s emphasized the desirability of black men while often ignoring how black women could fit into the politics of black beauty and value.

Although legal prohibitions on interracial marriages have not existed since the late 1960s, rates of interracial marriage remain relatively low, especially between blacks and whites. The color line separating black and white people remains a powerful predictor of marriage partners. In 2000 the Census Bureau reported that 2 percent of married couples were interracial. Of these couples, 363,000 were black/white couples. This signifies a small increase in the total number of married families but is significant nevertheless.[7] The most important question remains how to understand rates of black/white marriage. As I have worked on this project, numerous white and black liberals have commented that once we all intermarry, there will be no racial problems. What assumptions shape the arguments of those who advocate intermarriage as racial uplift?

The politics of interracial intimacy remains a central issue within black public-sphere politics. Orlando Patterson's *The Ordeal of Integration* advocates intermarriage as the final frontier of black civil rights politics. For Patterson,

> *Afro-American men and women . . . have every reason to outmarry: it will enrich the repertoire of childrearing practices among them; it will vastly expand their weak social ties and other social capital; it will help to solve the internal crisis of gender and marital relations among them; and it will complete the process of total integration as they become to other Americans not only full members of the political and moral community, but also people whom "we" marry. When that happens, the goal of integration will have been fully achieved.[8]*

Patterson's view on interracial intimacy advocates racial intermarriage as a strategy of assimilation. For him, the goals of integration are to realize a "color-blind" society in which race is not a salient category of identity.

Randall Kennedy similarly notes that interracial marriages signal racial progress for African Americans. "In my view, black-white intermarriage is not simply something that should be tolerated—it is a mode of partnership that should be applauded and encouraged . . . because it signals that newcomers or

outsiders are gaining acceptance in the eyes of those in the dominant population and are perceived by them as persons of value on whom it is worth risk-
ing one's future."[9]

Insofar as interracial marriages indicate a level of equality among black
and white people, Kennedy supports them as racial progress. While one
should celebrate any time two people fall in love, we should further interro-
gate Kennedy's and Patterson's arguments about the relationship of intermarriage to racial uplift. Given the absence of antimiscegenation laws since
the late 1960s, interracial marriages are today celebrated as indices of cultural
acceptance; Kennedy suggests that it signifies that blacks are seen as "persons
of value." In this sense, with the public act of interracial marriage no longer
legally prohibited, the new terrain is in the cultural debate over who is most
desirable. Yet these contemporary debates risk getting mired in the kind of
double standards that characterized black celebrations of GI intermarriages
after World War II. How does the contemporary hypervisibility of the black
male body in athletics and in popular culture shape cultural definitions of
who is most desirable? In an age where Strom Thurmond's legacy reminds us
of the regular interracial abuse of black women at the hands of white men,
in what ways do black women figure into Patterson's and Kennedy's formulations? Do gay and lesbian interracial couples who legally cannot get married also signify racial uplift?

Perhaps what is most striking about Kennedy's and Patterson's advocacy
of intermarriage is their lack of recognition of the contested nature of marriage within the public sphere today. Marriage continues to be a site of
contested notions of rights, as gay and lesbian people attempt to gain the
privileges of the institution. My focus on the spatial dimensions of racial and
sexual politics will assist those who attempt to understand the relationship
between the regulation of interracial intimacy and the regulation of same-sex
sexuality. These issues not only share a similar legal history, they are fundamentally related because of the ways they are determined by dominant formations of public and private spheres. The increasing access of interracial
heterosexuals to the public sphere in 1967 intersected with the diminishing
rights to privacy extended to same-sex couples. Similarly, the recent extension of a right to privacy for same-sex couples in the *Lawrence v. Texas* (2003)
decision was extended during an era when racial minorities are facing a
narrowing public sphere due to the attack on affirmative action. Gains in
one sphere of racial and sexual politics often signal retreats in other arenas.

One need not assume that race and sexuality are identical social identities to recognize how they are linked in the American juridical imagination.

First, we must consider how antimiscegenation laws differ from antigay marriage laws, for in claiming they are similar, I do not want to ignore how marriage has historically granted privileges only to heterosexuals. As we have already seen, antimiscegenation laws were passed to preserve the presumed integrity and purity of the white race. As protectors of white male dominance over women and people of color, antimiscegenation laws held together a vast system of privileges. When antimiscegenation laws were challenged, this was seen to interfere with the state's right to regulate marriage. Importantly, the attack on antimiscegenation laws did not challenge the presumed sanctity of marriage itself, although it did raise fundamental issues about the right to privacy and how the equal protection clause of the Constitution could apply to intimate matters.

Thirty-six years after *Loving*, the Supreme Court decided a case that, like the antimiscegenation cases, considered the role of federal regulation of intimacy. The ruling in *Lawrence v. Texas* reveals the similarities and differences between the history of antimiscegenation and antigay marriage laws. In *Lawrence*, the Court ruled that sodomy laws were unconstitutional. The decision articulated for the first time the right to sexual privacy among consenting adults. According to Justice Anthony Kennedy, "The petitioners are entitled to respect for their private lives. The state cannot demean their existence or control their destiny by making their private sexual conduct a crime."[10] The majority thus converted what had been a public policy matter in *Bowers v. Hardwick*—gay sexual behavior—into a protected privacy issue. It remains to be seen whether the *Lawrence* decision's focus on the right to privacy will extend a similar right to participate fully in the public sphere, in which marriage is a fundamental social and legal relationship.

What is most intriguing about *Lawrence* for our purposes is the specter of interracial intimacy in the case. The reason that the police barged into Lawrence's Houston home was because they were responding to a reported weapons disturbance. Lawrence's neighbors were disturbed that he had brought an African American man, Garner, into his home. Upon entering the home, the police found Lawrence and Garner engaged in consensual sex, at which point the police arrested them under a Texas statute making it a crime for same-sex couples to engage in "certain intimate sexual conduct." While the court's decision articulated a right to sexual privacy, the case also reveals the transparency of privacy when it comes to black bodies in white neighborhoods.[11]

The *Lawrence* decision's articulation of a right to privacy was quickly elaborated to a debate about rights within the public sphere. Concurrent with the decision, the Massachusetts supreme court ruled in favor of gay marriages. The court argued that because marriage was not solely a private matter but also a public act that carried all sorts of tax- and inheritance-related consequences, the state could not prevent same-sex couples' access to the institution. Immediately, conservative and liberal politicians came to the "defense" of marriage by claiming that marriage was fundamentally a private and religious matter. For social conservatives and many liberals, marriage is fundamentally a private relationship between a man and woman. Liberals, many of whom also believe in the inevitable heterosexual nature of marriage, advocate civil unions that grant all the rights of marriage without benefit of the legal term "marriage." Such formulations are problematic, however, for the very reason that any congressional debate about marriage illuminates marriage's public nature. That the federal government is considering a constitutional amendment to limit marriage to heterosexuals shows that marriage is, by definition, a civil issue and not just a religious and private affair.

It is useful to remember the history of the legal fight against antimiscegenation laws. This was a time when "activist judges" slowly, but steadily, undermined the legal institution of antimiscegenation laws. The *Loving* court argued that antimiscegenation laws were a violation of the equal protection clause of the Constitution and that marriage was fundamentally a public act. We should also remember, however, that *Loving* did not challenge the heterosexual nature of marriage and in this way must not be the final ruling on who has the right to marry.

Yet the history related in *Romance and Rights* ought to sound a note of caution for lesbian, gay, bisexual, and transsexual (LGBT) activists as well. Advocacy within black communities after World War II for the right to intermarry was fraught with all sorts of limits and complexities because of the ways that it privileged limited forms of interracial intimacy. Black soldiers' relationships with European women were celebrated, while black soldiers' relationships with Asian women were looked at with concern. Given the historical relationship of "profamily" politics to white heterosexuality, it remains to be seen how effective "profamily" politics can be for people of color and

LGBT activists. Perhaps the more radical struggle ought to include an attempt to divest marriage of all of its privileges so that it can become a human right that cannot be abridged by the state.

Obviously, the "right to privacy" articulated by the *Lawrence* court is not the same "right to privacy" accorded Strom Thurmond and countless other privileged white men who were able to have their illicit and violent sexual affairs hidden from public view. Such a comparison, however, invites more work on how privacy functions both as legal category and cultural norm and how legal definitions of privacy can act as rights in some cases and as enforced silence in others. Examining the private and public aspects of inter-racial intimacy shows how matters of race and sex, of romance and rights, are inextricably connected.

Notes

Introduction

1. See, for example, John Dower, *War without Mercy: Race and Power in the Pacific War* (New York: Pantheon, 1986); Tomas Engelhardt, *The End of Victory Culture: Cold War America and the Disillusioning of a Generation* (Amherst: University of Massachusetts Press, 1998); David W. Noble, *Death of a National Landscape: American Culture and the End of Exceptionalism* (Minneapolis: University of Minnesota Press, 2002).

2. All reviews come from Martin Duberman, *Paul Robeson* (New York: Knopf, 1988), 265.

3. Ibid., 279.

4. *Chicago Defender*, April 21, 1945. The "new world acomin'" prophesied by Burns was a reference to black journalist Roi Ottley's postwar study, *New World A-Coming: Inside Black America* (Boston: Houghton Mifflin, 1943). For a discussion of Burns's role as editor at *Ebony*, see Burns's autobiography, *Nitty Gritty: A White Editor in Black Journalism* (Jackson: University Press of Mississippi, 1996).

5. There are numerous historical studies of interracial sexuality, marriage, and romance that have been indispensable to this study. Among the most useful are Warner Sollors, ed., *Interracialism: Black-White Intermarriage in American History, Literature and Law* (New York: Oxford University Press, 2000); David Fowler, *Northern Attitudes towards Interracial Marriage: Legislation and Public Opinion in the Middle Atlantic and the States of the Old Northwest, 1780–1930* (New York: Garland, 1987); Martha Hodes, *White Women/Black Men: Illicit Sex in the Nineteenth-Century South* (New Haven, Conn.: Yale University Press, 1997); Paul Spickard, *Mixed Blood: Intermarriage and Ethnic Identity in Twentieth-Century America* (Madison: University of Wisconsin Press, 1989); Joel Williamson, *New People: Miscegenation and Mulattoes in the United States* (New York: Free Press, 1980); Kevin Mumford, *Interzones: Black/White Sex Districts in Chicago and New York in the Early Twentieth Century* (New York: Columbia University Press, 1997). There are also a growing number of critical texts that examine the history of hybridity and mixed-race identities that are central the issue of interracial intimacy. The most central to this study are Naomi Zack, *Race and Mixed Race* (Philadelphia: Temple University Press, 1993); Maria P.P. Root, *Racially Mixed People in America* (Newbury Park, Calif.: Sage, 1992); Gloria Anzaldua, *Borderlands: The New Meztiza/La Frontera* (San Francisco: Aunt Lute Press, 1987); Robert Young, *Colonial Desire: Hybridity in Theory, Culture, and Race* (New York: Routledge, 1995); Katya Gibel Azoulay, *Black, Jewish, and Interracial: It's Not the Color of Your Skin, But the Race of Your Kin, and Other Myths of Identity* (Durham, N.C.: Duke University Press, 1997).

6. See Mary L. Dudziak, *Cold War Civil Rights: Race and the Image of American Democracy* (Princeton, N.J.: Princeton University Press, 2000); Brenda Gayle Plummer, *Rising Wind: Black Americans and U.S. Foreign Affairs, 1935–1960* (Chapel Hill: University of North Carolina Press, 1996); Penny Von Eshen, *Race Against Empire: Black Americans and Anti-Colonialism, 1937–1957* (Ithaca, N.Y.: Cornell University Press, 1997); Ronald Takaki, *Double Victory: A Multicultural History of Americans in World War II* (Boston: Little, Brown, 2000).

7. Qtd. in Dudziak, *Cold War Civil Rights*, 100.

8. Peggy Pascoe, "Miscegenation Law, Court Cases, and Ideologies of 'Race' in Twentieth-Century America," in *Sex, Love, Race: Crossing Boundaries in North American History*, ed. Martha Hodes, 138 (New York: New York University Press, 1999).

9. George Lipsitz, *The Possessive Investment in Whiteness: How White People Profit from identity Politics* (Philadelphia: Temple University Press, 1998). See also Thomas Sugrue, *The Origins of the*

Urban Crisis: Race and Inequality in Postwar Detroit (Princeton, N.J.: Princeton University Press, 1996).

10. For a discussion of the Zoot Suit Riots, see Mauricio Mazon, *The Zoot Suit Riots: The Psychology of Symbolic Annihilation* (Austin: University of Texas Press, 1989); Eduardo Obregon Pagan, "Los Angeles Geopolitics and the Zoot Suit Riot 1943," *Social Science History* 24, no. 1 (2000): 223–256.

1. Legislating Love

1. It is important to note that laws regulating interracial intimacy were not called "antimiscegenation" laws until after 1864. The word "miscegenation," as I will discuss in this chapter, was not invented until the election of 1864, when Southern journalists coined the term as a political hoax meant to undermine Lincoln's presidential campaign. Prior to the invention of the word "miscegenation," laws regulating interracial intimacy were categorized as racial purity laws or antifornication laws. I use the term "antimiscegenation" realizing that such a term did not exist during some of the historical periods covered here.

2. It is difficult to identify the consequences of political containment after World War II through court cases. Because court rulings rely on previous courts' decisions, justices' opinions are not always a product of contemporary politics but instead signify minor adjustments to past rulings. Consequently, the antimiscegenation court cases discussed below show a slow evolution in ideas about interracial intimacy. What concerns us most, however, is how postwar antimiscegenation cases, even though they may have relied on the same logic as prewar antimiscegenation cases, held different meanings and consequences because of the changes wrought by the war and the civil rights movement.

3. For a discussion of the similarities between slaves and servants, see Edmund Morgan, *American Slavery American Freedom: The Ordeal of Colonial Virginia* (New York: W. W. Norton, 1975); Winthrop Jordan, *White Over Black: American Attitudes toward the Negro: 1550–1812* (Baltimore: Penguin, 1969); W.E.B. Du Bois, *Black Reconstruction: An Essay toward a History of the Part Which Black Folk Played in the Attempt to Reconstruct Democracy in America, 1860–1880* (New York: Harcourt, Brace, 1935). For a discussion of the Maryland legislation, see Hodes, *White Women/Black Men*; Carter G. Woodsen, "The Beginnings of Miscegenation of the Whites and Blacks," in Sollors, *Interracialism*.

4. Qtd. in Woodsen, "The Beginnings of Miscegenation," 45.

5. See Sydney Kaplan, *American Studies in Black and White: Selected Essays, 1949–1989* (Amherst: University of Massachusetts Press, 1991); David Roediger, *The Wages of Whiteness: Race and the Making of the American Working Class* (New York: Verso, 1991).

6. Kaplan, *American Studies*, 223.

7. Ibid.

8. Ibid.

9. For a discussion of this shift, see Hodes, *Black Men/White Women*.

10. See A. Leon Higginbotham Jr. and Barbara Kopytoff, "Racial Purity and Interracial Sex in the Law of Colonial and Antebellum Virginia," *Georgetown Law Journal* 77 (1989): 1967–2029.

11. Ibid., 1992.

12. James Hugo Johnson, *Race Relations in Virginia and Miscegenation in the South, 1776–1860* (Amherst: University of Massachusetts Press, 1970), 193–194.

13. It should be noted that Virginia's changing racial categories somewhat mirror two important moments in national racial formation. The 1785 law loosening the criteria for entrance into whiteness came a few years before the 1790 naturalization law that granted citizenship to all free white persons. The 1910 and 1924 laws restricting whiteness to no trace of "Negro blood" were enacted right around the 1924 Johnson-Reed Immigration Act, which sought, among other things, to preclude immigration of the undesirable "white races." For a brilliant analysis of these touchstones in

racial formation, see Matthew Frye Jacobsen, *Whiteness of a Different Color: European Immigrants and the Alchemy of Race* (Cambridge, Mass.: Harvard University Press, 1998).

14. For a discussion of *The Birth of Nation* and its racist implications, see Daniel T. Bernardi, *The Birth of Whiteness and the Emergence of U.S. Cinema* (New Brunswick, N.J.: Rutgers University Press, 1996); Thomas Cripps, *Slow Fade to Black: The Negro in American Film, 1900–1942* (New York: Oxford University Press, 1977); Ed Guerrero, *Framing Blackness: The African American Image in Film* (Philadelphia: Temple University Press, 1993).

15. For a discussion of how Griffith cast Gish as a "pure" white woman, see Richard Dyer, "The Color of Virtue: Lillian Gish, Whiteness, and Femininity," in *Women in Film: A Sight and Sound Reader*, ed. Pam Cook and Philip Dodd (Philadelphia: Temple University Press, 1993).

16. See Kevin Mumford's provocative study, *Interzones*. For more on the Progressive Era's construction of vice districts, see Peter Baldwin *Domesticating the Street: The Reform of Public Space in Hartford, 1850–1930* (Columbus: Ohio State University Press, 1999); John Burnham, "The Progressive Era Revolution in American Attitudes toward Sex," *Journal of American History* 59, no. 4 (1973): 885–908; Ivan Light, "The Ethnic Vice Industry, 1880–1994," *American Sociological Review* 42, no. 3 (1977): 464–479.

17. See George Hutchinson, *The Harlem Renaissance in Black and White* (Cambridge, Mass.: Harvard University Press, 1995); Victor A. Kramer and Robert A Russ, eds., *Harlem Renaissance Re-Examined* (Troy, N.Y.: Whitson, 1997); Bill Mullen and Sherry Lee Linkon, eds., *Radical Revisions: Rereading 1930s Culture* (Urbana: University of Illinois Press, 1996).

18. One of the most famous cases of white support of black cultural production was Carl Van Vechten's sponsorship of black writers like Chester Himes. See, for example, Hugh M. Gloster, "The Van Vechten Vogue," *Phylon* 6, no. 4 (1945): 310–314; Robert Hart, "Black-White Literary Relations in the Harlem Renaissance," *American Literature* 44, no. 4 (1973): 612–628; Mark Helbling, "Carl Van Vechten and the Harlem Renaissance," *Negro American Literature Forum* 10, no. 2 (1976): 39–47; George Schuyler "Phylon Profile, XXII: Carl Van Vechten," *Phylon* 11, no. 4 (1950): 362–368; Charles Scruggs, " 'All Dressed Up But No Place to Go': The Black Writer and His Audience during the Harlem Renaissance," *American Literature* 48, no. 4 (1977): 543–563.

19. See Mara L. Keire, "The Vice Trust: A Reinterpretation of the White Slavery Scare in the United States, 1907–1917," *Journal of Social History* 35, no. 1 (2001): 5–41; David Langum, *Crossing Over the Line: Legislating Morality and the Mann Act* (Chicago: University of Chicago Press, 1994).

20. On Jack Johnson and the Mann Act, see Robert H. DeCoy, *Jack Johnson: The Big Black Fire* (Los Angeles: Holloway House, 1991); Al-Tony Gilmore, "Jack Johnson and White Women: The National Impact," *Journal of Negro History* 58, no. 1 (1973): 18–38.

21. See Dudziak, *Cold War Civil Rights*; Takaki, *Double Victory*; Herbert Garfinkle, *When Negroes March: The March on Washington Movement in the Organization Politics for FEPC* (Glencoe, Ill.: Free Press, 1959).

22. Nat Brandt, *Harlem at War: The Black Experience in World War II* (Syracuse, N.Y.: Syracuse University Press, 1996), 98.

23. John Morton Blum, *V Was for Victory: Politics and American Culture during World War II* (New York: Harcourt Brace Jovanovich, 1976), 208.

24. John Silvera, *The Negro in World War II* (New York: Arno, 1969).

25. Russell Buchanan, *Black Americans in World War II* (Santa Barbara, Calif.: Clio Books, 1977), 21. See also Richard Dalfiume, *Desegregation of the U.S. Armed Forces: Fighting on Two Fronts, 1939–1953* (Columbia: University of Missouri Press, 1969).

26. Buchanan, *Black Americans in World War II*, 25. For a history of the March on Washington movement, see Garfinkle, *When Negroes March*.

27. See Lee Finkle, *Forum for Protest: The Black Press during World War II* (Rutherford, N.J.: Fairleigh Dickinson University Press, 1975); Takaki, *Double Victory*.

28. See Eileen Boris, "You Wouldn't Want One of 'Em Dancing with Your Wife': Racialized Bodies on the Job in WWII," *American Quarterly* 50, no. 1 (2000): 77–108; George Lipsitz, *Rainbow*

at Midnight: Labor and Culture in the 1940s (Urbana: University of Illinois Press, 1994); C.L.R. James et al., *Fighting Racism in World War II* (New York: Monad Press, 1980).

29. *Perez v. Sharp*, 198 P. 2d 17 (Calif., 1948).

30. It is telling that Traynor allows for racial discrimination in cases of national security, for in doing so, he was able to argue against antimiscegenation legislation without considering his state's contradictory internment of Japanese Americans during the war. For a good discussion of Blumenbach and Boas, see Jacobsen, *Whiteness of a Different Color*.

31. *Stevens v. United States*, 146 F.2d. 120 (1944).

32. For African American–Native American relations generally, see Wyatt Jeltz, "The Relations of Negroes and Choctaw and Chickasaw Indians," *Journal of Negro History* 33, no. 1 (1948): 24–37; Daniel Littlefield Jr. and Mary Ann Littlefield, "The Beams Family: Free Blacks in Indian Territory," *Journal of Negro History* 61, no. 1 (1976): 17–35; Patrick Minges, "Beneath the Underdog: Race, Religion, and the Trail of Tears," *American Indian Quarterly* 25, no. 3 (2001): 453–479; William McLoughlin, "Red Indians, Black Slavery and White Racism: America's Slaveholding Indians," *American Quarterly* 26, no. 4 (1974): 367–385.

33. Virginia's Racial Integrity Act of 1924.

34. See Higginbotham and Kopytoff, "Racial Purity."

35. Rachel Moran, *Interracial Intimacy: The Regulation of Race and Romance* (Chicago: University of Chicago Press, 2001), 90–91.

36. As George Lipsitz has argued, the federal government has played a crucial role in allowing whites to pass the material rewards of their racial privilege on to family members by allowing restrictive housing through federal loan programs. Here, Watts undermined his possessive investment by breaking the chain of inherited white wealth. See Lipsitz, *The Possessive Investment in Whiteness*.

37. This case underscores the ways that whiteness, to use Cheryl Harris's analysis, acts as a form of property. See Cheryl Harris, "Whiteness as Property," *Harvard Law Review* 106 (June 1993): 1709–1791; Ian Haney Lopez, *White By Law: The Legal Construction of Race* (New York: New York University Press, 1996).

38. Barbara J. Fields, "Ideology and Race in American History," in *Region, Race, and Reconstruction: Essays in Honor of C. Vann Woodward*, ed. J. Morgan Kouser and James M. McPherson (New York: Oxford University Press, 1991).

39. I am not here arguing that mistakenly admitted evidence is a minor matter. Certainly the procedural question determined that outcome of the case. Yet I think it prudent to speculate why Luby Griffith and Vena Mae Pendley received different verdicts given the seeming similarity of their cases. Moreover, one should not overlook the matter of Pendley giving up her child. As Rickie Solinger has argued in *Wake Up Little Susie*, middle-class white women could erase the fact of their extramarital sexual affairs in the 1950s by relinquishing their children. Not enough is known about Pendley's case to make conclusions, but it is interesting to speculate how ideologies of unwed pregnancy also shaped this case. See Rickie Solinger, *Wake Up Little Susie: Single Pregnancy and Race before Roe v. Wade* (New York: Routledge, 1992); Regina Kunzel, *Fallen Women, Problem Girls: Unmarried Mothers and the Professionalization of Social Work, 1890–1945* (New Haven, Conn.: Yale University Press, 1993).

40. Moran, *Interracial Intimacy*, 89.

2. Containing Contradictions

1. Michael Denning, *The Cultural Front: The Laboring of American Culture in the Twentieth Century* (New York: Verso, 1996). See also Bill Mullen, *Popular Fronts: Chicago and African American Politics* (Urbana: University of Illinois Press, 1999).

2. Robert Lee, *Orientals: Asian Americans in Popular Culture* (Philadelphia: Temple University Press, 2000), 7. See also Nancy Cott, *Public Vows: A History of Marriage and the Nation* (Cambridge, Mass.: Harvard University Press, 2002).

3. John Goldwater, *Americana in Four Colors: A Decade of Self-Regulation by the Comic Magazine Industry* (New York: Comics Magazine Association of America, 1974); Amy Kiste Nyberg, *Seal of Approval: The History of the Comics Codes* (Jackson: University Press of Mississippi, 1998); William Savage, *Commies, Cowboys, and Jungle Queens: Comic Books and America, 1945–1954* (Norman: University of Oklahoma Press, 1990).

4. See, for example, Andrew Ross, *No Respect: Intellectuals and Popular Culture* (New York: Routledge, 1989); Nyberg, *Seal of Approval*. On the blacklists and the House Un-American Activities Committee, see Richard Fried, *Nightmare in Red: The McCarthy Era in Perspective* (New York: Oxford, 1990); Walter Goodman, *The Committee: The Extraordinary Career of the House Committee on Un-American Activities* (New York: Farrar, Straus, and Giroux, 1968); Larry Ceplair and Steven Englund, *The Inquisition in Hollywood: Politics in the Film Community, 1930–1960* (Garden City, N.Y.: Anchor Press/Doubleday, 1980); David Cochran, *American Noir: Underground Writers and Filmmakers of the Postwar Era* (Washington, D.C.: Smithsonian Institution Press, 2000).

5. Goldwater, *Americana in Four Colors*, 34.

6. Ibid.

7. See, for example, James Gilbert, *A Cycle of Outrage: America's Reaction to the Juvenile Delinquent* (New York: Oxford University Press, 1986); Marjorie Heins, *Not in Front of the Children: "Indecency," Censorship, and the Innocence of Youth* (New York: Hill and Wang, 2001). For sources on the Kefauver committee, see Charles Fontenay, *Estes Kefauver, a Biography* (Knoxville: University of Tennessee Press, 1980); Joseph Gorman, *Kefauver, a Political Biography* (Cambridge: Oxford University Press, 1971).

8. Savage, *Commies, Cowboys, and Jungle Queens*, 97.

9. Edward Feder, *Comic Book Regulation* (Berkeley: Bureau of the Public Administration, University of California, 1955), 27.

10. Ibid., 42.

11. Ibid., 27.

12. Ibid., 42.

13. Ibid., 51.

14. Goldwater, *Americana in Four Colors*, 34.

15. The centrality of regulating women's behavior after World War II is explored in Solinger, *Wake Up Little Suzie*; Elaine Tyler May, *Homeward Bound: American Families in the Cold War Era* (New York: Basic Books, 1988); Kunzel, *Fallen Women*; Joann Meyerowitz, ed., *Not June Cleaver: Women and Gender in Postwar America, 1945–1960* (Philadelphia: Temple University Press, 1994).

16. See, for example, Robert F. Berkhofer Jr., *The White Man's Indian: Images of the American Indian from Columbus to the Present* (New York: Knopf, 1978); Reyna Green, "The Pocahontas Perplex: The Image of the Indian Woman in American Culture," *Massachusetts Review* 16 (1975): 698–714.

17. "My Parents Stood Between Us," *Heartthrobs* 29 (1954). Russel B. Nye Special Collections Library, Michigan State University, East Lansing.

18. *Confessions of the Lovelorn* (1952). Russel B. Nye Special Collections Library.

19. *Love Story* (1949). Russel B. Nye Special Collections Library.

20. Here I rely on the notion of "negotiation and dialogue" developed most clearly by George Lipsitz in *Time Passages: Collective Memory and American Popular Culture* (Minneapolis: University of Minnesota Press, 1990). Lipsitz argues that cultural forms are sites of negotiation and dialogue between audiences, the state, and producers of mass media. Each entity contains its own political agendas and desires. In the case of comic books, I suggest that they signify a negotiation between consumers and producers over social definitions of gender and class, while leaving unquestioned the status of race relations. In this way, the comics are a dialogue between white consumers and white producers. While there were a few comic books produced for people of color during the period of this study, I have been unable to find them in any archive.

21. Savage, *Commies, Cowboys, and Jungle Queens*, 77.

22. *First Love* 1, no. 9 (1952). Russel B. Nye Special Collections Library.

23. I draw on the work of Reyna Green, who, in "The Pocahontas Perplex," identifies the historical uses of the Pocahontas image as a mother/goddess figure. For discussions of minstrelsy, see Robert Toll, *Blacking Up: The Minstrel Show in 19th Century America* (New York: Oxford University Press, 1974); Eric Lott, *Love and Theft: Blackface Minstrelsy and the American Working Class* (New York: Oxford University Press, 1993); Susan Gubar, *Race Changes: White Skin, Black Face in American Culture* (New York: Oxford University Press, 1997); Roediger, *The Wages of Whiteness*; Alexander Saxton, *The Rise and Fall of the White Republic: Class, Politics, and Mass Culture in Nineteenth Century America* (New York: Verso, 1990).

24. For information about white consumption of black music in the 1950s, see Jeffrey Melnick, " 'Story Untold': The Black Men and White Sounds of Doo-Wop," in *Whiteness: A Critical Reader*, ed. Mike Hill; Ross, *No Respect*; Weinie Breines, *Young, White, and Miserable: Growing Up Female in the Fifties* (Boston: Beacon Press, 1992).

25. *True Stories* 5, no. 46 (1945). Russel B. Nye Special Collections Library.

26. Boris, " 'You Wouldn't Want One of 'Em Dancing with Your Wife.' "

27. *Women Outlaws* (1949). Russel B. Nye Special Collections Library.

28. *Girls Love Stories* (1953). Russel B. Nye Special Collections Library.

29. For a discussion of social-problem films, see Lipsitz, *Rainbow at Midnight*; Jim Hillier, ed., *Cashiers duCinema: The 1950s, Neo-Realism, Hollywood, New Wave* (Cambridge, Mass.: Harvard University Press, 1985); Michael Ryan and Douglas Kellner, *Camera Politica: The Politics and Ideology of Contemporary Hollywood Film* (Bloomington: University of Indiana Press, 1988).

30. There were many other films that also engage the matter of interracial intimacy or racism more broadly, such as *Show Boat, Pinky, Sayonara, Paisan* (Italian), *The Quiet One, Come to the Stable, No Way Out, Intruder in the Dust,* and *The Mullato* (Italian). For an analysis of passing in postwar films, see Gayle Wald, *Crossing the Line: Racial Passing in Twentieth-Century U.S. Literature and Culture* (Durham, N.C.: Duke University Press, 2000). For a good discussion of representations of Asian Americans in postwar films, see Gina Marchetti, *Romance and the "Yellow Peril": Race, Sex, and the Discursive Strategies in Hollywood Fiction* (Berkeley: University of California Press, 1993).

31. For a good discussion of the universalization of race, see Paul Gilroy, *Against Race: Imagining Political Culture Beyond the Color Line* (Cambridge, Mass.: Belknap Press of Harvard University Press, 2000); K. Anthony Appiah and Amy Gutman, *Color Conscious: The Political Morality of Race* (Princeton, N.J.: Princeton University Press, 1998).

32. Judith Smith, *Visions of Belonging: Family Stories, Popular Culture, and Postwar Democracy, 1940–1960* (New York: Columbia University Press, forthcoming).

33. David Palumbo Liu, *Asian/American: Historical Crossings of a Racial Frontier* (Stanford, Calif.: Stanford University Press, 1999); Marchetti, *Romance and the "Yellow Peril."*

3. Making Marriage Matter

1. Fred De Armond to Professor Roosevelt Williams, Howard University, August 15, 1956. Professor Williams was a fiction. The letter can be found in the Papers of the NAACP, Part 20, Reel 8, "White Resistance and Reprisals, 1956–1965." See also the NAACP pamphlet "A Fraud Unmasked: The Strange Fate of Roosevelt Williams," which reads, "For about a year now there has been widely circulated throughout the South tape recordings and mimeographed texts of a speech allegedly made at an NAACP meeting by one Roosevelt Williams. . . . This speech purports to set for 'the ultimate aim of the NAACP'—intermarriage." The pamphlet vehemently denies Cook's allegations.

2. See, for example, "The Ugly Truth About the NAACP," an address by Eugene Cook before the 55th Annual Convention of the Peace Officers Association of Georgia, held in Atlanta, 1955. See also Theodore Bilbo, *Take Your Choice: Separation or Mongrelization* (Poplarville, Miss.: Dream House Publishing, 1947).

3. *Time Magazine*, September 19, 1955.

4. Ottley, *New World A-Coming.*

5. *Ebony* 9, no. 3 (January 1954).

6. W.E.B. Du Bois, "Racial Intermarriage," *Crisis*, 1910.

7. W.E.B. Du Bois, "Marrying of Black Folk," *Independent* (October 13, 1910): 813.

8. NAACP to the Committee of Judiciary, State Senate of Madison, Wisconsin, January 25, 1917. Papers of the NAACP, Part 11, Series B: Special Subjects 1912–1939.

9. Senate Bill S. 4294, "Federal Marriage Bill," was introduced on January 23, 1923. NAACP responses to the proposed bill can be found in Papers of the NAACP, Part 11, Series B: Special Subjects 1912–1939.

10. Carl Murphy to James Weldon Johnson, January 24, 1924. Papers of the NAACP, Part 11, Series B: Special Subjects, 1912–1939.

11. "Argument Made by Mr. Butler B. Wilson, President of the Boston Branch of the NAACP, at the Hearing on the Anti-Intermarriage Bill introduced in the Massachusetts State Legislature." Papers of the NAACP, Part 11, Series B: Special Subjects, 1912–1939.

12. Letter concerning Bill Number 712 in the Massachusetts State House to forbid intermarriage, from Alice Stone Blackwell to Butler Wilson (Boston Branch of the NAACP), March 1927. Papers of the NAACP, Part 11, Series B: Special Subjects 1912–1939. Despite Blackwell's belief that antimiscegenation laws could be subverted and did not deter interracial sex, she was sure to suggest that "no doubt, it is generally wiser for people to marry within their own racial group; but that is a matter of personal choice."

13. Gunnar Myrdal, *An American Dilemma: The Negro Problem and Modern Democracy* (New York: Harper and Row, 1962), 62.

14. Horace Cayton and St. Clair Drake, *Black Metropolis: A Study of Negro Life in a Northern City*, vol. 1 (1945; reprint, New York: Harper and Row, 1962), 126.

15. Ibid., 120.

16. Oliver Cromwell Cox, *Caste, Class, and Race: A Study in Social Dynamics* (1948; reprint, New York: Modern Reader Paperbacks, 1970), 186.

17. Benjamin Mays, President of Morehouse College, to Garland Porter Southering Advertising and Publishing, December 19, 1954. Papers of the NAACP, Part 16, Series B, Reel 10.

18. Roy Wilkins to Benjamin Mays, December 23, 1954. Papers of the NAACP, Part 16, Series B, Reel 10.

19. "Peace Mission Movement Tenants," pamphlet. Father Divine Collection, Woodruff Library, Emory University, Atlanta.

20. See Divine Sermons, May 16, 1948. Father Divine Collection, Woodruff Library, Emory University.

21. This estimate is based on my own unscientific survey of Johnson's magazines from 1945 to 1954.

22. For a discussion of Johnson Publishing's use of interracial stories to sell magazines, see John Johnson, *Succeeding Against the Odds* (New York: Warner Books, 1989); Eliza G.C. Collins and Wanda A. Lankenner, "Failure Is a Word I Don't Accept," *Harvard Business Review* 54 (March/April 1976): 79–88; James A. Reichly, "How Johnson Made It," *Fortune*, January 1968; Burns, *Nitty Gritty*; Patricia Ann Friday Shaw, " 'Negro Digest,' 'Pulse,' and 'Headlines and Pictures' ": African American Periodicals as Informants, Morale Builders and Articulators of Protest during World War II" (Ph.D. diss., University of Maryland, 1994); Frank Miles, "Negro Magazines Come of Age," *Magazine World*, June 1, 1946; Walter C. Daniel, *Black Journals of the United States* (Westport, Conn.: Greenwood Press, 1982).

23. *Ebony* 5, no. 2. (December 1946).

24. Ibid.

25. *Chicago Defender*, September, 3, 1949.

26. *Ebony* 5, no. 2 (December 1946).

27. Ibid.

28. Ibid.

29. Ottley, *New World A-Coming*, 177.

30. Letters to the Editor, *Ebony* 7, no. 10 (August 1952).

31. Letters to the Editor, *Ebony* 2, no. 8 (June 1947).

32. *Jet* 3, no. 19 (March 19, 1953).

33. U.S. Census Bureau, http://www.census.gov/ population/socdemo/race/interractab1.txt.

34. *Ebony* 6, no. 1 (November 1950); see also Mumford, *Interzones.*

35. *Ebony* 6, no. 11 (September 1951).

36. *Jet* 4, no. 9 (July 9, 1953).

37. *Ebony* 9, no. 7 (May 1954).

38. *Chicago Defender*, January 19, 1946.

39. *Chicago Defender*, February 2, 1946.

40. *Chicago Defender*, July 29, 1950.

41. Ibid.

42. *Ebony* 6, no. 1 (November 1950).

43. *Chicago Defender*, January 2, 1950.

44. *Jet* 4, no. 1 (May 14, 1953).

45. Ibid.

46. Benjamin Mays to Garland Porter, December 18, 1954. Papers of the NAACP, Part 16, Series B, Reel 10.

47. *U.S. News and World Report*, September 19, 1958.

4. At Home and Abroad

1. Lawrence Levine, *Black Culture and Black Consciousness: Afro-American Folk Thought from Slavery to Freedom* (New York: Oxford University Press, 1997), 341.

2. Graham Smith, *When Jim Crow Met John Bull: Black American Soldiers in World War II Britain* (New York: St. Martin's, 1988); David Reynolds, *Rich Relations: The American Occupation of Britain, 1942–1945* (New York: Random House, 1995). Both Smith and Reynolds suggest that what fueled concern over black GI interracial romances were white soldiers' fears that they had lost a competitive struggle over foreign women. This view, while partially correct, does not fully elucidate the role of interracial romances as a subtext to the entire wartime and postwar eras. On black participation in World War II, see Neil A. Wynn, *The Afro-American and the Second World War* (New York: Holmes and Meier, 1975); Brandt, *Harlem at War*; Blum, *V Was for Victory*; Buchanan, *Black Americans in World War II*; Dalfiume, *Desegregation of the U.S. Armed Forces.*

3. Ronald Takaki makes a similar point in *A Different Mirror: A History of Multicultural America* (Boston: Little, Brown, 1994). See also Williamson, *New People*; Timothy Tyson, *Radio Free Dixie: Robert F. Williams and the Roots of Black Power* (Chapel Hill: University of North Carolina Press, 1999); Dudziak, *Cold War Civil Rights*; Plummer, *Rising Wind.*

4. David Reynolds has convincingly argued that the War Department made all GI marriages difficult irrespective of race. Yet he also suggests that interracial couples faced even more difficult obstacles. See Reynolds, *Rich Relations.*

5. A description of the film, and others like it, can be found in Smith, *When Jim Crow Met John Bull*, 88; and Wynn, *The Afro-American and the Second World War*, 33. See also Reynolds, *Rich Relations.*

6. Qtd. in Brandt, *Harlem at War*, 106.

7. Qtd. in Reynolds, *Rich Relations*, 218.

8. *Chicago Defender*, August 18, 1945.

9. Cited in Elfrieda Shukert and Barbara Smith Scibetta, *War Brides of WWII* (Novato, Calif.: Presidio Press, 1988), 20.

10. Howard Peterson, Assistant Secretary of War, to Alice Rivkin, Director, League of Women Shoppers, Inc. N.Y., May 17, 1947. Papers of the NAACP, Part 9, Series B: Discrimination in the U.S. Armed Forces, 1918–1955. It is nearly impossible to estimate the number of marriages among white and black GIs in Europe and Asia. The Immigration and Naturalization Service (INS) recorded the number of war brides who were admitted into the United States from 1945 to 1951. Yet the INS didn't

account for the race of the soldier in these statistics. Moreover, the War Department did not record evidence of GI marriage proposals that were denied. And finally, rates of wartime marriage, which can only be estimated at best, do not account for the number of interracial sexual liaisons between black GIs and foreign women. More ethnographic work needs to be done on black soldiers' intimate relations while serving abroad. David Reynolds provides the best evidence about the number of war brides when he estimates 70,000. See Reynolds, *Rich Relations*.

11. Cited in Shukert and Scibetta, *War Brides of WWII*, 47.

12. Marion T. Frederick, Attorney at Law, Columbus, Ohio, to the National Office of the NAACP, March 16, 1945. Papers of the NAACP, Part 9, Series B: Discrimination in the U.S. Armed Forces, 1918–1955.

13. Robert Carter, Legal Assistant of the NAACP, to Leslie Perry, Administration Assistant NAACP, July 7, 1945. Papers of the NAACP, Part 9, Series C: Soldier Complaints.

14. Leslie Perry, NAACP, to James Evans, Civilian Assistant Officer of the Secretary of Defense. Papers the NAACP, Part 9, Series C: Soldier Complaints.

15. Cpl. Ceophas J. Randall to Mother, November 3, 1945. Papers of the NAACP, Part 9, Series C: Soldier Complaints.

16. NAACP to James Evans, Advisor to the Secretary of Defense, April 29, 1948. Papers of the NAACP, Part 9, Series C: Soldier Complaints.

17. John McMorris to NAACP, March 1948. Papers of the NAACP, Part 9, Series C: Soldier Complaints.

18. Giana Del Prede, Naples, Italy, to Director of the NAACP, February 4, 1946. Papers of the NAACP, Part 9, Series C: Soldier Complaints.

19. Hildegard Lousie Kaiser, Nuremberg, to Jess Dedmon, December 7, 1946. Papers of the NAACP, Part 9, Series C, Soldier Complaints.

20. Marie Draux, France, to NAACP, October 14, 1946. Papers of the NAACP, Part 9, Series C: Soldier Complaints.

21. Shukert and Scibetta, *War Brides of WWII*, 13.

22. Smith, *When Jim Crow Met John Bull*, 118. This kind of protest should be viewed not simply as antiracist but, perhaps more powerfully, as anti-American. Smith and Reynolds suggest that British civilians resented the American military presence in their communities and may have waged these protests against the military's color line as a way to protest the American military and not as a way to support black soldiers. Europe was not devoid of racism, as some of the examples that follow will suggest.

23. Smith, *When Jim Crow Met John Bull*, 121.

24. NAACP to Secretary of the Navy James Forestall, December 20, 1945. Papers of the NAACP, Part 9, Discrimination in the U.S. Armed Forces, 1918–1955.

25. *Ebony* 1, no. 11 (October 1946). The article in which this poem appears is about black GIs and their German girlfriends. The story suggests that these relationships would be short-lived because of considerable obstacles to interracial relationships constructed by the U.S. Department of War.

26. *Chicago Defender*, July 28, 1945.

27. One could also look at a number of other *Defender* stories about race relations in Russia to make this point. See, for example, Chatwood Hall, "No Race Hatred in Russia: CIO Union Leader Finds," *Chicago Defender*, January 12, 1946; "Soviets Invite 99th Pilots to Postwar Jobs; No Color Line in USSR," *Chicago Defender*, March 10, 1945; "Race Supremacy Ideas Just 'Popycock' to Reds," *Chicago Defender*, April 7, 1945.

28. "Germany Meets the Negro Soldier," *Ebony* 1, no. 11 (October 1946).

29. "Wanted: Negro Husbands and Wives: Germans Forget Aryan Doctrine, Seek Colored Mates in America," *Ebony* 6, no. 5 (September 1951). Although the title suggested that German men wanted African American women, the story focused entirely on black men and German women.

30. "Why German Women Want Negro Husbands," *Jet* 1, no. 12 (January 17, 1952).

31. "Britain's Brown Babies: Illegitimate Tots a Tough Problem for England," *Ebony* 2, no. 1 (November 1946).

32. *Chicago Defender*, July 14, 1945.

33. "What Europe's Women Think of Negro Men," *Tan Confessions*, 5, no. 1 (1954).

34. "How Europe's Women Make Love," *Jet* 4, no. 11 (July 23, 1953).

35. Letters to the Editor, *Ebony* 6, no. 6 (April 1949).

36. *Chicago Defender*, January 25, 1947.

37. Blum, *V Was for Victory*, 183. See also Reginald Kearney, *African American Views of the Japanese: Solidarity or Sedition?* (Albany: State University of New York Press, 1998); Marc Gallichio, *The African American Encounter with Japan and China: Black Internationalism in Asia: 1895–1945* (Chapel Hill: University of North Carolina Press, 2000).

38. Englehardt, *The End of Victory Culture*. See also Dower, *War without Mercy*.

39. Letters to the Editor, *Ebony* 7, no. 1 (December 1951).

40. "Is Vice Menacing Our GIs?" *Jet* 2, no. 2 (May 8, 1952).

41. *Chicago Defender*, November 18, 1950.

42. *Chicago Defender*, November 4, 1950.

43. "The Truth About Japanese War Brides: Hundreds of GIs Defy Red Tape to Marry Beautiful Nipponese Girls," *Ebony* 7, no. 4 (March 1952). See also Alex Wilson, "Why Tan Yanks Go for Japanese Girls," *Chicago Defender*, November 11, 1950. In this story, Wilson suggests that the answer to his question is that Japanese women are submissive and that Japan offered jobs to "tan yanks." Yet Wilson also suggested that many married black GIs had Japanese girlfriends, thereby heightening concerns by black women that GI interracial intimacy threatened their own relationships.

44. "Do Japanese Women Make Better Wives?" *Jet* 5, no. 1 (November 12, 1953).

45. Letters to the Editor, *Tan Confessions* 3, no. 1 (1952).

46. Letters to the Editor, *Ebony* 2, no. 2 (December 1946).

47. Letters to the Editor, *Ebony* 2, no. 3 (January 1947).

48. These three letters to the editor can be found in *Ebony* 2, no. 3 (January 1947).

49. "White Women in Negro Society," *Jet* 2, no. 7 (June 12, 1952).

50. *Ebony* 7, no. 12 (November 1951).

51. "Negro Women with White Husbands," *Jet* 1, no. 17 (February 21, 1952).

52. *Ebony* 8, no. 8 (June 1953). This was also the argument posed in "How Negro Beauties Charm Europe's Men," *Jet* 1, no. 2 (November 8, 1951): "No place on earth are Negro Beauties more eulogized and exalted than among Europe's men. Openly courted and chased by counts and dukes, admired and idolized by men in the street, more and more good-looking U.S. Negro women have gone to the continent in recent years to captivate cosmopolitan Europeans." Similarly, "Are Europe's Men Stealing Our Women?" *Jet* 3, no. 26 (May 7, 1953) argued, "In the past decade a host of America's most ravishing chocolate-hued entertainers, students and tourists have returned home with extravagant stories of romances shared with some of the top personages on the continent."

5. From the Outside Looking In

1. Gilroy, *Against Race*, 111–112.

2. See Gilroy, *Against Race*; Paul Gilroy, *The Black Atlantic: Modernity and Double Consciousness* (Cambridge, Mass.: Harvard University Press, 1993); Lipsitz, *A Rainbow at Midnight*.

3. See Frank Yerby, *The Foxes of Harrow* (New York: Dial Press, 1946); Yerby, *The Vixens* (New York: Dial Press, 1947); Yerby, *The Golden Hawk* (New York: Dial Press, 1948); Clifton Cuthbert, *The Robbed Heart* (New York: L. B. Fisher, 1945); Nevil Shute, *The Chequer Board* (New York: W. Morrow, 1947); Worth Tuttle Hedden, *The Other Room* (New York: Crow, 1947); Margaret Halsey, *Color Blind: A White Woman Looks at the Negro* (New York: Simon and Schuster, 1946); Marjorie Sinclair, *The Wild Wind* (New York: J. Day, 1950).

4. Tyler Stovall, *Paris Noir: African Americans in the City of Light* (Boston: Houghton Mifflin, 1996).

5. This experience is described in LeRoy S. Hodges, *Portrait of an Expatriate: William Gardner Smith, Writer* (Westport, Conn.: Greenwood Press, 1985), 11.

6. William Gardner Smith, *Last of the Conquerors* (1948, reprint, Chatham, N.J.: Chatham Booksellers, 1973), n.p.

7. Ibid., 238.

8. Ibid., n.p.

9. See Heather Hicks, "'This Strange Communion': Survellance and Spectatorship in Ann Petry's *The Street*," *African American Review* 37, no. 1 (Spring 2003): 21–38; Hicks, "Rethinking Realism in Ann Petry's *The Street*," *Melus* (Winter 2002): 89–106; Jacqueline Bryant, "Postures of Resistance in Ann Petry's *The Street*," *CLA Journal* 45, no. 4 (June 2002): 444–460; Michael Barry, "'Same Train Be Back Tomorrer': Ann Petry's *The Narrows* and Repetition," *Melus* (Spring 1999): 141–160; Keith Clark, "A Distaff Dream Deferred? Ann Petry and the Art of Subversion," *African American Review* 26, no. 3 (Fall 1992): 495–506.

10. Ann Petry, *The Street* (New York: Houghton Mifflin, 1998), 40.

11. Ibid., 45.

12. Ibid., 68.

13. *Oxford English Dictionary*, online edition. http://dictionary.oed.com

14. Petry, *The Street*, 275.

15. Ibid., 16.

16. Ibid., 45.

17. Ibid., 315.

18. Ibid., 322.

19. Ibid., 435.

20. Ibid., 436.

21. See Gilroy, *Against Race*.

22. Ann Petry, *The Narrows* (New York: Mariner Books, 1999), 145.

23. Ibid., 143.

24. Ibid., 85. Here Petry acknowledges that black urban neighborhoods can function as complex interzones, to use Kevin Mumford's term. The Narrows is a site of black domesticity, production, and white escape.

25. Here I am inspired by a paper presented by Bill Mullen on *The Street* at the Center for Working-Class Studies Conference in Youngstown, Ohio, 2003.

26. Petry, *The Narrows*, 280.

27. Ibid., 399.

28. Gilroy, *The Black Atlantic*.

29. Chester Himes, *Black on Black* (New York: Doubleday, 1973), 5.

30. Ed Margolies and Michael Fabre, *The Several Lives of Chester Himes* (Jackson: University Press of Mississippi, 1997), 34.

31. This admission can be found in Himes's first autobiography, *The Quality of Hurt, the Early Years: The Autobiography of Chester Himes* (New York: Thunder's Mouth Press, 1972).

32. For example, in *Gay New York: Gender, Urban Culture, and the Making of the Gay Male World, 1890–1940* (New York: Basic Books, 1994), George Chauncey argues that by the 1940s, heterosexuality came to be seen as normative and homosexuality as perverse. This was a historical shift from the 1920s and 1930s, where a wider range of sexual practices could be considered normative. Moreover, Allan Berube's *Coming Out Under Fire: The History of Gay Men and Women in World War Two* (New York: Free Press, 1990) illustrates the shifting definitions of normative sexuality, which, by the 1940s, would lead to the criminalization of homosexuality. For another analysis of definitions of homosexuality in the 1940s and 1950s, see Robert Corber, *Homosexuality in Cold War America: Resistance and the Crisis of Masculinity* (Durham, N.C.: Duke University Press, 1997).

33. Chester Himes to Carl Van Vechten, June 1946. Beinecke Library, Yale University, New Haven, Conn.

34. Chester Himes to Richard Wright, February 1953, Beinecke Library, Yale University. Himes wrote to Carl Van Vechten, who supported Himes financially and emotionally, that "[*Cast*] is written in three books, one of which is a homo-sexual love story which takes place in prison. The book has been around a great deal (since I wrote it several years ago) and has aroused a great deal of comment, mostly complimentary on the writing, but the homo-sexual story seems to have killed it."

35. Margolies and Fabre, *The Several Lives*, 53.

36. Himes, *The Quality of Hurt*, 48.

37. Margolies and Fabre, *The Several Lives*, 5.

38. Chester Himes, *If He Hollers Let Him Go* (1945; reprint, New York: Thunder's Mouth Press, 1986), 19.

39. Ibid., 41.

40. Ibid., 75.

41. Ibid., 125.

42. Chester Himes, *Lonely Crusade* (1947; reprint, New York: Thunder's Mouth Press, 1986), 26.

43. Ibid., 89.

44. Ibid., 140.

45. Ibid., 144, 150.

46. Ibid., 196.

47. Ibid., 70.

48. Ibid., 69.

49. Chester Himes to Carl Van Vechten, February 18, 1957. Beinecke Library, Yale University.

50. Chester Himes to Richard Wright, October 19, 1952. Beinecke Library, Yale University. In this letter, Himes thanked Wright for writing a favorable review of the French version of *Lonely Crusade*. Himes considered Wright to be among the greatest black writers alive. "As you know, I consider it a great honor your writing the preface for this book which so many people have continued to hate and abuse, and I am deeply elated that you have continued to like it as well as you first did. . . . I will never change on the book—with all its faults it still tells the truth as I saw it then and as I see it now." As for Wright, he wrote a flattering introduction to *Crusade* in which he said, "If I had the power, I'd pass a law requiring that every Liberal, Socialist, and Communist read and reread Chester Himes's novel, LONELY CRUSADE, for in this book they can see themselves as Negroes see them. . . . Because Himes tells the brutal truth, because he has courage, and because of his straight realism, I say, Long Live Chester Himes." Letter from Alfred Knopf publishers to Carl Van Vechten, August 5, 1947, Beinecke Library, Yale University.

51. Himes to Van Vechten, February 18, 1947.

52. Chester Himes, "Dilemma of the Negro Novelist," in *Beyond the Angry Black*, ed. John Williams, 54 (New York: Cooper Square, 1966). In *The End of a Primitive*, Jesse Robinson faces the problem of white publishers who expect African American writers to avoid discussion of racism. Upon rejecting his manuscript, Jesse's editor suggests, "You're a hell of a good writer, Jesse. Why don't you write a black success novel? An inspirational story? The public is tired of the plight of the poor downtrodden Negro" (124).

53. *Kirkus Reviews*, July 15, 1947, 372.

54. Qtd. in Margolies and Fabre, *The Several Lives*.

55. James Baldwin, "History as Nightmare," *New Leader*, October 25, 1947, 11, 15.

56. *Ebony* 7, no. 1 (November 1941).

57. Lloyd Brown, "White Flag—Chester Himes' Banner Is More Than a Symbol of Surrender—Under It He Joins His People's Foes," *New Masses*, September 9, 1947, 19.

58. Himes wrote his most scathing critique of middle-class African Americans involved in interracial sex in *Pinktoes* (1961), a scandalous tale of interracial parties in which African American elites engage in adulterous interracial sex as a means to "solve the Negro Problem."

59. Himes, *Dilemma*, 55.

Conclusion

1. *Washington Post*, December 7, 2002.

2. May, *Homeward Bound*; Meyerowitz, *Not June Cleaver*.

3. Manning Marable, *Race, Reform, and Rebellion: The Second Reconstruction in Black America, 1945–1982* (Jackson: University Press of Mississippi, 1984).

4. Denning, *The Cultural Front*.

5. See Marjorie Bryers, "Representing the Nation: Pinups, *Playboy*, Pageants, and Racial Politics, 1943–1966" (Ph.D. diss., University of Minnesota, 2003).

6. "Why I Quit My TV Show," *Ebony* 13, no. 4 (February 1958). See also Herman Grey, *Watching Race: Television and the Struggle for "Blackness"* (Minneapolis: University of Minnesota Press, 1995).

7. U.S. Census bureau, http://www.census.gov/population/socdemo/race/interractab1.txt.

8. Orlando Patterson, *The Ordeal of Integration: Progress and Resentment in America's "Racial" Crisis* (Washington, D.C.: Civitas, 1997), 198.

9. Randall Kennedy, "How Are We Doing With *Loving*?: Race, Law, and Intermarriage," in *Mixed Race America and the Law: A Reader*, ed. Kevin R. Johnson, 66 (New York: New York University Press, 2003).

10. http://caselaw.lp.findlaw.com/scripts/getcase.pl?court=US&vol=000&invol=02-102

11. Ibid.

Bibliography

Primary Sources

Beinecke Library, Yale University, New Haven, Connecticut
    Papers of James Weldon Johnson
    Papers of Richard Wright
    Papers of Carl Van Vechten, "Correspondence with Blacks"

National Association for the Advancement of Colored People Papers
    Part 11, Series B: Special Subjects, 1912–1939
    Legal Defense Committee, Special Subjects
    Part 9, Series B: Discrimination in the U.S. Armed Forces, 1918–1955
    Part 9, Series C: Soldier Complaints
    Part 16, Series B
    Part 20, Reel 8, "White Resistance and Reprisals, 1956–1965"

Russel B. Nye Special Collections Library, Michigan State University, East Lansing
    Comic Book Collections

U.S. Senate
    Juvenile Delinquency (Comic Books) Hearings before the Subcommittee to Investigate Juvenile Delinquency of the Committee of the Judiciary. 83rd Congress, 2nd Session. Pursuant to S190. Washington, D.C., Government Printing Office, 1954

Woodruff Library, Emory University, Atlanta
    Papers of Father Divine

Court Cases

Agnew v. State of Alabama, 54 So. 2d 89 (Ala., 1951)
Bowers v. Hardwick, 478 U.S. 186 (1986)
Dees et al. v. Metts, 17 So. 2d 137 (Ala., 1944)
Griffith v. State of Alabama, 23 So. 2d 22 (Ala., 1945)
Jackson v. State of Alabama, 72 So. 2d 114 (Ala., 1954)
Knight v. State of Mississippi, 42 So. 2d 747 (Miss., 1941)
Lawrence v. Texas 41 S.W. 3d 349 (2003)
Loving v. Commonwealth of Virginia, 87 S.Ct. 1817 (1967)
Naim v. Naim, 90 S.E. 2d 849 (Va., 1956)
Perez v. Sharp, 198 P. 2d 17 (Calif., 1948)
Plessy v. Ferguson, 163 U.S. 537 (1896)
Stevens v. United States, 146 F.2d 120 (1944)

Secondary Sources

Anzaldua, Gloria. *Borderlands: The New Meztiza/La Frontera*. San Francisco: Aunt Lute Press, 1987.

Appiah, K. Anthony, and Amy Gutman. *Color Conscious: The Political Morality of Race*. Princeton, N.J.: Princeton University Press, 1998.

Baldwin, Peter C. *Domesticating the Street: The Reform of Public Space in Hartford, 1850–1930*. Columbus: Ohio State University Press, 1999.

Berkhofer, Robert F. *The White Man's Indian: Images of the American Indian from Columbus to the Present*. New York: Knopf, 1978.

Bernardi, Daniel, ed. *The Birth of Whiteness Race and the Emergence of U.S. Cinema*. New Brunswick, N.J.: Rutgers University Press, 1996.

Berson, Judith. *Neither White Nor Black: The Mulatto Character in American Fiction*. New York: New York University Press, 1978.

Berube, Allan. *Coming Out Under Fire: The History of Gay Men and Women in World War Two*. New York: Free Press, 1990.

Bilbo, Theodore. *Take Your Choice; Separation or Mongrelization, by Theodore G. Bilbo*. Poplarville, Miss.: Dream House Publishing, 1947.

Blum, John Morton. *V Was for Victory: Politics and American Culture during World War II*. New York: Harcourt Brace Jovanovich, 1976.

Boris, Eileen. " 'You Wouldn't Want One of 'Em Dancing with Your Wife': Racialized Bodies on the Job in WWII." *American Quarterly* 50, no. 1 (2000): 77–108.

Brandt, Nat. *Harlem at War: The Black Experience in World War II*. Syracuse N.Y.: Syracuse University Press, 1996.

Breines, Winnie. *Young, White, and Miserable: Growing Up Female in the Fifties*. Boston: Beacon Press, 1992.

Brown, Lloyd. "White Flag—Chester Himes' Banner Is More Than a Symbol of Surrender-Under It He Joins His People's Foes." *New Masses*, September 9, 1947.

Bryer, Marjorie. "Representing the Nation: Pinups, *Playboy*, Pageants, and Racial Politics, 1943–1966." Ph.D. diss., University of Minnesota, 2003.

Buchanan, A. Russell. *Black Americans in World War II*. Santa Barbara, Calif.: Clio Books, 1977.

Burnham, John C. "The Progressive Era Revolution in American Attitudes toward Sex." *Journal of American History* 59, no. 4 (1973): 885–908.

Burns, Ben. *Nitty Gritty: A White Editor in Black Journalism*. Jackson: University Press of Mississippi, 1996.

Cayton, Horace, and St. Clair Drake. *Black Metropolis: A Study of Negro Life in a Northern City*. Vol. 1. 1945. Reprint, New York: Harper and Row, 1962.

Ceplair, Larry, and Steven Englund. *The Inquisition in Hollywood: Politics in the Film Community, 1930–1960*. Garden City, N.Y.: Anchor Press/Doubleday, 1980.

Chauncey, George. *Gay New York: Gender, Urban Culture, and the Making of the Gay Male World, 1890–1940*. New York: Basic Books, 1994.

Cochran, David. *American Noir: Underground Writers and Filmmakers of the Postwar Era*. Washington, D.C.: Smithsonian Institution Press, 2000.

Collins, Eliza G. C., and Wanda A. Lankenner. "Failure Is a Word I Don't Accept." *Harvard Business Review* 54 (March/April 1976): 79–88.

Corber, Robert. *Homosexuality in Cold War America: Resistance and the Crisis of Masculinity*. Durham, N.C.: Duke University Press, 1997.

Cott, Nancy. *Public Vows: A History of Marriage and the Nation*. Cambridge, Mass.: Harvard University Press, 2002.

Cox, Oliver Cromwell. *Caste, Class, and Race: A Study in Social Dynamics*. 1948. Reprint, New York: Modern Reader Paperbacks, 1970.

Cripps, Thomas. *Slow Fade to Black: The Negro in American Film, 1900–1942*. New York: Oxford University Press, 1977.

Cuthbert, Clifton. *The Robbed Heart.* New York: L. B. Fisher, 1945.

Dalfiume, Richard. *Desegregation of the U.S. Armed Forces: Fighting on Two Fronts, 1939–1953.* Columbia: University of Missouri Press, 1969.

Daniel, Walter C. *Black Journals of the United States.* Westport, Conn.: Greenwood Press, 1982.

DeCoy, Robert H. *Jack Johnson: The Big Black Fire.* Los Angeles: Holloway House, 1991

Denning: Michael. *The Cultural Front: The Laboring of American Culture in the Twentieth Century.* New York: Verso, 1996.

Dower, John. *War without Mercy: Race and Power in the Pacific War.* New York: Pantheon, 1986.

Duberman, Martin. *Paul Robeson.* New York: Knopf, 1988.

Du Bois, W.E.B. *Black Reconstruction: An Essay toward a History of the Part Which Black Folk Played in the Attempt to Reconstruct Democracy in America, 1860–1880.* New York: Harcourt, Brace, 1935.

Dudziak, Mary. *Cold War Civil Rights: Race and the Image of American Democracy.* Princeton, N.J.: Princeton University Press, 2000.

Dyer, Richard. "The Color of Virtue: Lillian Gish, Whiteness, and Femininity." In *Women in Film: A Sight and Sound Reader,* ed. Pam Cook and Philip Dodd. Philadelphia: Temple University Press, 1993.

Edelstein, Tilden. "*Othello* in America: The Drama of Racial Intermarriage." In *Region, Race and Reconstruction: Essays in Honor of C. Vann Woodward,* ed. J. Morgan Kouser and James M. McPherson. New York: Oxford University Press, 1991.

Engelhardt, Tom. *The End of Victory Culture: Cold War America and the Disillusioning of a Generation.* Amherst: University of Massachusetts Press, 1998.

Feder, Edward L. *Comic Book Regulation.* Berkeley: Bureau of the Public Administration, University of California, 1955.

Fields, Barbara J. "Ideology and Race in American History." In *Region, Race, and Reconstruction: Essays in Honor of C. Vann Woodward,* ed. J. Morgan Kouser and James M. McPherson. New York: Oxford University Press, 1991.

Finkle, Lee. *Forum For Protest: The Black Press during World War II.* Rutherford, N.J.: Fairleigh Dickinson University Press, 1975.

Fonteney, Charles. *Estes Kefauver, a Biography.* Knoxville: University of Tennessee Press, 1980.

Fowler, David. *Northern Attitudes towards Interracial Marriage: Legislation and Public Opinion in the Middle Atlantic States of the Old Northwest, 1780–1930.* New York: Garland, 1987.

Fried, Richard. *Nightmare in Red: The McCarthy Era in Perspective.* New York: Oxford University Press, 1990.

Gallichio, Marc. *The African American Encounter with Japan and China: Black Internationalism in Asia: 1895–1945.* Chapel Hill: University of North Carolina Press, 2000.

Garfinkle, Herbert. *When Negroes March: The March on Washington Movement in the Organization Politics for FEPC.* Glencoe, Ill.: Free Press, 1959.

Gibel Azoulay, Katya. *Black, Jewish, and Interracial: It's Not the Color of Your Skin, But the Race of Your Kin, and Other Myths of Identity.* Durham, N.C.: Duke University Press, 1997.

Gilbert, James. *A Cycle of Outrage: America's Reaction to the Juvenile Delinquent in the 1950s.* New York: Oxford University Press, 1986.

Gilmore, Al-Tony. "Jack Johnson and White Women: The National Impact." *Journal of Negro History* 58, no. 1 (1973): 18–38.

Gilroy, Paul. *Against Race: Imagining Political Culture Beyond the Color Line.* Cambridge, Mass.: Belknap Press of Harvard University Press, 2000.

———. *The Black Atlantic: Modernity and Double Consciousness.* Cambridge, Mass.: Harvard University Press, 1993.

Gloster, Hugh M. "The Van Vechten Vogue." *Phylon* 6, no. 4 (1945): 310–314.

Goldwater, John. *Americana in Four Colors: A Decade of Self-Regulation by the Comic Magazine Industry.* New York: Comics Magazine Association of America, 1974.

Goodman, Walter. *The Committee: The Extraordinary Career of the House Committee on Un-American Activities.* New York, Farrar, Straus, and Giroux, 1968.

Gorman, Joseph. *Kefauver, a Political Biography*. Cambridge: Oxford University Press, 1971.

Gray, Herman. *Watching Race: Television and the Struggle for "Blackness."* Minneapolis: University of Minnesota Press, 1995.

Green, Reyna. "The Pocahontas Perplex: The Image of the Indian Woman in American Culture." *Massachusetts Review* 16 (1975): 698–714.

Gubar, Susan. *Race Changes: White Skin, Black Face in American Culture*. New York: Oxford University Press, 1997.

Guerrero, Ed. *Framing Blackness: The African American Image in Film*. Philadelphia: Temple University Press, 1993.

Halsey, Margaret. *Color Blind: A White Woman Looks at the Negro*. New York: Simon and Schuster, 1946.

Harris, Cheryl. "Whiteness as Property." *Harvard Law Review* 106 (June 1993): 1709–1791.

Hart, Robert C. "Black-White Literary Relations in the Harlem Renaissance." *American Literature* 44, no. 4 (1973): 612–628.

Hedden, Worth Tuttle. *The Other Room*. New York: Crow, 1947.

Heins, Marjorie. *Not In Front of the Children: "Indecency," Censorship, and the Innocence of Youth*. New York: Hill and Wang, 2001.

Helbling, Mark "Carl Van Vechten and the Harlem Renaissance." *Negro American Literature Forum* 10, no. 2 (1976): 39–47.

Hernton, Calvin. *Sex and Racism in America*. New York: Grove Press, 1988.

Higginbotham, A. Leon, and Barbara K. Kopytoff. "Racial Purity and Interracial Sex in the Law of Colonial and Antebellum Virginia." *Georgetown Law Journal* 77 (1989): 1967–2029.

Hillier, Jim, ed. *Cashiers du Cinema: The 1950s: Neo-Realism, Hollywood, New Wave*. Cambridge, Mass.: Harvard University Press, 1985.

Himes, Chester. *Black on Black*. New York: Doubleday, 1973.

———. *Cast the First Stone*. 1953. Reprint, New Jersey: Chatham Booksellers, 1973.

———. "Dilemma of the Negro Novelist in the U.S.A." In *Beyond the Angry Black*, ed. John Williams. New York: Cooper Square, 1966.

———. *The End of a Primitive*. 1955. Reprint, New York: Norton, 1997.

———. *If He Hollers Let Him Go*. 1945. Reprint, New York: Thunder's Mouth Press, 1986.

———. *Lonely Crusade*. 1947. Reprint, New York: Thunder's Mouth Press, 1986.

———. *Pinktoes*. 1961. Reprint, Jackson: University Press of Mississippi, 1996.

———. *The Quality of Hurt, the Early Years: The Autobiography of Chester Himes*. New York: Thunder's Mouth Press, 1972.

———. *The Third Generation*. 1953. Reprint, New York: Thunder's Mouth Press, 1989.

———. *Yesterday Will Make You Cry*. New York: Norton, 1988.

Hodes, Martha. *White Women/Black Men: Illicit Sex in the Nineteenth-Century South*. New Haven, Conn.: Yale University Press, 1997.

———, ed. *Sex, Love, Race: Crossing Boundaries in North American History*. New York: New York University Press, 1999.

Hodges, LeRoy. *Portrait of an Expatriate: William Gardner Smith, Writer*. Westport, Conn.: Greenwood Press, 1985.

Hutchinson, George. *The Harlem Renaissance in Black and White*. Cambridge, Mass.: Belknap Press of Harvard University Press, 1995.

Jacobsen, Matthew Frye. *Whiteness of a Different Color: European Immigrants and the Alchemy of Race*. Cambridge, Mass.: Harvard University Press, 1998.

James, C.L.R. *American Civilization*. Cambridge: Blackwell, 1993.

James, C.L.R., et al. *Fighting Racism in World War II*. New York: Monad Press, 1980.

Jeltz, Wyatt F. "The Relations of Negroes and Choctaw and Chickasaw Indians." *Journal of Negro History* 33, no. 1 (1948): 24–37.

Johnson, James Hugo. *Race Relations in Virginia and Miscegenation in the South, 1776–1860*. Amherst: University of Massachusetts Press, 1970.

Johnson, John. *Succeeding Against the Odds*. New York: Warner Books, 1989.

Jordan, Winthrop. *White Over Black: American Attitudes toward the Negro: 1550–1812*. Baltimore: Penguin, 1969.

Kaplan, Sydney. *American Studies in Black and White: Selected Essays, 1949–1989*. Amherst: University of Massachusetts Press, 1991.

Kearney, Reginald. *African American Views of the Japanese: Solidarity or Sedition?* Albany: State University of New York Press, 1998.

Keire, Mara L. "The Vice Trust: A Reinterpretation of the White Slavery Scare in the United States, 1907–1917." *Journal of Social History* 35, no. 1 (2001): 5–41.

Kennedy, Randall. *Interracial Intimacies: Sex, Marriage, Identity, and Adoption*. New York: Pantheon, 2003.

———. "How Are We Doing With *Loving*?: Race, Law, and Intermarriage." In *Mixed Race America and the Law: A Reader*, ed. Kevin R. Johnson. New York: New York University Press, 2003.

Kramer, Victor A., and Robert A. Russ, eds. *Harlem Renaissance Re-Examined*. Troy, N.Y.: Whitson, 1997.

Kunzel, Regina. *Fallen Women, Problem Girls: Unmarried Mothers and the Professionalization of Social Work, 1890–1945*. New Haven, Conn.: Yale University Press, 1993.

Langum, David J. *Crossing Over the Line: Legislating Morality and the Mann Act*. Chicago: University of Chicago Press, 1994.

Lee, Robert. *Orientals: Asian Americans in Popular Culture*. Philadelphia: Temple University Press, 2000.

Levine, Lawrence. *Black Culture and Black Consciousness: Afro-American Folk Thought from Slavery to Freedom*. New York: Oxford University Press, 1997.

Light, Ivan. "The Ethnic Vice Industry, 1880–1944." *American Sociological Review* 42, no. 3 (1977): 464–479.

Lipsitz, George. *The Possessive Investment in Whiteness: How White People Profit from identity Politics*. Philadelphia: Temple University Press, 1998.

———. *Rainbow At Midnight: Labor and Culture in the 1940s*. Urbana: University of Illinois Press, 1994.

———. *Time Passages: Collective Memory and American Popular Culture*. Minneapolis: University of Minnesota Press, 1990.

Littlefield, Daniel F., Jr., and Mary Ann Littlefield. "The Beams Family: Free Blacks in Indian Territory." *Journal of Negro History* 61, no. 1 (1976): 17–35.

Lopez, Ian Haney. *White By Law: The Legal Construction of Race*. New York: New York University Press, 1996.

Lott, Eric. *Love and Theft: Blackface Minstrelsy and the American Working Class*. New York: Oxford University Press, 1993.

Marable, Manning. *Race, Reform, and Rebellion: The Second Reconstruction in Black America, 1945–1982*. Jackson: University Press of Mississippi, 1984.

Marchetti, Gina. *Romance and the "Yellow Peril": Race, Sex, and the Discursive Strategies in Hollywood Fiction*. Berkeley: University of California Press, 1993.

Margolies, Ed, and Michael Fabre. *The Several Lives of Chester Himes*. Jackson: University Press of Mississippi, 1997.

May, Elaine Tyler. *Homeward Bound: American Families in the Cold War Era*. New York: Basic Books, 1988.

Mazon, Mauricio. *The Zoot-Suit Riots: The Psychology of Symbolic Annihilation*. Austin: University of Texas Press, 1989.

McClintock, Anne. *Imperial Leather: Race, Gender, and Sexuality in the Colonial Contest*. New York: Routledge, 1995.

McLoughlin, William G. "Red Indians, Black Slavery and White Racism: America's Slaveholding Indians." *American Quarterly* 26, no. 4 (1974): 367–385.

Melnick, Jeffrey. " 'Story Untold': The Black Men and White Sounds of Doo-Wop." In *Whiteness: A Critical Reader*, ed. Mike Hill. New York: New York University Press, 1997.

Meyerowitz, Joann, ed. *Not June Cleaver: Women and Gender in Postwar America, 1945–1960*. Philadelphia: Temple University Press, 1994.

Miles, Frank. "Negro Magazines Come of Age." *Magazine World*, June 1, 1946.

Minges, Patrick. "Beneath the Underdog: Race, Religion, and the Trail of Tears." *American Indian Quarterly* 25, no. 3 (2001): 453–479.

Moran, Rachel. *Interracial Intimacy: The Regulation of Race and Romance*. Chicago: University of Chicago Press, 2001.

Morgan, Edmund. *American Slavery, American Freedom: The Ordeal of Colonial Virginia*. New York: W. W. Norton, 1975.

Morrison, Toni. *Playing in the Dark: Whiteness and the Literary Imagination*. New York: Vintage, 1993.

Mullen, Bill. *Popular Fronts: Chicago and African American Politics*. Urbana: University of Illinois Press, 1999.

Mullen, Bill, and Sherry Lee Linkon. *Radical Revisions: Rereading 1930s Culture*. Urbana: University of Illinois Press, 1996.

Mumford, Kevin. *Interzones: Black/White Sex Districts in Chicago and New York in the Early Twentieth Century*. New York: Columbia University Press, 1997.

Myrdal, Gunnar. *An American Dilemma: The Negro Problem and Modern Democracy*. New York: Harper and Row, 1962.

Noble, David W. *Death of a Nation: American Culture and the End of Exceptionalism*. Minneapolis: University of Minnesota Press, 2002.

Nyberg, Amy Kiste. *Seal of Approval: The History of the Comics Codes*. Jackson: University Press of Mississippi, 1998.

Omi, Michael, and Howard Winant. *Racial Formation in the United States: From the 1960s to the 1980s*. New York: Routledge, 1986.

Ottley, Roi. *New World A-Coming: Inside Black America*. Boston: Houghton Mifflin, 1943.

Pagan, Eduardo Obregon. "Los Angeles Geopolitics and the Zoot Suit Riot 1943." *Social Science History* 24, no. 1. (2000): 223–256.

Palumbo-Liu, David. *Asian/American: Historical Crossings of a Racial Frontier*. Stanford, Calif.: Stanford University Press, 1999.

Pascoe, Peggy. "Miscegenation Law, Court Cases and Ideologies of 'Race' in Twentieth-Century America." In *Sex, Love, Race: Crossing Boundaries in North American History*, ed. Martha Hodes. New York: New York University Press, 1999.

Patterson, Orlando. *The Ordeal of Integration: Progress and Resentment in America's "Racial" Crisis*. Washington, D.C.: Civitas, 1997.

Petry, Ann. *The Narrows*. New York: Mariner Books, 1999.

——. *The Street*. New York: Houghton Mifflin, 1998.

Plummer, Brenda Gayle. *Rising Wind: Black Americans and U.S. Foreign Affairs, 1935–1960*. Chapel Hill: University of North Carolina Press, 1996.

Pratt, Mary Louise. *Imperial Eyes: Travel Writing and Transculturation*. New York: Routledge, 1992

Reichly, James. "How Johnson Made It." *Fortune*, January 1968.

Reynolds, David. *Rich Relations: The American Occupation of Britain, 1942–1945*. New York: Random House, 1995.

Roediger, David. *Black on White: Black Writers on What It Means to Be White*. New York: Schocken Books, 1998.

——. *The Wages of Whiteness: Race and the Making of the American Working Class*. New York: Verso, 1991.

Romano, Renee. *Race Mixing: Black-White Marriage in Postwar America*. Cambridge, Mass.: Harvard University Press, 2003.

Root, Maria P. P. *Love's Revolution: Interracial Marriage*. Philadelphia: Temple University Press, 2001.

———. *The Multiracial Experience: Racial Borders as the New Frontier*. Thousand Oaks, Calif.: Sage, 1996.

———. *Racially Mixed People in America*. Newbury Park, Calif.: Sage, 1992.

Ross, Andrew. *No Respect: Intellectuals and Popular Culture*. New York: Routledge, 1989.

Ryan, Michael, and Douglas Kellner. *Camera Politica: The Politics and Ideology of Contemporary Hollywood Film*. Bloomington: University of Indiana Press, 1988.

Savage, William. *Commies, Cowboys, and Jungle Queens: Comic Books and America, 1945–1954*. Norman: University of Oklahoma Press, 1990.

Sawyer-Laucanno, Christopher. *The Continual Pilgrimage: American Writers in Paris, 1944–1969*. San Francisco: City Lights Publishers, 1997.

Saxton, Alexander. *The Rise and Fall of the White Republic: Class, Politics, and Mass Culture in Nineteenth Century America*. New York: Verso, 1990.

Schuyler, George S. "Phylon Profile, XXII: Carl Van Vechten." *Phylon* 11, no. 4 (1950): 362–368.

Scruggs, Charles. "'All Dressed Up But No Place to Go': The Black Writer and His Audience during the Harlem Renaissance." *American Literature* 48, no. 4 (1977): 543–563.

Shaw, Patricia Ann Friday. "'Negro Digest,' 'Pulse,' and 'Headlines and Pictures': African American Periodicals as Informants, Morale Builders and Articulators of Protest during World War II." Ph.D. diss., University of Maryland, 1994.

Shukert, Elfrieda, and Barbara Smith Scibetta. *War Brides of WWII*. Novato, Calif.: Presidio Press, 1988.

Shute, Nevil. *The Chequer Board*. New York. Morrow, 1947.

Silvera, John. *The Negro in World War II*. New York: Arno, 1969.

Sinclair, Marjorie. *The Wild Wind: A Novel*. New York: J. Day, 1950.

Sitkoff, Harvard. *The Struggle for Black Equality, 1954–1992*. New York: Hill and Wang, 1981.

Smith, Graham. *When Jim Crow Met John Bull: Black American Soldiers in World War II Britain*. New York: St. Martin's, 1988.

Smith, Judith. *Visions of Belonging: Family Stories, Popular Culture, and Postwar Democracy, 1940–1960*. New York: Columbia University Press, forthcoming.

Smith, William Gardner. *Last of the Conquerors*. 1948. Reprint, Chatham, N.J.: Chatham Booksellers, 1973.

Solinger, Rickie. *Wake Up Little Susie: Single Pregnancy and Race before* Roe v. Wade. New York: Routledge, 1992.

Sollors, Werner. *Neither Black Nor White But Both: Thematic Explorations of Interracial Literature*. New York: Oxford University Press, 1997.

———. *Interracialism:: Black-White Intermarriage in American History, Literature, and Law*. New York: Oxford University Press, 2000.

Spickard, Paul. *Mixed Blood: Intermarriage and Ethnic Identity in Twentieth-Century America*. Madison: University of Wisconsin Press, 1989.

Stoval, Tyler. *Paris Noir: African Americans in the City of Light*. Boston: Houghton Mifflin, 1996.

Sugrue, Thomas J. *The Origins of the Urban Crisis: Race and Inequality in Postwar Detroit*. Princeton, N.J.: Princeton University Press, 1996.

Takaki, Ronald. *A Different Mirror: A History of Multicultural America*. Boston: Little, Brown, 1994.

———. *Double Victory: A Multicultural History of Americans in World War II*. Boston: Little, Brown, 2000.

Toll, Robert. *Blacking Up: The Minstrel Show in 19th Century America*. New York: Oxford University Press, 1974.

Tyson, Timothy. *Radio Free Dixie: Robert F. Williams and the Roots of Black Power*. Chapel Hill: University of North Carolina Press, 1999.

Von Eshen, Penny. *Race Against Empire: Black Americans and Anti-Colonialism, 1937–1957*. Ithaca, N.Y.: Cornell University Press, 1997.

Wald, Gayle. *Crossing the Line: Racial Passing in Twentieth-Century U.S. Literature and Culture.* Durham, N.C.: Duke University Press, 2000.

Wallace, Michelle. *Black Macho and the Myth of the Superwoman.* New York: Verso, 1990.

West, Cornel. *Race Matters.* Boston: Beacon Press, 1993.

Williamson, Joel. *New People: Miscegenation and Mulattoes in the United States.* New York: Free Press, 1980.

Woodsen, Carter G. "The Beginnings of Miscegenation of the Whites and Blacks." In *Inter-racialism:: Black-White Intermarriage in American History, Literature, and Law,* ed. Werner Sollers. New York: Oxford University Press, 2000.

Wynn, Neil A. *The Afro-American and the Second World War.* New York: Holmes and Meier, 1975.

Yerby, Frank. *The Foxes of Harrow.* New York: Dial Press, 1946.

———. *The Golden Hawk.* New York: Dial Press, 1948.

———. *The Vixens.* New York: Dial Press, 1947.

Young, Robert. *Colonial Desire: Hybridity in Theory, Culture, and Race.* New York: Routledge, 1995.

Zack, Naomi. *Race and Mixed Race.* Philadelphia: Temple University Press, 1993.

Index